HELLENISTIC PHILOSOPHY

CLASSICAL LIFE AND LETTERS

General Editor: HUGH LLOYD-JONES

Regius Professor of Greek in the University of Oxford

Cicero   *D. R. Shackleton Bailey*
Homer   *C. M. Bowra*
The Presocratics   *Edward Hussey*
Neoplatonism   *R. T. Wallis*
Plutarch   *D. A. Russell*
Xenophon   *J. K. Anderson*

Epicurus

Chrysippus

Carneades

HELLENISTIC PHILOSOPHY

STOICS, EPICUREANS, SCEPTICS

A. A. Long

CHARLES SCRIBNER'S SONS
NEW YORK

Contents

Preface

THE purpose of this book is to trace the main developments in Greek philosophy during the period which runs from the death of Alexander the Great in 323 B.C. to the end of the Roman Republic (31 B.C.). These three centuries, known to us as the Hellenistic Age, witnessed a vast expansion of Greek civilization eastwards, following Alexander's conquests; and later, Greek civilization penetrated deeply into the western Mediterranean world assisted by the political conquerors of Greece, the Romans. But philosophy throughout this time remained a predominantly Greek activity. The most influential thinkers in the Hellenistic world were Stoics, Epicureans and Sceptics. In this book I have tried to give a concise critical analysis of their ideas and their methods of thought.

As far as I am aware, the last book in English to cover this ground was written sixty years ago. In the interval the subject has moved on, quite rapidly since the last war, but most of the best work is highly specialized. There is a clear need for a general appraisal of Hellenistic philosophy which can provide those who are not specialists with an up-to-date account of the subject. Hellenistic philosophy is often regarded as a dull product of second-rate thinkers who are unable to stand comparison with Plato and Aristotle. I hope that this book will help to remove such misconceptions and arouse wider interest in a field which is fascinating both historically and conceptually.

One reason for the misunderstanding from which Hellenistic philosophy has suffered is the scarcity of primary evidence. Nearly all the writings of the early Stoics have perished, and their theories must be reconstructed from quotations and summaries by later writers. The limitations of evidence are also a problem in dealing with Epicureans and Sceptics. In this book I have devoted little space to the evaluation of sources which technical work on Hellenistic philosophy requires. But the evidence is so scattered and so variable in quality that I have not hesitated to give references in the text for most theories which I attribute to particular philosophers. Many of the subjects which are discussed can be interpreted in different ways. I have not attempted to refer to more than a few divergent opinions, and some of my own conclusions will prove controversial. My aim throughout has been to make the best philosophical sense of the evidence, and at the same time to indicate which theories are most vulnerable to criticism. I have been liberal with quotations and the discussion of details is based wherever possible upon the extracts which I have translated.

The subject which I have treated at greatest length is Stoicism. In giving the Stoics so much space I have been influenced by two considerations: they were, in my judgment, the most important philosophers of the Hellenistic period, and at the present time their thought is less accessible to the general reader than Epicureanism or Scepticism. I have tried to keep conceptual rather than historical issues before the reader's mind in much of the book. But historical background is the main theme of the first chapter, and I have concluded the book with a short survey of the later influence of Hellenistic philosophy, which was extensive. I have also discussed some characteristics of earlier Greek thought which help to explain concepts accepted and rejected by Hellenistic philosophers.

The work of Usener, von Arnim, Brochard, Bailey and Pohlenz is indispensable to anyone who studies Hellenistic philosophy, and I have also learnt much from contemporary scholars. My thanks are also due to my pupils, my colleagues and to those who have given me many opportunities to read papers on the subject at meetings in Britain and other countries. In particular, I have benefited greatly from my membership of University College London where I taught throughout the time this book was being prepared. To George Kerferd, who commented on Chapters 2 and 3, and to Alan Griffiths, who scrutinized the whole typescript, I am especially grateful. Lastly, I thank my wife, Kay, who helped me in more ways than I can indicate with any acknowledgment.

For permission to reproduce the frontispiece photographs I am grateful to the following: for Epicurus to the Metropolitan Museum, New York; for Chrysippus to the Trustees of the British Museum; for Caneades to the Antikenmuseum, Basel.

A.A.L.

Abbreviations

Acad.	Cicero, *Academica*
Adv. math.	Sextus Empiricus, *Adversus mathematicos* (Against the dogmatic philosophers)
Comm. not.	Plutarch, *De communibus notitiis contra stoicos* (On universal conceptions against the Stoics)
DK	*Die Fragmente der Vorsokratiker*, ed. H. Diels and W. Kranz
D.L.	Diogenes Laertius
De an.	Aristotle, *De anima* (On the soul)
De div.	Cicero, *De divinatione* (On divination)
De nat.	Epicurus, *De natura* (On nature)
De off.	Cicero, *De officiis* (On duties)
E.N.	Aristotle, *Nicomachean ethics*
Ep.	Seneca, *Epistulae morales* (Moral letters)
Ep. Hdt.	Epicurus, *Letter to Herodotus*
Ep. Men.	Epicurus, *Letter to Menoeceus*
Ep. Pyth.	Epicurus, *Letter to Pythocles*
Fin.	Cicero, *De finibus bonorum et malorum* (On the chief things which are good and bad)
K.D.	Epicurus, *Kuriai doxai* (Principal doctrines)
Met.	Aristotle, *Metaphysics*
N.D.	Cicero, *De natura deorum* (On the nature of the gods)
P.H.	Sextus Empiricus, *Pyrrhoneioi hypotyposeis* (Outlines of Pyrrhonism)
Plac.	Galen, *De placitis Hippocratis et Platonis* (On the opinions of Hippocrates and Plato)
R.E.	Pauly-Wissowa, *Real-Enzyklopädie der klassischen Altertumswissenschaft*

Rep.	Cicero, *De republica* (On the state)
Sent. Vat.	Epicurus, *Sententiae Vaticanae* (Epicurean aphorisms from a Vatican manuscript)
Stoic. rep.	Plutarch, *De Stoicorum repugnantiis* (On the contradictions of the Stoics)
SVF	*Stoicorum Veterum Fragmenta* (Fragments of the early Stoics, ed. H. von Arnim)
Tusc.	Cicero, *Tusculan disputations*
Us.	*Epicurea,* ed. H. Usener

CHAPTER ONE

Introduction

SIGNIFICANT stages in the history of philosophy are seldom identifiable with the same precision as political events, but there are good reasons for bringing the new movements of thought which developed in the Greek world at the end of the fourth century B.C. under a single description. Hellenistic is a term which refers to Greek, and later, Graeco-Roman civilization in the period beginning with the death of Alexander the Great (323 B.C.) and ending, by convention, with the victory of Octavian over Mark Antony at the battle of Actium in 31 B.C. During these three centuries it is neither Platonism nor the Peripatetic tradition established by Aristotle which occupied the central place in ancient philosophy, but Stoicism, Scepticism and Epicureanism, all of which were post-Aristotelian developments. These are the movements of thought which define the main lines of philosophy in the Hellenistic world, and 'Hellenistic philosophy' is the expression I use in this book to refer to them collectively. Their influence continued into the Roman empire and later times, but in the first century B.C. Platonism began a long revival and an interest in Aristotle's technical writings was also re-awakened. The detailed treatment of Hellenistic philosophy in this book comes to an end with these developments. They are both a cause and a symptom of an eclectic stage in Greek and Roman thought, during which the Hellenistic systems become only of secondary importance to the historian of philosophy.

In this introductory chapter our interest is chiefly in the beginning of Hellenistic philosophy, and it is useful to glance initially at the social and political circumstances which provided the framework for intellectual life at this period. Alexander's eastern empire disintegrated in the wars and dynastic struggles which followed his early death. But it prepared the ground for an unparalleled extension of Greek culture. Alexandria in Egypt and Antioch in Syria were Greek foundations, capitals respectively of the Ptolemaic and Seleucid kingdoms secured by two of Alexander's generals. The soldiers, civil servants and businessmen who settled in Asia and Egypt transplanted the social institutions of the Greek mainland. A common culture, modified by different influences in different places, and above all, a common language (the *koinê*), gave them a sense of unity. Alexandria under the Ptolemys became a new centre of arts and sciences, which had such power to attract eminent men of letters and scholars that it outshone Athens in the diversity of its culture. Athens remained pre-eminent in philosophy. But Antioch, Pergamum and Smyrna were other flourishing cities whose rulers competed with one another as patrons of poets, philosophers, historians and scientists.

For about a hundred years it was an age of remarkable intellectual achievement. The extension of the social and political horizon of classical Greece was matched by a widening of interest in subjects such as history and geography. Great advances were made in philology, astronomy and physiology. Learning affected literature, and most of the notable literary figures were scholars. One of the consequences of this scholarly activity was a narrower definition of subject boundaries. Aristotle and his immediate followers took in a very wide range of subjects under 'philosophy', including studies that we would designate scientific or literary or historical. The scope of Hellenistic philosophy is much more limited on the whole. Strato of Lampsachus (died 270/68), one of Aristotle's successors, was a philosopher whose primary interests might be called scientific. Much later, the Stoic Posidonius (died 51/50) made staunch efforts to associate philosophy with history, geography, astronomy and mathematics. But these are exceptions. The special sciences were vigorously studied in our period, but not primarily by leading members of the Hellenistic philosophical schools. In their hands philosophy came to acquire something of its modern connotations, with a division drawn between logic, ethics and general investigation of 'nature'. This distinction between philosophy and science was underlined by place as well as time. The major figures of early Hellenistic philosophy—Epicurus, Zeno, Arcesilaus, and Chrysippus—all migrated to Athens from elsewhere. Those who are most noteworthy for their scientific achievements—Archimedes, Aristarchus, the astronomer, and the medical scientists, Herophilus and Erasistratus, had no strong association that we know of with Athens.

Without Alexander there would have been no Alexandria. Many of the characteristics of the Hellenistic world can undoubtedly be traced to his imperial ambitions and their subsequent effects. Philosophy, so

many have said, responded to the unsettled age of the Hellenistic
monarchs by turning away from disinterested speculation to the provision of security for the individual. Stoicism has been described as
'a system put together hastily, violently, to meet a bewildered world'.[1]
It would certainly be wrong to isolate Stoicism and Epicureanism from
their milieu. Epicurus' renunciation of civic life and the Stoics' conception of the world itself as a kind of city may be viewed as two
quite different attempts to come to terms with changing social and
political circumstances. But many of the characteristics of Hellenistic
philosophy were inherited from thinkers who were active before the
death of Alexander. The needs of people in the Hellenistic world for
a sense of identity and moral guidance can help to explain why Stoicism
and Epicureanism rapidly gained adherents at Athens and elsewhere.
But the Peloponnesian War a hundred years previously probably
caused greater suffering to Greece than Alexander and his successors.
Economically, Athens was a prosperous city at the end of the fourth
century and new public works absorbed capital and energy. It is
difficult to find anything in early Hellenistic philosophy which answers
clearly to a *new* sense of bewilderment.

Alexander, it is true, helped to undermine the values which the
declining city-states had once so proudly asserted, and Aristotle's
ethics assumes as its social context a city-state like Athens. But Diogenes the Cynic was already challenging the basic conventions of
classical Greek civic life many years before the death of Alexander.
These three men, Alexander, Diogenes and Aristotle, all died within
a year or two of each other (325–322), and this is worth mentioning
because it emphasizes the need to take account of continuity as well as
change in the interpretation of Hellenistic philosophy. The young
Alexander was taught in Macedonia by Aristotle, and in later years
Alexander, who knew the free-speaking Diogenes, is reputed to have
said, 'If I had not been Alexander, I should like to have been Diogenes'
(D.L. vi 32). Alexander set out to conquer the external world; Diogenes
aimed to show men how to conquer their own fears and desires.
Aristotle and Diogenes were contemporaries but they had little else
in common. Moralist, iconoclast, preacher, these are descriptions
which catch something of Diogenes' posture. He shared none of

[1] E. Bevan, *Stoics and Sceptics* (Oxford 1913) p. 32. Contrast with this kind of
explanation L. Edelstein's reference to a 'new consciousness of man's power that
arose in the fourth century, the belief in the deification of the human being', which
he finds influential on Stoicism and Epicureanism, *The Meaning of Stoicism*
(Cambridge, Mass. 1966) p. 13.

Aristotle's interest in logic or metaphysics, and attacked the city-state as an institution by advocating an ascetic life based upon 'human nature', the rationality of which was at variance, he argued, with the practice of Greek society. This repudiation of accepted customs was backed up by reference to the supposed habits of primitive men and animals.

Behind Diogenes' exhibitionism and deliberate affront to convention lay a profound concern with moral values which looks back to Socrates. The Stoics refined Diogenes' ideas, and there were men in the Hellenistic world and the Roman empire who called themselves Cynics, modelling their preaching and life on the uncompromising style of Diogenes. Unlike Socrates however he acknowledged no allegiance to any city, whether it was Sinope on the Black Sea, his native town, or Athens where he spent much of his later life. His ethical values took no account of social status and nationality, and this emphasizes the radical character of Diogenes' criticism of traditional attitudes. A study of Aristotle's painful defence of slavery in *Politics* Book I should make the point beyond doubt. What mattered to Diogenes was the individual human being and the well-being he might achieve purely by his natural endowments. This strong emphasis upon the individual and a 'nature' which he shares with humanity at large is one of the characteristics of Hellenistic philosophy. It becomes most prominent among Stoics, at the time of Rome's expansion from the second century B.C. onwards; but the early Stoics, Sceptics and Epicureans were supremely confident that a man's inner resources, his rationality, can provide the only firm basis for a happy and tranquil life. The city recedes into the background, and this is a sign of the times. But Diogenes had pointed the way before the dawn of the Hellenistic age.

When Zeno, the founder of Stoicism, and Epicurus began teaching at Athens in the last years of the fourth century the city already had two illustrious philosophical schools. A few years before 369, Plato had established the Academy, a society which seems to have had much less in common with a general centre of learning than later uses of the name might suggest.[1] Its senior members pursued a wide range of interests, but formal teaching may have been limited to mathematics and certainly is not likely to have gone beyond the curriculum, which includes dialectic for those over thirty, described in Book vii of the

[1] cf. Harold Cherniss, *The Riddle of the Early Academy* (Berkeley and Los Angeles 1945) pp. 61–72.

Republic. What the numbers of the Academy were at any one time is not known. The juniors in its early days must have been a small group of upper-class young men, not exclusively Athenians, for Aristotle who spent the years 367–347 as student and teacher in the Academy came from Macedonia. In founding the Academy Plato may have hoped among other things to educate men who could be expected to become prominent in public life. The published dialogues were his principal method of reaching a wider audience.

After Plato's death (347) the headship of the Academy passed first to his nephew, Speusippus, then to Xenocrates and thirdly to Polemo, a contemporary of Epicurus and Zeno. Aristotle remained formally a member for the rest of his life, but he left Athens for reasons which are open to conjecture on the appointment of Speusippus. He spent the next twelve years in various cities of Asia Minor and Macedonia, returning to Athens in 335. During his absence from Athens, Aristotle probably devoted much of his time to biological research, the fruits of which bulk so large in his writings. Following Alexander's accession to the Macedonian throne, Aristotle began his second prolonged stay in Athens, now teaching not in the Academy but in the Lyceum, a grove just outside the civic boundaries. Theophrastus and other Academicians, who had accompanied Aristotle on his travels, joined him there; and after Aristotle's death in 322, Theophrastus established the Lyceum (often called the Peripatos) as a school in its own right. He continued to direct its work until his death in 288/4.

The activities of the later Academy are not well documented. Aristotle often associates Speusippus with 'the Pythagoreans' (e.g. *Met.* 1072b30; *E.N.* 1096b5). The transmission of so-called Pythagoreanism is a complex and controversial subject. What seems to have happened, very briefly, is that Speusippus and Xenocrates developed certain metaphysical and mathematical principles which were not called Pythagorean by Plato. In their hands Plato's theory of Forms underwent considerable transformation.[1] They also wrote copiously on ethical subjects. Here again the details largely escape us, but it is certain that they accepted such basic Platonic notions as the necessary connexion between virtue and human well-being. Speusippus took up the extreme position of denying that pleasure in any sense or form can be something good (Aristotle, *E.N.* vii 14), and he attacked the hedonist philosopher, Aristippus, in two books. Several doctrines attributed to Xenocrates recur in Stoicism. One text is of particular

[1] cf. Cherniss, op. cit. p. 33.

interest: 'The reason for discovering philosophy is to allay that which causes disturbance in life' (fr. 4, Heinze). Xenocrates' name in this passage, which comes from Galen, depends on an emendation of the name 'Isocrates'. But the statement harmonizes well with the general aims of Hellenistic philosophy, especially Epicureanism and Pyrrhonism.

Xenocrates probably saw himself chiefly as a scholarly exponent of Plato's philosophy. Under his leadership the Academy professed Platonism, a systematic account of ideas which Plato himself, however positively he held them, may never have intended to be presented as a firm body of doctrine.

In the ancient biographical tradition Xenocrates is presented as a grave figure who had such an effect on Polemo, who eventually succeeded him, that the latter turned from a life of dissipation to philosophy. Polemo became head of the Academy in 314, three or four years before Zeno's arrival in Athens. With its fourth head the Academy seems to have moved away from mathematics, metaphysics and dialectic to concentrate upon ethics. Polemo is reported to have said that 'a man should train himself in practical matters and not in mere dialectical exercises' (D.L. iv 18). Plato regarded dialectic as the best moral training, on the grounds that it prepared its practitioners for an insight into the nature of goodness. But Hellenistic philosophy strove to make itself relevant to a wider social group than Plato or Aristotle had influenced. This is proved, to my mind convincingly, by the number of rival philosophers who were active at the end of the fourth century, all of them offering their own solution to the question already asked and answered by Plato and Aristotle: 'What is happiness or well-being and how does a man achieve it?' One answer, advanced by the first Sceptic, Pyrrho, was equanimity born of a refusal to make any definite judgments, but Epicureans and Stoics were the new philosophers who tackled the question most successfully. They succeeded not because they abandoned theory for practice, but because they offered a conception of the world and human nature which drew its support from empirical observations, reason and a recognition that all men have common needs. In saying this I do not mean to imply that they restricted the scope of philosophy to ethics. This is a frequent misconception about Hellenistic philosophy. Epicurus wrote thirty-seven books *On Nature*. The Stoics made contributions of great interest in logic, theory of language and natural philosophy. Both systems adopted the important assumption that happiness depends upon an understanding of the universe and what it is to be a man.

There were a number of minor philosophical movements in the early Hellenistic period all claiming descent from Socrates. We know or think we know Socrates so well from Plato that it is easy to forget the other Socratics who went their own way in the first part of the fourth century. They are shadowy figures whose views are preserved only in occasional references by contemporary writers and the bald summaries compiled in late antiquity. But they established traditions which anticipate certain aspects of Hellenistic philosophy and which influenced or even competed briefly with the new schools.[1]

I have said a little about Diogenes the Cynic, and will return to him in Chapter 4. Ancient historians of philosophy liked to concoct tidy master-pupil relationships, and they make Diogenes a pupil of Antisthenes. This man was an Athenian associate of Socrates. It is difficult to say how far Diogenes was positively influenced by Antisthenes. Perhaps twenty years older then Plato, Antisthenes himself is attacked by Aristotle for his naïveté (*Met.* 1024b33) and his followers ('Antistheneans') are criticized for their lack of culture (ibid. 1043b23). Sniping at traditional education was part of Diogenes' platform; and if Diogenes Laertius is to be trusted, Antisthenes himself claimed that virtue (*aretê*) is something practical, needing neither copious words nor learning (D.L. vi 11). In fact, Antisthenes was a voluminous writer whose style was highly regarded by a number of ancient critics. The titles of his books show that he was interested in literature, problems of knowledge and belief, and especially dialectic (D.L. vi 15ff.). The later Cynic tradition has coloured Diogenes Laertius' biography. It is reasonable, however, to suppose that Antisthenes advocated Socratic strength of mind as much by personal example as by teaching and writing. The little that we know of his logic and theories of language suggests that he was strongly at variance with Plato. But it was not for contributions to theoretical philosophy that Antisthenes became famous. His importance in this book rests on certain moral propositions in which he certainly foreshadowed and may have directly influenced the Stoics. Especially striking are the following fragments: virtue can be taught and once acquired cannot be lost (Caizzi fr. 69; 71); virtue is the goal of life (22); the sage is self-sufficient, since he has (by being wise) the wealth of all

[1] For a detailed account of the minor Socratics cf. W. K. C. Guthrie, *A History of Greek Philosophy* vol. iii (Cambridge 1969).

men (80). Probably Antisthenes, like Diogenes, dispensed with any detailed theory which might support such statements. It was left to the Stoics to build them into a systematic treatment of ethics.

A second Socratic, whose followers were active in the early Hellenistic age, is Aristippus of Cyrene (*c*. 435–355). Xenophon records conversations between Socrates and Aristippus (e.g. *Mem*. 3.8, 1–7; 2.1) and Aristotle also mentions him (*Met*. 996a29). Aristippus' importance rests on his claim that pleasure is the goal of life. He advanced this thesis long before it was adopted by Epicurus, and Epicurean hedonism, though possibly influenced by Cyrenaic views, differs from them in significant respects. By pleasure Aristippus meant bodily gratification, which he conceived as a 'smooth movement', 'rough movements' producing pain (D.L. ii 86). Unlike the Epicureans the Cyrenaics denied absence of pain to be pleasure—it was an intermediate condition—and they rated pleasing bodily sensations above mental pleasures (ibid. 89–90). Our sources do not distinguish clearly between the theories of Aristippus himself and those of his followers, two of whom, Theodorus and Hegesias, flourished at the end of the fourth century. From Aristotle (*Met*. 996a29) we learn that Aristippus scorned mathematics because it took no account of good or bad; and it may be inferred from this that the main concern of his teaching was ethical. Here it is possible to see the influence of Socrates, and Socratic influence may also be evident in Aristippus' dismissal of speculation about the physical world (D.L. 92), which he perhaps developed into a sceptical attitude towards knowledge of external reality.

Eucleides of Megara was a third follower of Socrates whose adherents were still prominent in the early Hellenistic period. It is unfortunate that our knowledge of Eucleides is so slight, for he seems to have been a philosopher of greater significance than Antisthenes or Aristippus. The Megarian school was particularly interested in the kind of arguments first developed by Parmenides and Zeno of Elea in the fifth century. Parmenidean monism was also taken over by Eucleides who held that 'the good is one thing, called under many names' (D.L. ii 106). In the same context, Diogenes Laertius observes that Eucleides denied the existence of that which is contradictory to the good. In seeking to reduce everything to one thing, which is good, Eucleides may have been as much influenced by Socrates as by Parmenides. (Socrates' interest in teleological explanations for phenomena is well attested in Plato's *Phaedo* 97c). But we cannot say how Eucleides worked out the implications of this proposition. Later Megarians were largely renowned for their skill at dialectic, and they had an important influence on Stoic logic. Zeno the Stoic studied with two eminent Megarian philosophers, Stilpo and Diodorus Cronus.

To later antiquity these minor Socratic schools were of only marginal interest. It would be a mistake to regard them as insignificant in their own day. We tend to think that Plato and Aristotle completely overshadowed rival contemporary philosophers because their work has not survived or proved influential. It is unlikely that an educated Greek at the end of the fourth century would have formed the same judgment. Stilpo is reputed to have won followers from Aristotle, Theophrastus and many others (D.L. ii 113f.). Platonists and Peripatetics never exercised a monopoly in Greek philosophy, and they were soon outdone in the extent of their influence by the new Stoic and Epicurean schools.

When these schools were founded, the Academy had ceased to be outstanding in mathematics and theoretical philosophy. Its intellectual vitality was restored about the year 265 in a very different form by Arcesilaus, who turned the Academy from dogmatism to scepticism. But the Lyceum remained a vigorous society down to the death of Strato in 270/68. Theophrastus was a scholar of great versatility who maintained the research tradition established by Aristotle. He refined and expounded Aristotelian doctrines, but was also quite prepared to challenge Aristotle, as may be seen in the work which has come down to us with the title, *Metaphysics*. There Theophrastus discusses a series of problems which arise out of Aristotle's metaphysics. He made important advances in logic, and was particularly interested in the collection and analysis of data in natural history and geology. The importance of empirical checking is frequently stressed in two of his surviving works, *Inquiry into plants* and *On the causes of plants*. His ethical theory seems to have been closely based on Aristotle. Theophrastus was no radical and can hardly have found Epicurean and Stoic views on man and society congenial. Epicurus wrote a book *Against Theophrastus*, the content of which is not known, and through the writings of Theophrastus and other Peripatetics the technical works of Aristotle, which he did not prepare for general circulation, must have become more widely known.

This last point is important. Some scholars have argued that Epicurus and Zeno could have read only Aristotle's 'published' literary works and not the technical treatises which form the bulk of the work which survives today. Strabo, writing in the early Roman empire, relates that after Theophrastus' death Aristotle's manuscripts were dispatched to a man called Neleus, who lived at Skepsis, a town near Pergamum in Asia Minor (xiii 1, 54). When Neleus himself died the books were hidden in a cellar, for reasons of security, only to be recovered and edited in the early first century B.C. Too much has been based on this curious story. It has been held to show that Aristotle's technical treatises were completely unknown for about two centuries. But the conclusion does not follow. It is difficult to believe that only one version of these works was available in Athens at the time of Theophrastus. That Epicurus and the early Stoics had some knowledge of Aristotle's principal doctrines is both a reasonable and, I think, a necessary assumption. Nor is it only an assumption. We have one piece of evidence which connects Epicurus by name with Aristotle's *Analytics* and a work on Nature (see p. 29). But the decline of the Lyceum from the middle of the third century B.C. makes it unlikely that much of Aristotle's technical philosophy was known during the next hundred and fifty years.[1]

Ever since Eduard Zeller wrote his monumental *Philosophie der Griechen* over a hundred years ago, many scholars have contrasted Hellenistic philosophy unfavourably with Plato and Aristotle. But by any standards the achievement of Plato and Aristotle is virtually without parallel in the history of western thought. In assessing Hellenistic philosophy we need to remember that little of Epicurus and no complete work by an early Greek Stoic have survived. Moreover our knowledge of Carneades' sceptical methodology is also derived from secondary sources. We know the broad outlines of early Stoicism and Epicureanism. The details and the arguments are often missing. Plato and Aristotle have a head-start over the Hellenistic philosophers in terms of work which we can evaluate today.

Much of our evidence comes from hand-books written centuries after the time of the early Stoics, Epicureans and Sceptics. The absence of so much first-hand evidence makes the study of these philosophers a very different enterprise from work on Plato and Aristotle. Considerable care must be taken over comparing and assessing different sources,

---

[1] Little is known about the Peripatetic philosophers at this time. Their activities seem to have centred largely upon rhetoric, biography and works of popular moralizing. Theophrastus himself wrote on such subjects as marriage, piety and drunkenness. For the ancient evidence see F. Wehrli, *Die Schule des Aristoteles* (Basel 1944–), a series of volumes on individual philosophers.

and this preparatory work, if it is allowed too much room in the presentation and analysis of the subject-matter, can easily make Hellenistic philosophy seem tedious, inaccessible and lacking in conceptual interest. This is a false impression. We can now see that Epicurus and Zeno were philosophers whose ideas evolved gradually as a considered reaction against theories in vogue at the end of the fourth century and earlier. It is also true that they felt passionately about the truth of their own theories and the implications of them for human well-being. The same might be said of Plato. But philosophy advances by criticism, and Epicurus and Zeno were critical of current dogmas concerning the structure of the physical world, the sources of knowledge, the nature of man and the grounds of his happiness. The Sceptics challenged the basis of all objective statements, and Carneades' criticism of the Stoics provides ample evidence of his sharp mind. We can argue about the merits of the alternative Stoic and Epicurean theories, but there is no justification for regarding them as a sudden impoverishment of Greek philosophy.

The Stoics and Epicureans however interpreted the scope of philosophy more narrowly and dogmatically than Aristotle, and by the middle of the first century B.C. onwards, which is the period of our earliest secondary sources, both schools had taken up entrenched positions. But two hundred and fifty years is a long time, and our loss of philosophical writing from this period is almost total. Possibly, as is often said, Epicurus' followers were largely content from early days to accept the teachings of their founder. They certainly revered him as the saviour of mankind, but we know of developments in Epicurean logic, to take only one example, which probably occurred long after his death. The Stoics, who have far more in common with Plato and Aristotle, were more self-critical than the Epicureans, and such leading figures as Chrysippus and Diogenes of Babylon elaborated logic and other subjects in great detail, turning Stoicism into a highly technical philosophy. Stoics and Epicureans criticized each other and were criticized in turn by the Academic Sceptics. But until the time of Panaetius and Posidonius, few very significant amendments to fundamental Stoic doctrines seem to have been made, and the extent of their modifications was less substantial than has sometimes been supposed. Perhaps the new Hellenistic systems were too successful in gaining popular support to channel the development of philosophy into new directions. The Academic Sceptics, who had no 'system' to defend, were very able critical philosophers, but their influence was naturally restricted and often negative. Stoicism and Epicureanism could be understood in a rudimentary sense by almost anyone, and they could also provide intellectual satisfaction for those who wanted more than a message. The early Academy and Lyceum were less flexible in terms of general appeal. They did not make the world intelligible in a manner which could be found satisfying at many different levels.

Both the Epicureans and the Stoics were prepared to popularize their teaching. In his *Letter to Herodotus*—the name refers to a friend, not the fifth-century historian—Epicurus opens by remarking that he has prepared an epitome of his philosophy for those unable to study his technical writings (D.L. x 35). He also compiled a set of ethical maxims which set out the cardinal doctrines and were learnt by heart. But within the school itself there were those like Epicurus himself who devoted their main energies to philosophy. The Stoics assigned a special place to what they called 'suasions and dissuasions', the purpose of which was moral advice. The serious student will have been expected to advance far beyond such things, much as Lucilius, in Seneca's *Moral letters*, is conducted from the rudiments of ethics to problems about the meaning of 'good'. Under Chrysippus a course at the Stoa must have included a considerable assignment of logic and natural philosophy.

We should not think of professional Stoics and Epicureans as men in whom freedom of thought had ossified. But they became the transmitters of doctrines which provided many people throughout the Hellenistic world with a set of attitudes that religion and political ideologies might also have supported. The decline of the Greek cities accelerated the decline of the Olympian gods. Stoics attempted to accommodate the Olympians by interpreting them as allegorical references to natural phenomena. The Epicureans denied the gods any influence over the world. Eastern religious ideas infiltrated into the Mediterranean world. Some embraced them; others chose Stoicism or Epicureanism instead. Stoic and Epicurean philosophers, particularly the latter, made it their business to win supporters, but the market was open to be developed. The price which they paid for entering it with such success was dogmatism, at least outwardly, and the divorce of philosophy from scientific research. Epicurus' attitude to science was naïve and reactionary. The Stoics defended out-of-date theories in astronomy and physiology against the new discoveries of Aristarchus and Erasistratus. The Sceptics were unsympathetic to science, and only

Posidonius in the later Hellenistic period made a serious effort at re-uniting philosophy with mathematics and other scientific studies.

But Epicurus and especially the Stoics were clearly interested in many problems for their own sake. The humanist focus of their philosophy is one of its most interesting features, and it leads to very different results in the two systems. In neither case is it narrowly moralistic because the ethical values of both philosophies are related to two fully developed, if divergent, conceptions of the universe.

In the period covered by this book philosophy became thoroughly institutionalized and practically synonymous with higher education. Epicureanism was the exception. For a brief period at the time of Lucretius and Julius Caesar, it was fashionable and influential in Rome. But it never achieved the public respectability of Stoicism. Philosophers were among the most eminent members of the community and some of the men who feature in this book were chosen to represent their cities as ambassadors. From the middle of the second century B.C., philosophers are found in Rome, but no school was permanently set up there. Some Romans during this period took up Hellenistic philosophy, but they made few original contributions to it. Most of the impetus and the ideas came from Athens and the eastern Mediterranean cities in which many of the Hellenistic philosophers were born.

CHAPTER TWO

Epicurus and Epicureanism

We must not make a pretence of doing philosophy, but really do it; for what we need is not the semblance of health but real health (Usener 220).

IT has often been said that Epicurus was primarily a moralist, and if by this we mean someone who strives by theory and practice to advocate a particular way of life the description is appropriate. Epicurus thought that he could trace the causes of human unhappiness to mistaken beliefs in his society, beliefs about the gods, the destiny of the soul, and the objects in life which are truly valuable. Ultimately all his teaching has the aim of discrediting such beliefs and replacing them with those which he holds to be true. By his adherents Epicurus was regarded as a 'saviour', as the bringer of 'light', words which we naturally associate with Judaism and Christianity. But Epicurus was not a preacher, even if he sometimes preaches. He wished ardently to persuade, and to convince; it would be quite wrong to try to make him into a purely academic philosopher. But he was a philosopher. Arguments and evidence are the instruments by which he hoped to persuade those who would listen, and it is with the theory rather than the practical aspects of Epicureanism that I shall be concerned here. Beginning, after some introductory remarks, with Epicurus' theory of knowledge I propose to consider the details of his system in an order which seems to be both coherent and representative of his own methodology. Ethics proper is dealt with last, for other topics have ethical implications which can be noted *en passant* and moral conclusions are the ultimate goal of Epicurus' philosophy.

(i) Life and works
Epicurus was born on the island of Samos in 341 B.C. (D.L. x 14). His father, who held Athenian citizenship, had settled there some ten years earlier. The first philosophical influence on Epicurus may have come in Samos itself from Pamphilus, a Platonist (Cic. *N.D.* i 72; D.L. x 14). But Epicurus' own philosophy is strikingly at odds with Platon-

ism, and perhaps while still an adolescent he began an association with Nausiphanes on the neighbouring island of Teos (Herculaneum papyrus 1005) which nipped in the bud any positive allegiance to Plato. Nausiphanes was a Democritean (D.L. i 15; Cic. *N.D.* i 73), and it is likely that Epicurus first became acquainted with the basic principles of atomism through the teaching of Nausiphanes. In later life Epicurus denounced Nausiphanes in highly vitriolic language (D.L. x 7–8). It is not clear what prompted these attacks, but they are typical of Epicurus' attested attitudes towards other philosophers.

At the age of eighteen Epicurus went to Athens to do his two years of military and civilian service alongside the comic poet Menander (Strabo xiv 638). We know little in detail of his activities during the next fifteen years. He may have taught for some time as an elementary school teacher in Colophon, a small town to the north-west of Samos on the Persian mainland, where his family had now taken up residence (D.L. x 1; 4). Later he established his own philosophical circle first in Mytilene (on Lesbos) and then in Lampsacus (D.L. x 15), a port near the site of ancient Troy, returning to Athens at the age of thirty-four in 307/6. Here he remained for the rest of his life. The return to Athens indicates that Epicurus was now confident of attracting followers in the main centre of philosophy. Between Athens and Piraeus Epicurus bought a house the garden of which came to stand as the name of the Epicurean school.

The community which Epicurus founded differed in important respects from the Academy and Lyceum. Its modern analogue is not a college or research institution but a society of friends living according to common principles, in retreat from civic life. Friendship has particular ethical significance in Epicureanism, and the Garden provided a setting for its realization. Women and slaves were admitted, and scraps of several private letters are preserved in which Epicurus expresses deep affection for his friends and followers. It is doubtful whether the Garden during Epicurus' lifetime offered much that might be called formal training to would-be Epicureans. Those who committed themselves to Epicurus were not so much students 'reading for a course' as men and women dedicated to a certain style of life. Seneca quotes the revealing maxim: 'Act always as if Epicurus is watching' (*Ep.* 25, 5). The similarity to George Orwell's 'Big brother is watching you' could scarcely be more misleading. Epicurus clearly inspired the strongest regard in his associates and personified the values of his own philosophy. But if the Garden lacked the formal curriculum of the Academy we can safely assume that its members devoted much time to reading and discussing Epicurus' books; his *Principal doctrines* (see below) were probably learnt by heart; some members must have been engaged in the preparation and copying of works both for internal consumption and for dissemination to Epicureans outside Athens; and Epicurus' chief adherents, such as Metrodorus, will have engaged in advanced study with the master himself.[1] Book xxviii of Epicurus' *On Nature* refers to Metrodorus in the second person, and the fragments which survive record parts of a discussion between the two philosophers on problems of language and theory of knowledge. Epicurus kept in touch with his followers outside Athens by correspondence, and the opening of his *Letter to Pythocles* is worth quoting for the attitudes it reveals of Epicurus himself and one of his disciples:

> Cleon brought me a letter from you in which you continue to show good-will towards me matching my own love for you. You are trying not ineffectively to memorize the arguments which are directed at a life of sublime happiness, and you ask me to send you a brief summary of the argument about astronomical phenomena so that you can easily get it by heart. For you find my other writings difficult to remember even though, as you say, you are always using them. I was delighted to receive your request and it caused me joyous expectations.[2]

Consistent with these principles Epicurus preferred the company of a few intimates to popular acclaim (Sen. *Ep.* 7, 11). He did not however withdraw completely from civic life. In a letter cited by Philodemus Epicurus says that he has participated in all the national festivals (Us. 169); his slogan 'live quietly' was not a revolutionary denunciation of contemporary society but a prescription for attaining tranquillity. Opponents of Epicureanism vilified the founder as a libertine and voluptuary, but this is inconsistent both with his teaching on pleasure, as we shall see, and with his own professed attitudes. He claimed to derive great pleasure from a subsistence diet which cheese would turn into a feast (Us. 181f.). On his death in 271 B.C., Epicurus bequeathed his house and garden to his follower, Hermarchus, for the benefit of the Epicurean community, and succeeding heads of the school probably nominated their own successor. On the twentieth of

[1] Epicurus probably first encountered Metrodorus, his junior by about ten years, at Lampsachus, the latter's native town.

[2] The authenticity of this letter has been questioned, but there is no reason to doubt its reliability as a statement of Epicurus' attitudes and doctrine.

every month Epicurus' memory and that of Metrodorus were celebrated at a festival within the Garden. This and other arrangements which are recorded in Epicurus' will (D.L. x 16–21) throw an interesting light on the character of the man himself.

Epicureanism has rightly been called 'the only missionary philosophy produced by the Greeks'.[1] Before he took up residence at Athens, Epicurus had established a following in Lampsachus and Mytilene, and his disciples helped to propagate the Epicurean gospel throughout the Mediterranean world. Antioch and Alexandria are two major cities in which Epicureanism established itself at an early date. Later, it spread widely into Italy and Gaul. Cicero in the middle of the first century B.C. could write, and it gave him no pleasure to do so, 'The [Roman] Epicureans by their writings have seized the whole of Italy' (*Tusc.* iv 6–7). This was a time when Epicureanism briefly claimed the allegiance of some prominent Romans including Calpurnius Piso and Cassius. Julius Caesar may have been sympathetic and Cicero's Atticus was an Epicurean. The fortunes of the movement fluctuated. Political opposition was not unknown, but the main antagonists were first rival philosophers, especially Stoics, and later Christianity.

In the Roman world Epicureanism seems to have been at its strongest immediately before the fall of the Republic. But it suffered no sudden decline. Seneca quotes with approval many Epicurean moral maxims; Lucian's *Alexander*, written in the second century A.D., gives a fascinating account of Epicurean and Christian reactions to persecution in the area south of the Black Sea. And most remarkable of all, about A.D. 200 in the interior of modern Turkey, at a place called Oenoanda in antiquity, an old man named Diogenes had erected a huge philosophical inscription carved on a great stone wall. Between 1884 and the present day many fragments of his work have been recovered, and it constitutes a summary of Epicurus' teaching which Diogenes bestowed on his countrymen and humanity at large for their happiness.[2] Apart from adding valuable information to our knowledge of Epicureanism, Diogenes' inscription proves the vitality of Epicurus' gospel five hundred years after the foundation of the Garden.

Epicurus himself was a prolific writer. Diogenes Laertius, who records forty-one titles of Epicurus' 'best books', says that his writings

[1] N. W. De Witt, *Epicurus and his Philosophy* (Minneapolis 1954) p. 329. The last chapter of this book should be consulted for a survey of the later fortunes of Epicureanism.
[2] For the evidence see Bibliography.

ran to three hundred rolls (x 26), and that he exceeded all previous writers 'in the number of his books'. Many of these consisted of short popular tracts and letters. Epicurus' major work was the series of thirty-seven books *On Nature*, a treatise *On the criterion* or *kanôn*, and a collection of ethical books which included *On lives*; *On the goal*; *On choice and avoidance*. He also wrote polemical works *Against the physicists*, *Against the Megarians*, and *Against Theophrastus*. Many of the letters, as we know from our own evidence, summarized points of doctrine or discussed these in some detail. Of all this writing only a small fraction has survived. Three letters are preserved which Diogenes Laertius included in his Life of Epicurus. The longest and most important of these, *To Herodotus*, gives a compressed and difficult summary of the main principles of atomism. Astronomical phenomena are the subject of the *Letter to Pythocles*, and the third letter, *To Menoeceus*, presents a clear if somewhat over-simplified account of Epicurean moral theory. In addition to these letters, Diogenes gives us a collection of forty *Kuriai doxai*, 'Principal doctrines', and a further set of maxims (*Vaticanae sententiae*) survives in a Vatican manuscript. Excavation at Herculaneum during the eighteenth century brought to light many charred rolls of papyrus which originally formed the library of some wealthy Roman. He was probably an adherent of Epicureanism, since most of the papyri which have been unrolled and read are fragmentary works by Philodemus of Gadara, an Epicurean philosopher and poet contemporary with Cicero. The rolls also contain fragments of some of the books of Epicurus *On Nature*. These are formidably difficult to read and reconstruct, but an invaluable supplement to earlier knowledge. Much work remains to be done on them.[1]

For our information about details of Epicurus' doctrine we are heavily dependent upon secondary sources. The most important of these is the Roman poet Lucretius, who wrote more than two hundred years after Epicurus' death. It is perhaps misleading to describe Lucretius as a secondary source. His poem, *De rerum natura*, is a work of genius which preceded the *Aeneid* and challenges it as a literary masterpiece. Lucretius, whose life and character are virtually unknown to us, was a fervid proponent of Epicureanism who presents Epicurus' teaching as the only source of human salvation. But Lucretius is no

[1] Nearly all the Herculaneum papyri belong to the Biblioteca Nazionale of Naples; but the British Museum has substantial fragments of Epicurus *On Nature* Book ii.

mere panegyrist. His six books set out in great detail Epicurean arguments concerning the basic constituents of things, the movement of atoms, the structure of body and mind, the causes and nature of sensation and thought, the development of human culture, and natural phenomena. At the same time, there is no reason to regard Lucretius himself as an original thinker. His work amplifies and explains points that we can find in Epicurus' own writings. Even where Lucretius reports theories, for instance the swerve of atoms (ii 216–93), which cannot be checked against Epicurus' own words, he was probably drawing on original sources which we cannot recover. Epicurus' own immediate successors were not noted for any major innovations. Certain refinements were doubtless made, and Philodemus' treatise *On signs* (preserved partially on papyrus) incorporates logical work by Zeno of Sidon (*c.* 150–70 B.C.) which may well go beyond anything worked out by Epicurus himself. But for the most part Epicurus' own writings remained canonical throughout the history of the school.

After Lucretius the best secondary sources are Diogenes Laertius, Cicero, Seneca and Plutarch. Cicero and Plutarch intensely disliked Epicureanism, and their criticism is of interest for understanding the adverse reception which the school often encountered. Seneca, though officially a Stoic, concludes most of his first *Moral letters* with an Epicurean maxim which he recommends to his correspondent, Lucilius. Sextus Empiricus, to whom Epicureanism was the most congenial of the dogmatic schools of philosophy, provides a useful supplement to our direct knowledge of Epicurean empiricism. Finally, as I have already mentioned, we have substantial fragments from the inscription of Diogenes of Oenoanda.

(ii) The scope of Epicurus' philosophy
Epicurus' philosophy is a strange mixture of hard-headed empiricism, speculative metaphysics and rules for the attainment of a tranquil life. There are links between these aspects of his thought, some of which are clearer than others. But one thing which certainly unites them is Epicurus' concern to set the evidence of immediate sensation and feeling against the kind of logical analysis which is characteristic of Platonic and Aristotelian methodology. Epicurus rejected many of the fundamental principles in terms of which Plato and Aristotle described the world. But more important than his disagreement concerning what is to be said about the world is his dismissal of certain logical and metaphysical concepts which are basic to Plato and Aristotle.

Epicurus recognized the distinction between universal and particular; but he did not regard universals as having existence in their own right, like Plato; nor apparently was he interested, as Aristotle had been, in classifying things under genera and species. He did not set up principles such as Plato's *same* and *different*, or Aristotle's *substrate* and *form*, for the analysis of objects and their properties. Philosophers who proceed in this way, he held, are merely playing with words, setting up empty assumptions and arbitrary rules. He did not deny that philosophy uses language and logic as its tools (Us. 219). But he vehemently rejected the view that linguistic analysis by itself can tell us anything about the world which is true or relevant to a happy life. The value of words is to express those concepts which are clearly derived from sensations and feelings. These latter give us our only hold on facts and the only secure foundation for language.

One might suppose from this that Epicurus would have dispensed with metaphysics altogether. In fact, his account of what exists does not stop short at the objects of which we are made aware by immediate sensations and feelings. Our senses report to us things which we call sheep, grass, cats etc., but for Epicurus all such things are compounded out of atoms and void, neither of which is something that we can sense or feel. In asserting atoms and void to be the ultimate entities which constitute the world, Epicurus is making a metaphysical statement. This is not something which he can prove or verify directly from sensations with or without the help of experiment. He has to establish it by setting up certain axioms and assuming the validity of certain methods of inference.

The first atomist explanation of things was advanced more than a century before Epicurus began his philosophical career. Epicurus clearly believed it to be a theory for which he could offer new and improved proof. But while providing an elegant and economical answer to such questions as 'What is the structure of physical objects?' or 'How are bodies able to move?', the atomist theory attracted Epicurus on other than purely theoretical grounds. If all events and all substances are ultimately explicable by reference to atoms necessarily moving in empty space, both divine causation as popularly conceived and its sophisticated equivalents—Plato's Forms and Demiurge or World-Soul, Aristotle's Prime Mover and Heavenly Intelligences—become superfluous. Epicurus held that beliefs in divine management of the cosmos and of human destiny were a major cause of human failure to live a tranquil life. On an atomist analysis of the world, supposing this to be demonstrable, consequences would follow which could not fail to affect beliefs about a man's own place in the world.

Epicurus often asserts that philosophy has no value unless it helps men to attain happiness. This applies with particular force to his moral theory, but there is no necessary connexion between atomism and hedonism. The claim that pleasure is the only thing which is good as an end is compatible with all manner of metaphysical hypotheses. Epicurus has various ways of establishing his hedonism, none of which draws direct support from atoms and void. In this he differs markedly from the Stoics whose moral theory is intrinsically related to their metaphysics. But Epicurus thought he could show the validity of hedonism by appeal to immediate experience which, less directly, he held to support atomism. If labels can be usefully applied to a philosopher, Epicurus should be called an empiricist. That at least is what he would like to be remembered as, and empiricism provides the clearest internal connexion between his different ideas.

(iii) *Theory of knowledge*

If you fight against all sensations, you will have nothing by reference to which you can judge even those which you say are deceptive (*K.D.* xxiii).

The foundation of Epicurus' theory of knowledge is sense-perception. He starts from the fact that all men have sensations (*aisthêseis*), and asserts, without proof, that these must be caused by something other than themselves (D.L. x 31). It does not of course follow from this assertion that sensations are caused by things external to the percipient, and Epicurus would acknowledge that a feeling such as hunger (a *pathos* in his terminology) has an internal cause. But he takes it as self-evident that sensations of colour, sound, smell etc. must be caused by actual objects which possess these properties. 'We must suppose that it is when something enters us from things which are external that we perceive . . . their shapes' (*Ep. Hdt.* 49). This statement at once raises questions which the Sceptics did not hesitate to ask about mirages, hallucinations and the like. But Epicurus has an answer to put forward, as we shall see later.

Suppose we accept that sensations cannot lie concerning their causes: in other words, that if I have the sensation of hearing there must be something sounding which causes my sensation. Does this support the further proposition that there is some object like a motor-car horn or a train whistle which corresponds precisely to the content of my sensation? For Epicurus the inference may or may not be warranted. That about which our sensations cannot deceive us is not a motor-car horn but a sense-impression (*phantasia*). What enters me from things outside is not a motor-car horn, if that is what I do genuinely hear, but a cluster of atoms (*eidôla*) thrown off the outer surface of such objects. Provided that these 'effluences', as we may call them, enter the sense organ without experiencing any change of structure the impression they produce on us will be an accurate image of the object.[1] If on the other hand their structure is disrupted in transit, the effluences will cause us to sense something which corresponds not to some actual characteristic of the object itself but to their own modified structure.

Sensations therefore are necessarily good evidence only of effluences. This raises the problem of how we can distinguish between those sensations which report to us accurately about objects and those which do not. For we cannot get at objects independently of effluences. Epicurus tackles this problem in an interesting way. He distinguishes sharply between the sense-impression itself and judgments, or the identification of sense-impressions with objects (*Ep. Hdt.* 50–1). Our sense-impressions are not judgments, nor are they dependent upon reason. We are not to say that this sense-impression is reliable, that one untrustworthy, for to do so presupposes an object which can test the validity of sensation, and our sole knowledge of objects is derived from sensations. Considered as an item of information about that which affects our senses every impression is of equal validity (D.L. x 31–2).

Nevertheless, sense-impressions can be distinguished from one another in terms of clarity or vividness. Sounds may be sharp or faint, visual images both clear and blurred. Epicurus was also aware of the fact that as we move away from the apparent source of many sensations our impressions change, and may decrease in clarity. Putting these facts together he concluded that sensations provide reliable evidence about objects if and only if they are characterized by clear and distinct impressions (*enargeia, Ep. Hdt.* 52, cf. *K.D.* xxiv). Other impressions 'await confirmation' by those which are clear. This conclusion could also seem to derive some support from Epicurus' explanation of the physical processes by which sensation takes place.

---

[1] Epicurus did not invent the 'effluence' theory of sense-perception. It goes back to Democritus and still earlier, in a different form, to Empedocles.

If we are near the ultimate source of our sensations the effluences which affect us are less likely to encounter disruption. It is only from a distance, supposedly, that the tower which is square looks round (Us. 247).

Epicurus does not specify conditions which establish the clarity of a sense-impression. He probably regarded this as something which would entail an infinite regress. He could take it as a datum of experience that we do distinguish within limits between that which is clear and that which is blurred or obscure. Clarity however is not a sufficient guarantee that we see things as they really are. Epicurus was grossly misled by 'clear views' when he argued that the sun is about the same size as it is seen to be (*Ep. Pyth.* 91).

Close attention to clear impressions is the first stage in acquiring knowledge. But Epicurus did not regard it as sufficient by itself. However clear our sense-impressions may be they do not constitute knowledge. They do not tell us what something is. Before judgments about objects can be made, our sense-impressions must be classified, labelled and so marked off from one another. Epicurus proposed to satisfy these conditions by what he called *prolépseis*, 'preconceptions'.[1] These are general concepts or mental pictures produced by repeated sense-impressions which are both clear and similar in kind. They persist after particular sensations cease and constitute a record of our experience of the world. We acquire a concept or *prolépsis* of man by repeated and remembered experience of particular men. Hence we are able to interpret new sensations by comparing them with preconceptions, and all our judgments about objects are made on this basis of recorded experiences, which we classify by using language (D.L. x 33). Epicurus agreed broadly with Aristotle who asserted that 'science comes to be when out of many ideas born of experience a general concept which is universal arises concerning things that are similar' (*Met.* A 981a5 ff.). For Epicurus, preconceptions are the foundations of judgments and language. 'We should not have named anything unless we had previously learnt its form by a preconception' (D.L. ibid.). Language is a method of signifying those preconceptions which seem to us to fit the present object of experience. Because preconceptions themselves are supposed to possess 'clarity', they establish, in association with the appropriate new sense-impressions, what it is that we see,

---

[1] Cicero (*N.D.* i 44) says that Epicurus was the first to use the word *prolépsis* in this sense.

hear and so on.[1] Error arises when we use words which signify a preconception that does not correspond with the phenomenon (*De nat.* xxviii fr. iv col. 3). This may happen through confusing unclear with clear impressions, and Epicurus also recognized that the ambiguity of many words can be a cause of misassociating sense-impressions and preconceptions.[2]

Epicurus probably thought that all other concepts, including those which have no empirical reference, are derived from preconceptions. Preconceptions can be combined with one another, or they can be used as a basis for inference (see D.L. x 32). But, with a few exceptions, preconceptions seem to be direct derivatives of sensation, and Epicurus recommended that the meaning of words should always be established by reference to 'the first mental image' (*Ep. Hdt.* 37). In this way he hoped to forge a firm bond between statements and immediate experience, though he gave no sufficient reasons why people's preconceptions should be regarded as similar and therefore identifiable by the same words.

So far Epicurus can claim to be a rigorous empiricist. But we must now note a number of curious exceptions to the principle that our ideas about the world are all derived ultimately from sense-impressions. Apart from those effluences which cause our sense-impressions, Epicurus also supposed that there are 'images' which somehow bypass the sense organs and penetrate directly to the mind. In nature these too are atomic clusters, but their density is much finer than the effluences which affect our senses. They are *tenuia simulacra*, as Lucretius called them (iv 722ff.), and account both for dream-images, phantoms, visions of the dead, and for such ordinary objects of thought as lions. Such 'images' may be direct effluences from the surface of an object. But many of them are simply chance combinations of individual atoms; others may consist of real effluences which are compounded and then produce images of Centaurs and monsters (*Ep. Hdt.* 48; Lucret. iv 130–42). Instead of accounting for dreams and hallucinations by reference to images entirely created or brought to consciousness by some psychological faculty, Epicurus supposed that dreams and hallucinations too are explicable by the mind's contact with atoms that enter it from outside.

[1] Clement of Alexandria (Us. 255) reports Epicurus as saying that 'it is impossible for anyone to investigate . . . or to form a judgment . . . independently of preconception'.

[2] For further evidence and discussion see my article in *Bulletin of the Institute of Classical Studies* 18 (1971) 114–33.

If we ask how dreams and visions are to be distinguished from sense-impressions, the answer is not entirely clear. Lucretius looks for a distinction in terms of continuity. 'Real' sense-impressions are produced by a steady stream of effluences; but the mind can be moved by a single 'image' (iv 746), and thus presumably catch a momentary vision. Also, dream-images are said to move by a series of effluences perishing one after another; Lucretius' description makes one think of the staccato movement of early cinema. Clearly such criteria are inadequate for Epicurus' purpose. In effect he is saying that a hallucinated person really does see something which is there, but mistakenly takes it to correspond with an actual solid object (cf. Us. 253).

The gods are a further object of direct mental perception. Postponing for the present consideration of their physical structure, we may observe here that Epicurus posits a series of fine effluences from the gods which penetrate directly to the mind. The texts which describe these divine 'images' are difficult; Epicurus put forward theoretical reasons, as well as the evidence of such visions, to justify his claims about the divine nature (Cic. *N.D.* i 43–55). But he seems to have given no adequate arguments in favour of divine 'images'. It is no help to this queer thesis to invoke the supposed universality of human belief in gods. The real difficulty is however that of the grounds for verification. By the concept of 'clear' view Epicurus has a standard for verifying perceptual judgments which has some claims to be called objective. Only in a special philosophical sense could people's perception of dogs be said to depend on their beliefs. How we may conceive of gods, on the other hand, is something which cannot be assimilated to perception of empirical objects. Epicurus' theory of divine 'images' puts religious belief in the same category as empirical observation.

Some scholars have argued that Epicurus posited a special mental faculty, 'apprehension by intellect' (*epibolê tês dianoias*), which somehow guarantees the veracity both of impressions of the gods and the validity of scientific concepts. If Epicurus had held such a theory he would have been an intuitionist in much of his philosophical activity. This interpretation was defended at great length by Cyril Bailey, whose work on Epicurus and Lucretius has held authority in the English-speaking world. According to Bailey, Epicurus supposed that the 'clear' sense-impression, of which I have already spoken, is obtained by the 'attention of the senses', and correspondingly, clear visions of the gods and clear concepts concerning, for instance, atoms and void,

are obtained by the 'attention' of the mind. If Bailey were merely
arguing that we cannot be aware of any object or thought unless we
'attend' to something, he would be ascribing nothing remarkable to
Epicurus. But Bailey meant much more than this. On his interpretation, Epicurus supposes that 'the concepts of science are built up
step by step by the juxtaposition of previous concepts, each in their
turn grasped as "clear"... by the immediate apprehension of the mind'.[1]

Epicurus' use of the expression 'apprehension by intellect' does not
justify Bailey's view. Any explanation of Epicurus as an intuitionist
is on quite the wrong tack. Probably what he means by 'apprehension',
whether by the mind or the senses, is concentration or attention: we
need to concentrate, if we are to grasp the images which can be received
by the sense organs or the mind. I shall return to this subject in the
discussion of Epicurean psychology (p. 56).

In order to use the evidence of the senses as material for establishing
true propositions about the world, Epicurus assumed the validity of
certain axioms. One of these has been stated already: 'Sense-impressions
which are "clear" provide accurate information about the external
appearance and properties of objects.'[2] These sense-impressions
confirm or *bear witness against* the truth of judgments about objects
which we may make provisionally on evidence lacking the requisite
clarity. But Epicurus also allowed a weaker form of confirmation, 'lack
of contrary evidence'. And this we may state as a further axiom:
'Judgments about non-evident objects are true if they are consistent
with clear sense-impressions.' This second axiom is of the utmost
importance to Epicurus. If positive confirmation by clear impressions
were the sole ground for true objective statements, Epicurus would be
unable to advance beyond the description of sensible objects. As it
is, he assumes that the validity of clear impressions is such that they
provide indirect evidence of things which are imperceptible, or for
which a clear view is unobtainable in the nature of the case. Here is an
example preserved by Sextus Empiricus (cited n. 21): If void does not
exist (something non-evident) then motion should not exist since *ex
hypothesi* all things are full and dense; so that since motion does exist
the apparent does not contradict the judgment about that which is
non-evident. (As stated, of course, the argument is invalid since it

---

[1] *The Greek Atomists and Epicurus* (Oxford 1928) p. 570.
[2] Formal statements of these 'axioms' are to be found in Sextus Empiricus,
Adv. math. vii 212–13 (Us. 247). Epicurus writes of them more informally in
Ep. Hdt. 51 and *K.D.* xxiv.

assumes that void is a necessary condition of movement, having full-ness as its contradictory.)

Epicurus associates the axiom concerning non-contradiction with a further proposition (*X*), which may be treated as an implication of the second axiom: If more than one explanation of non-evident phenomena is consistent with observation then all such explanations are to be treated as equally valid (*Ep. Pyth.* 87). Let us state this more formally. Suppose that *p* is an evident fact, *q* a problem requiring explanation which cannot be solved directly by reference to *p*, and *s, t, u* three different statements about *q* which are all consistent with *p*. Then, independently of any other criterion or axiom, it follows from pro-position *X* that *s, t,* and *u* are all equally acceptable explanations. This argument is formally valid, and Epicurus applied it rigorously to all statements concerning astronomical phenomena. In order to reject any of the hypotheses *s, t* and *u* it would be necessary to introduce some further principle of verification over and above the second axiom. Epicurus declined to do this on the grounds that it would be a depar-ture from that which is definitely knowable, that is, the state of objects as given by clear sense-impressions.

Epicurus applies this principle regularly in the *Letter to Pythocles*, as the following excerpt shows (94):

The repeated waning and waxing of the moon may come about owing to the rotation of this celestial body; equally it may be due to configurations of air; or again by reason of the interposition of other bodies; it may happen in any of the ways in which things manifest to us invite us to account for this phenomenon, provided that one does not become so attached to a single explanation that one rules out others for no good reason, failing to consider what it is possible for a man to observe and what impossible, and therefore desiring to discover the indiscoverable.

Up to a point this is admirable as a scientific principle. One thinks of the current debate concerning different explanations of the origin of the universe (big bang, steady state etc.) which has not yet been resolved by empirical data. Epicurus could argue, with considerable justification, that the astronomy of his own day claimed to know more than its source of evidence, the naked eye, justified. What he seems to have wholly failed to appreciate is the valid check on immediate observations which some astronomers were already trying to make by reference to systematic records and by mathematical calculations.

In application to celestial phenomena, Epicurus' use of the axiom of non-contradiction has the largely negative function of leaving open a plurality of possible explanations. But the Epicureans used the principle positively as grounds to support general statements arrived at by induction. Philodemus records this example: from the proposition 'Men in our experience are mortal' we infer that 'men everywhere are mortal'. The general statement is based on the empirical fact that we know no exception to it *and therefore* it is consistent with experience (*On signs* col. xvi). The Stoics objected to this kind of reasoning on the grounds that it presupposes the non-evident (unobserved men) to be similar in kind to the evident. The Epicureans replied that their inference does not make a presupposition that all men are mortal. It is the absence of any man known to be immortal which justifies the general inference about human mortality.

Epicurus assumes, as any scientist must, that there are certain uniformities in nature which hold for what is evident and non-evident alike. Of course, it does not follow by the second axiom that a proposition which is consistent with some evident phenomenon *must* also be true concerning something non-evident. But science cannot operate merely by propositions which are necessarily true. It must proceed by empirical generalizations which are rejected as and when new evidence refutes previous hypotheses. The Stoics held that all inferences must be established by arguments which are deductively valid. But deductive reasoning by itself can never be sufficient to establish a scientific statement. For the premises which entail a deductive conclusion about observable data must either be empirical generalizations, or be ultimately based upon statements of this form. At some point the scientist must make an inductive inference on the basis of evidence, and for Epicurus that point is reached when observation seems to support the belief that no instances are likely to be found which will contradict a general statement.

Epicurus and Lucretius often appeal to 'analogy' or 'similarity' to support an inference from the visible to the invisible. Thus Epicurus takes the (allegedly) observed fact that no parts can be distinguished in the smallest visible magnitude to support the inference that the same is true of the smallest invisible magnitude, the minimum part of an atom (*Ep. Hdt.* 58f.). The main subject of Philodemus' *On signs* is 'analogical inference', and we might suppose that this requires a further axiom for its justification. None of our secondary sources nor Epicurus himself gives any independent discussion of 'analogy', and it is not needed. The justification for inference by analogy is provided by the two axioms already discussed.[1] By the first axiom we are justified in asserting that 'clear impressions' give evidence that men are mortal. All the men of whom we have reliable experience are similar in respect of mortality. From this positive evidence Epicurus infers that men of whom we have no experience are equally similar in respect of mortality. The inference is justified by the second axiom which allows us to assert *p* if there is no evidence against it. Philodemus even states that it is 'inconceivable' that there should be something which possesses nothing in common with empirical evidence (*On signs* col. xxi 27ff.). The Epicurean test of the 'conceivable' is sense-perception and the problematic mental 'images' already discussed (p. 24).

Epicurus' method of indirect proof can be illustrated by copious passages from Lucretius. It is the poet's regular practice to refute a proposition by appeal to what is clear, what we actually see, and thus infer the contradictory of the rejected proposition. I give just one example. In Book i Lucretius argues towards the atomist thesis by stages. He begins by dismissing the proposition 'Something can be created from nothing'. For, if this were so, every type of thing could be produced out of anything; nothing would require a seed. But we see (*videmus*) that cultivated land produces better yield than uncultivated land, which proves the existence in the soil of primary bodies stirred to birth by the plough. 'If there were no primary bodies you would see (*videres*) each thing coming to birth much more successfully of its own accord' (159–214).

Like this Lucretian argument Epicurus' methodology seems imprecise and informal when judged by the criteria of stricter logic. I have no doubt that it is proper to describe as 'axioms' the two principles concerning confirmation and non-contradiction. But Epicurus does not *call* them axioms. He almost certainly knew Aristotle's *Analytics*, if a fragment of Philodemus has been correctly deciphered.[2] But although Aristotle's inductive methodology may have been an influence on Epicurus, the later philosopher did not share Aristotle's interest in logic for its own sake; and he seems to have thought that any kind of demonstrative science, based upon deductive reasoning, was mere word-play. Since most of Aristotle's *Analytics* is concerned with the analysis of deductive argument in the form of syllogisms and

---

[1] See Philodemus, *On signs* col. xvi ed. Ph. and E. A. De Lacey (Pennsylvania 1941).
[2] *Adversus sophistas* frs. 1, 3 ed. Sbordone (Naples 1947).

with specifying the sufficient conditions of necessary truths, Epicurus cannot have liked what he read. Above all, he rejected any kind of logical inquiry which was not applied to the understanding of empirical data. He did not, apparently, see that empirical science, if it is to be well-grounded, cannot advance very far solely on the guidance of 'clear' sense-impressions.

The reader will be able to extend the criticism of Epicurus' methodology for himself. What should be added is a warning against taking at face value off-hand remarks in ancient writers, which would imply that Epicurus had no interest in logic and scientific method. These views are to be found in many modern hand-books and they are incorrect. Epicurus, in order to shock, sometimes writes as if he despised all learning; but this is rhetoric, an expression of contempt for what he regarded as pedantic and positively harmful in the culture of his own day. Fortunately, sufficient of the twenty-eighth book of *On Nature* survives to give us a glimpse of Epicurus when he is not merely summarizing or exhorting. In this work Epicurus discussed induction, using Aristotle's technical term *epagôgê*, problems of meaning and ambiguity, the distinction between universal and particular, problems connected with the designation of individuals, and linguistic puzzles of the sort propounded by the Megarians. Unfortunately the text is too badly damaged to let us see how he treated all of these subjects in detail.[1] But it gives us sufficient evidence to judge that parts of the following statement by Cicero are grossly misleading: 'Epicurus rejects definitions [he did not]; gives no instruction concerning division [classification into genus and species]; fails to show how an argument is to be constructed; does not point out how sophisms are to be resolved nor how ambiguities are to be distinguished' (*Fin.* i 22). It is salutary to remember that Epicurus wrote thirty-seven books *On Nature*, and that we can observe Cicero's prejudice by studying fragments from just one of these.

(iv) The structure of things

The nature of the universe is bodies and void (*On Nature* i).

Epicurus claimed to be self-taught, but atomism was more than a century old in Greece by the time he re-asserted its central principles. First Leucippus and then Democritus, in the second half of the fifth century, had argued that what really exists is ultimately reducible to

[1] For more details see the article cited in n. 2, p .24.

two and only two kinds of thing: the full (indivisible bodies) and the empty (space). How such a thesis came to be propounded is itself a fascinating story, but it belongs to the history of Presocratic philosophy. I will touch on it here only in so far as it is essential to understanding Epicurus' atomism.

Our starting-point is once again the *Letter to Herodotus*. There, in a few paragraphs of highly succinct argumentation, Epicurus discloses the essential features of the atomist theory (38–44). The problem which that theory purports to solve may be stated as follows: What principles derived from empirical evidence are necessary and sufficient to account for the physical world as it presents itself to our senses? The answer is highly economical: an infinite number of indivisible bodies moving in infinite empty space.

Epicurus arrives at this answer by a series of metaphysical propositions, which he then uses to support inferences about the underlying structure of the changing objects of experience. (A) Nothing can come out of nothing. (B) Nothing can be destroyed into nothing. (C) The universe never was nor will be in a condition which differs from its present one.[1] The first two propositions are established indirectly by what I have called the second axiom. It would controvert experience to suppose that nothing pre-exists or survives the objects which we observe to grow and decay. Things are seen to grow *out of* something; they do not just emerge at random. Secondly, there *is* something *into* which things pass away. Otherwise there would be no limit to destruction and everything would have perished into non-being. The third proposition (C) is treated by Epicurus as analytic. Since the universe embraces all that there is, nothing exists outside the universe which could cause it to change. (He does not consider the possibility that any internal cause of change might bring about different conditions of the universe as a whole at different times.)

From (C) it follows that any explanation of things in general which holds now is eternally valid.

It is an evident fact that bodies exist; empty space must therefore also exist, since bodies must be *in* something and have something through which to move.[2] Epicurus next asserts that apart from bodies and void nothing can be conceived of as an independent entity: all

---

[1] Lucretius develops (A) and (B) at length, i 159–264; he deals with (C) at ii 294–307.

[2] For Lucretius' arguments concerning void, see i 329–97. Aristotle denied the necessity of void to explain motion, as did the Stoics.

things must be reducible to body and mind. Bodies are of two kinds, compounds and the units out of which compounds are formed. From (B) it follows that one class of bodies, non-compounds, must be limited with respect to change and destruction. Epicurus expresses this thus: 'And these bodies [*sc.* non-compounds] are indivisible and changeless, if all things are not to be destroyed into *non*-being but are to persist secure in the dissolution of compounds; they are solid in nature and cannot be divided at any place or in any manner. Hence the first principles must be bodies which are indivisible' (*Ep. Hdt.* 39–41).

Question-begging though this argument is, in Epicurus' abbreviated formulation, its main points are wholly clear. We do not see atoms, but what we see, birth and death, growth and decay, is taken to require the existence of bodies which are themselves changeless and wholly impenetrable.

What else is to be said about atoms and empty space? Epicurus proceeds to argue that the universe is 'unlimited' in itself and also in the number of atoms which it contains, and in the extent of empty space. If the universe were limited it would have extremities; but there is nothing to limit the universe. And if the universe itself is unlimited its constituents must also be unlimited. For a limited number of atoms in infinite empty space would not be sufficient to hold one another together; they could not form the plurality of compounds which we experience; and an unlimited number of atoms could not be accommodated in limited space (*Ep. Hdt.* 41–2).

Since all the objects of experience are compounded out of atoms and void, Epicurus held that the atoms themselves must have innumerable, though not infinitely, different shapes, in order to account for the variety of things. Besides shape, all atoms are necessarily subject to continuous movement, a fact which will require further discussion shortly. They also possess weight, and of course bulk or mass. All other properties of which we have experience are accounted for by the arrangements which come into being when a plurality of atoms and void combine. Atoms as such are not hot or cold, coloured or resonant, and so forth (*Ep. Hdt.* 42–4; 68–9).

It is now time to consider in more detail what Epicurus meant by the 'indivisibility' of the atom. As has been shown already, the concept of an atom is arrived at by elimination of a contradictory hypothesis, that bodies are ultimately divisible into *non*-being. If Epicurus supposed that the infinite divisibility of a body must lead to its reduction to nothing at all he was guilty of an elementary fallacy. Infinite divisibility implies nothing about reduction to sheer non-existence. Lucretius however sets out an argument for indivisible bodies which avoids this fallacy, and which, we may presume, goes back to Epicurus himself.

The argument runs thus: body and empty space are mutually exclusive, otherwise there would not be *two* kinds of real things (i.e. all things could be reduced to either body or empty space). Body therefore cannot include as part of itself empty space. Anything which does include as part of itself empty space must be bounded by that which is solid—body. Created things are of this kind, that is, compounds of body and empty space. But the particular bodies which help to form such compounds must consist of that which is wholly solid and indivisible. For nothing can be divided unless it contains within itself empty space. And nothing can contain within itself empty space unless it has components which are themselves wholly indivisible (Lucret. i 503–35).

The force of this argument turns on the assumption that empty space is a necessary condition of divisibility. The earlier atomists had spoken of empty space as '*non*-being' and of body as 'being': empty space is non-body. If we take Epicurus' reference to *non*-being as a legacy of this earlier usage his argument becomes compatible with the passage summarized from Lucretius. Just as what-is cannot be ultimately reduced to what-is-not, so body cannot be reduced to non-body, i.e. empty space.

The Epicurean atoms cannot be split into smaller bodies. They are physically indivisible. But they are not the smallest units of extension. The atom itself consists of minimal parts which are not merely physically unsplittable but indivisible in thought: nothing beyond these *minima* can be conceived of. Epicurus supposed that there is a finite number of such minimal parts for every atom. Atoms vary in size, and their size is determined by the number of their minimal parts. Again, atoms vary in shape and their shape is determined by the arrangement of their minimal parts.

This doctrine of minimal parts raises many difficulties and will only be discussed briefly here. Epicurus apparently regarded each atom as something composed of minimum units of magnitude which are not separable from one another, and therefore not separable from the whole atom which they compose (*Ep. Hdt.* 56–9).[1] The notion is obscure and may be clarified by a concrete analogy. Suppose we take a

---

[1] See also Lucretius i 599–634.

cubic centimetre of solid metal and mark it off in three dimensions by millimetres. Then, the minimal parts stand to the atom as each cubic millimetre to the whole cube of metal, with this proviso: each square millimetre must be taken as the smallest unit which can be distinguished on any surface of the whole cube. The Epicurean atom is the smallest magnitude which can exist as a discrete independent body. Epicurus seems to have thought that this left something to be accounted for—namely, the atom's boundary points, or the fact, to put it another way, that the atom is a three-dimensional object and as such possesses shape. He sought an explanation by reference to its having minimal parts.

In giving the atoms minimal parts Epicurus almost certainly modified earlier atomism. The atoms of Leucippus and Democritus were physically indivisible but also, in all probability, without parts, and therefore theoretically indivisible as well. Simplicius, the Aristotelian commentator, distinguishes Epicurus from the earlier atomists thus: Epicurus, he says, appealed merely to the changelessness of his primary bodies, whereas Leucippus and Democritus also referred to their smallness and lack of parts (Us. 268).

Our knowledge of early atomism is largely derived from Aristotle. Modern research has shown that he was right to connect the fifth-century atomists with the slightly older Eleatic philosophers, Parmenides and Zeno.[1] This is not the place to offer any detailed account of the Eleatics. Very briefly, Parmenides, in his poem *The way of truth*, had set out arguments of quite remarkable subtlety concerning what can be said about that which exists. He concluded that the following predicates are inadmissible: subject to creation and destruction, subject to divisibility, subject to change of place, and change of quality; what exists is 'whole, immobile, eternal, all together, one and continuous'. Zeno reinforced Parmenides' arguments by seeking to show that the proposition 'Things are many and subject to motion' leads to insoluble dilemmas. Zeno's puzzles turn chiefly on the notion of partition or divisibility. The interpretation of them is extremely difficult and controversial. One point only concerns us here. Zeno argued that if a unit of magnitude can be divided at all it must be infinitely divisible. This conclusion was unpalatable to the early atomists who wished to give an explanation of the world which would

---

[1] The most penetrating study of Democritean and Epicurean atomism is by D. J. Furley, *Two Studies in the Greek Atomists* (Princeton 1967). His first study deals with the notion of minimal parts.

be compatible, as far as possible, with Parmenides' logic. Hence they adopted as their primary bodies partless, and therefore indivisible, units of magnitude, which satisfied most of the predicates deduced by Parmenides to belong to what really exists. Lacking parts, the atoms of Democritus would not even be theoretically divisible.

Epicurus modified this doctrine by ascribing parts to the atom but making these parts themselves *minima*, i.e. physically and theoretically indivisible. He seems to have supposed that it is a necessary condition of the atom itself, the minimum discrete body, that it possesses parts— but parts which rule out theoretical divisibility to infinity for the atom itself. Minimal parts satisfied this condition, and they also provided a means of accounting for differences in the shape, size and weight of particular atoms. Lucretius asserts that 'things which are not augmented by parts do not have the diversities of properties which creative matter must have' (i 631–3). Finally, Aristotle had pointed out a number of difficulties in the notion of a partless atom which Epicurus' new thesis may have been intended to resolve (*Physics* vi 231b25–232a17; 240b8–241a6). We shall come back to minimal parts in the next section.

(v) *The motion of atoms and formation of compound bodies*

One modification of earlier atomism by Epicurus has just been discussed. He also differed from Democritus concerning the motion of atoms. Both agreed that the atoms are always in motion, but Democritus almost certainly supposed that the course which any one atom takes relative to any other is wholly random.[1] In fact, most of our evidence for the motion of Democritus' atoms clearly refers to motion derived from collisions with other atoms, and we can only speculate about what he might have said of the original motion of an atom. He probably did not attribute weight to the atom, and if so, cannot have used weight as a cause of motion. Furthermore, it is unlikely that he would have thought it proper to ascribe any direction to the movement of atoms since he said of infinite void that it has neither top nor bottom, centre or extremity (Cic. *Fin.* i 17). Void provided Democritus with a condition which he certainly regarded as necessary for motion, and he may have simply taken it as a fact about the atom that it does necessarily move in the void.

---

[1] This is supported by Aristotle's words, quoted by Simplicius (DK 68 A 37); cf. W. K. C. Guthrie, *History of Greek Philosophy* vol. ii (Cambridge 1965) pp. 400–2.

Against Democritus Epicurus held that weight is a necessary property of the atom. His reasons for this assertion cannot be established
by any direct testimony, but they are almost certainly founded on the
hypothesis that a weightless body cannot move. Aristotle devoted
considerable attention to the analysis of weight as a determining factor
of motion. Indeed, in the *De caelo* Aristotle defines heavy and light
as 'the capacity for a certain natural motion' (307b32), and a little later
says: 'There are certain things whose nature it is always to move away
from the centre, and others always towards the centre. The first I speak
of as moving upwards, the second downwards' (308a14). Now Epicurus recognized that in an infinite universe one cannot strictly speak
of a centre, nor of up and down (*Ep. Hdt.* 60). But he thought that
one could speak of up and down relative to some fixed point, and that
in this relative sense the natural motion of atoms is downwards as a
consequence of their weight. Any other motion than perpendicular
fall requires other factors than weight alone to account for it. In all
probability, Aristotle's discussion of weight as a determinant of movement influenced Epicurus' modification of Democritus.

If an atom is unimpeded by collision with other atoms its speed and
direction of motion are invariant. Epicurus grasped the important
fact that differences of weight make no difference to the velocity of
bodies falling in a vacuum: 'When they are moving through the void
and encounter no resistance the speed of the atoms must be equal.
Neither will heavy ones travel faster than light ones . . .' (*Ep. Hdt.* 61).
At what speed then do free-falling atoms move? Epicurus sometimes
expresses this in the graphic phrase 'as quick as thought'. But that does
not help us very much. In fact, he seems to have supposed that time,
like extension, is not infinitely divisible. Just as the atom is the minimum discrete body and consists of minimal parts, so time is divisible
into 'minimum continuous periods' which themselves consist of
indivisible temporal units, 'times distinguishable only in thought' (*Ep.
Hdt.* 62). Epicurus probably supposed that the time which an atom
takes to move the minimum distance, that is the minimum of extension,
is the minimum temporal unit. This temporal unit, being indivisible,
is not such that a movement can take place *during* it. 'Has moved' not
'is moving' is the relation which a moving body has to the indivisible
units that constitute time and space (Us. 278). As Aristotle saw, such
a theory turns movement into a series of jerks (*Phys.* vi 231b25–
232a17). The atom has to hop, as it were, from one set of spatial units
into the next. For there is no time or space in which its progression

from one unit into the next can be said to occur. The minimum distance by which an atom can alter its location at any moment is the measure of any one minimal part.

Epicurus could have avoided these consequences if he had seen that the infinite divisibility of any *quantum*, whether of space or time, can be asserted without its entailing the consequence that these *quanta* are, as a matter of fact, divisible into infinite parts. He chose instead to predicate physical indivisibility of the atom and a limit to the theoretical division of its parts. Having wrongly concluded that the extremities of the atom must be accounted for by positing minimal spatial units, he accepted as a corollary the indivisibility of time and movement as well. He countered Aristotle's objection, that this makes differences of speed impossible, by arguing that apparent differences in the speed of the compound bodies which we see can be explained as a function of the collective movements at constant speed of individual atoms within each compound; the speed of a moving compound is determined by the collisions which occur between its internal atoms. The more its atoms tend to move in the same direction over a short period of time the greater the speed of the compound body. If the movement of some atoms in one direction is balanced by a movement of others in a different direction the compound body will be stationary (*Ep. Hdt.* 47; 62).[1]

Let us now return to consider the falling atom in more detail. Given that this fall is at constant speed for any atom, and in the same direction, how can a world be formed which consists of atoms in conjunction, atoms which have collided and formed compound bodies? Oddly enough, no word of the answer to this problem survives by Epicurus himself. But his theory can be reconstructed from Lucretius and other later writers. Lucretius writes as follows: 'At this point I wish you to learn this too: when bodies are being carried straight down through the void by their own weight, at an undetermined time and at undetermined places they push a little from their course—only as much as you might call a change of direction. If they were not accustomed to swerve, all things would fall down through the deep void like raindrops, nor could collision come about nor would the atoms experience blows. And so nature would never have created anything' (ii. 216–24).

This swerve which atoms make at no determined time or place has always intrigued the readers of Lucretius. It apparently builds into

[1] For a detailed treatment, to which I am much indebted, see Furley, *Two Studies in the Greek Atomists*, pp. 111–30.

the universe, as Epicurus conceives of this, a principle of relative indeterminacy. The movements of an atom, and therefore any consequences of its movement, are not entirely predictable. Our further information about the swerve in this context merely confirms Lucretius' words, and they must be taken at face value.[1] It follows then that an atom, independently of any secondary motion which may result from collisions, has both a unidirectional movement and an unpredictable tendency to deviate from this.

The atomic swerve is also important to Epicurus' theory of human action. But that will require discussion later (p. 57). The effect of the swerve with which we are concerned here is the collision between two or more atoms which it may bring about. Since every atom is solid through and through, the effect of a collision between atoms is a momentary check on atomic movement followed by a rebound (at the same speed), and hence a further change of direction. But it may sometimes happen that colliding atoms in spite of their tendency to rebound become intertwined and form a temporary and apparently stable compound. The compound so formed is in fact a dynamic entity, a collection of atoms moving both in their normal downward manner and from the effect of blows or swerves. But it will often present the appearance of something stable. Lucretius reports that the different densities of objects are determined by the relation between the atoms and void which they contain. Iron consists of close-packed atoms which are unable to move and rebound any great distance. Air, on the other hand, is composed of atoms which are interspersed with large areas of void (ii 100–8).

We have seen that for Epicurus all properties of things beyond size, shape, weight and movement are secondary. That is to say, they are properties which cannot be predicated of atoms but only of the compound bodies which atoms may form. This does not mean that colour, sound etc. are merely human ways of ordering and interpreting sense-impressions. Democritus had argued thus, but Epicurus did not agree (*Ep. Hdt.* 68–71). His discussion of secondary qualities is condensed and obscure, but seems basically to amount to this: colour, sound etc. cannot exist independently of bodies, nor are they 'parts' out of which compound bodies arise. Rather, any secondary property which is a permanent attribute of some object (compound body) is a *constituent* of the object in the sense that the object would not be what it is without this attribute. We might illustrate this point by saying

[1] The gist of what Lucretius says is repeated by Cicero, *Fin.* i 18–20.

that a man does not arise out of a combination of hands, legs, colour and so forth. He arises from a combination of atoms and void. But the effect of this combination is the production of hands, legs, pink or black colour etc., and these, or some of them, are necessary attributes of any man.

Although Epicurus' basic distinction between bodies is the simple disjunction, atom or compound, he may have supposed that certain compounds function as molecules or basic complexes which serve as 'seeds' for the production of more complex things.[1] Lucretius writes of 'seeds of water' or 'seeds of fire', and though he may mean simply 'that out of which water or fire is composed' the specific property of water or fire is something which only arises through the combination of atoms. It is probable, though not certain, that Epicurus would have regarded a pool of water as a compound of smaller compounds— molecules of water. If the molecule were broken down we should of course be left only with atoms and void. Epicurus firmly rejected the four-element theory which persists through Greek philosophy in various forms from Empedocles to Neoplatonism.

I have called the compound body a dynamic entity. This description applies not merely to its internal atoms but also to those atoms which constitute its surface. An object which persists over any length of time does not retain the same atoms throughout that time. Epicurus supposed that atoms are constantly leaving the surface of objects and having their place taken by further atoms which bombard the object and may then get caught up on its structure.[2] The notion that atoms are constantly leaving the surface of objects is fundamental to the explanation of sensation. As observed already, we sense something when effluences enter our sense organs. If these are 'real' images they are simply the outer surface or skin of objects which is 'sloughed off', to use a Lucretian metaphor, in a continuous stream of 'films'.

Epicurus took over his fundamental principles of atoms and void from earlier atomists but we have seen that he was no slavish imitator. The atomist system seemed to him to provide an explanation of the structure of things which was both compatible with empirical data and psychologically comforting, in that it did away with the need for divine causation and any form of teleology. Whether or not men find

[1] Good arguments in favour of this have been advanced by G. B. Kerferd, *Phronesis* 16 (1971) 88–9.
[2] See in particular *Ep. Hdt.* 48. The regular replenishment of 'lost' atoms explains why objects are not (normally) seen to diminish in bulk.

it more or less comforting to suppose that the world is determined by a supernatural being or beings, seems to be very much a matter of personal temperament. Lucretius praises Epicurus for delivering mankind from 'the weight of religion' (i 62ff.). He means popular religion, superstitious beliefs in the gods as direct arbiters of human destiny and fears of divine anger as expressed in thunder and lightning. But Epicurus cannot have taken popular superstitions as his only target. He was also concerned to reject the sophisticated theology of Plato and probably Aristotle too.

How he did so and what he put in its place will be the subject of the next few pages. Before discussing this, however, we should notice how Epicurus rejects out of hand the method of teleological explanation which bulks so large in Plato and Aristotle. Plato makes Socrates complain that Presocratic thinkers fail to show why it is best for things to be as they are (*Phaedo* 99a–d).[1] What Socrates is alleged to have found a defect—the concentration on mechanical explanations— Epicurus regarded as a positive merit. Things are not 'good for anything', he argued; this is merely a piece of learned superstition. There is no purpose which the world as a whole or things in particular are designed to fulfil. For design is not a feature of the world; it is manifestly imperfect.[2] Given the fact that the number of atoms is infinite and that their shapes are immensely various, it is not remarkable that similar combinations of things arise. Indeed, Epicurus held that the number of worlds is infinite, some of which are like our own while others vary (*Ep. Hdt.* 45). All of them however are ultimately explicable by reference to the purposeless combination and separation of discrete and inanimate physical entities moving in empty space.

Epicurus' cosmology denies the foundation of the Platonic and Aristotelian world-picture. The fossilized Aristotelianism of the schoolmen came under attack in the Renaissance, and Epicurean atomism was given a new relevance by the French mathematician and opponent of Descartes, Pierre Gassendi. The history of later science has amply vindicated Epicurus' rejection of final causes. But it is arguable that Epicurus' renunciation of teleology, in its historical context, went too far. His principle of explanation in terms of accidental arrangement of atoms will hardly serve to account adequately for such phenomena as biological reproduction. Why, to give the question

---

[1] Plato himself attacks purely mechanistic theories of causation, probably with Democritus in mind, in the tenth book of his *Laws* 889b.

[2] Lucretius attacks 'final' causes at length, v 195–234.

an Aristotelian tone, does man produce man? Lucretius, it is true, offers an answer to this question: the characteristics of a species are transmitted to the offspring through its own seed (iii 741ff.), and he repeatedly emphasizes that each thing has its own fixed place; that there are natural laws determining biological and other events (i 75–7; ii 700ff.; iii 615ff. etc.). But the basis of these laws does not seem to rest firmly on anything implied by Epicurus' atomist principles. His physical theory has to explain too much by too little. These complaints are legitimate if we judge Epicurus by Aristotelian standards. But in making them it is necessary to remember that Epicurus did not set out to be a purely disinterested investigator of things. According to his own words, 'the purpose of studying nature is to gain a sharp understanding of the cause of those things which are most important' (*Ep. Hdt.* 78). By 'most important' he means fundamental to human well-being.

The two subjects on which he thought it most important to have correct beliefs were theology and psychology. Having now discussed Epicurus' basic physical principles I turn to consider how he applied these to his treatment of the gods and the human mind.

(vi) The gods of Epicurus

That which is sublimely happy and immortal experiences no trouble itself nor does it inflict trouble on anything else, so that it is not affected by passion or partiality. Such things are found only in what is weak (*K.D.* i).

Nothing disquieted Epicurus more profoundly than the notion that supernatural beings control phenomena or that they can affect human affairs. That there are gods he did not deny. But he repeatedly and vociferously rejected the belief that gods are responsible for any natural events. His rejection of this belief is expressed most pointedly in contexts concerning astronomical phenomena.

Moreover we must not suppose that the movement and turning of the heavenly bodies, their eclipses and risings and settings and similar movements are caused by some being which takes charge of them and which controls or will continue to control them, while simultaneously enjoying complete bliss and immortality. For occupation and supervision, anger and favour, are not consistent with sublime happiness. . . . Nor again must we suppose that those things which are merely an aggregate of fire possess sublime happiness and direct these (celestial) movements deliberately and voluntarily (*Ep. Hdt.* 76–7).

The object of Epicurus' polemic in these lines is any theology which ascribes divine control to the heavenly bodies. By denying the survival of the personality in any form after death Epicurus thought he could remove the source of one basic human anxiety—fear of divine judgment and eternal punishment. And I will discuss this feature of his philosophy in the next section. But he held that it was equally false and disturbing to credit gods with any influence over human affairs here and now. Thereby he denied the foundations of popular Greek religion. The notion that human well-being and adversity are dispensed by the gods was fundamental to popular Greek religion. Language reflected the belief: a happy man was *eudaimōn*, 'one who has a favourable deity'; *kakodaimōn*, 'unhappy', literally means 'having a harmful deity'. For the majority perhaps, belief in the gods of mythology had generally been a matter of civic or private ritual rather than any inner experience. But many Greeks, educated and uneducated alike, subscribed to mystery cults which promised salvation to the initiated, and fears of pollution and divine intervention remained strong. Theophrastus' portrait of the Superstitious Man, overdrawn though it is, would lose all point if it had no basis in everyday experience.[1]

But Epicurus' attack on divine management of the cosmos was more specifically directed, we may suppose, against the cosmology of Plato and Aristotle. Plato, in his later works, constantly refers to the regularity of celestial movements as evidence of intelligent direction by divine beings. In the *Timaeus* we are told that the purpose of sight for men is to observe the 'revolutions of intelligence in the heavens, so that we may use their regular motions to guide the troubled movements of our own thinking'; we are to 'imitate the invariant movements of God' (47b–c.) This concept of divine ordination of the heavens was developed by Plato with much more detail in the *Laws*, his last major work.[2] There he defends the thesis that the heavenly bodies have as their cause virtuous souls or gods (x 899b). Their virtue is proved by the regularity of the movements which they cause. Disorderly movements, whether in the heavens or on earth, must be accounted for by a soul which is bad (897d).

Not only, according to Plato, are the stars directed by gods. Man-

[1] The reference is especially relevant because it is a contemporary one. Theophrastus' *Characters* are a set of short vignettes of character types: complaisance, boorishness, miserliness etc.

[2] The development of Plato's theology is a complex subject; for a well-balanced account see F. Solmsen, *Plato's Theology* (Ithaca, N.Y. 1942).

kind and the universe as a whole are the 'possessions' of the gods (902b–c). In the *Laws* Plato emphasizes that the control which gods exercise over men is providential. But he states equally strongly that it is absolute. Plato thought he could legislate for a reformed religion by banishing the discreditable gods of tradition and replacing them with new gods whose excellence was manifested in the mathematical perfection of celestial physics. But to Epicurus Plato's astral gods were quite as repugnant as the traditional Olympian pantheon. His refusal to regard the movements of the stars as a consequence of divine intentions is an explicit rejection of Plato's own language. In the *Epinomis,* the title of which means 'after the laws', astronomy is made the key to this new theology.[1] The heavenly bodies are there said to be the source of our knowledge of number, which itself is the foundation of intelligence and morality. This queer assertion is put forward in all seriousness, and it leads to a reiteration of the divinity of the stars. These beings possess wondrous powers of mind; they know our own wills; they welcome the good and loathe the bad (984d–985b).

Epicurus regarded such beliefs as a prime source of human anxiety. To him they seemed to compound old superstitions and to make the heavenly bodies, with their watching brief over human affairs, an object of utter terror. He can have been little less disquieted by Aristotle's theology. For Aristotle too regarded the heavenly bodies as intelligent, divine beings whose movements are voluntary. We know that Aristotle expressed such views in an early work designed for popular consumption.[2] It is also true that Aristotle's views about celestial movements developed during his lifetime and that he does not in any extant treatise make the heavenly bodies personal arbiters of human destiny. But it is a basic doctrine of his *Metaphysics* that all movement and life are ultimately dependent upon the Unmoved Mover, pure Mind or God, whose activity of eternal self-contemplation promotes desire and motion in the heavenly bodies, each governed by its own intelligence. Aristotle approved of popular

---

[1] Doubts about the Platonic authorship of this work have been expressed from antiquity onwards. If not by Plato himself, which is likely enough, it should be ascribed to a younger contemporary Academic, perhaps Philip of Opus (D.L. iii 37).

[2] Cic. *N.D.* ii 42–4. Comparison with Book i 33 of Cicero's treatise suggests the reference may be to Aristotle's third book 'On philosophy'. On Aristotle's theology see W. K. C. Guthrie, *Classical Quarterly* 27 (1933) 162–71; 28 (1934) 90–8.

beliefs in the divinity of the heavens, even though he denied their traditional mythological trappings (*Met.* 1074a38ff.). The Unmoved Mover, like Epicurus' own gods, is not personally concerned with the universe. But unlike Epicurus' gods the Unmoved Mover is the prime cause of all things. He does not determine human affairs by his own fiat. They are none the less dependent upon events, such as the sun's diurnal rotation and seasonal change, of which he is the ultimate cause.[1]

Epicurus rejects divine management of the world by an argument based upon the meaning and implications of the words 'sublimely happy' and 'immortal'. He accepts that these predicates, traditionally ascribed to the gods, express real attributes of divine beings (*Ep. Men.* 123). But he denies that sublime happiness and immortality are compatible with any involvement in 'our affairs' (Cic. *N.D.* i 51–2). In his view happiness, whether human or divine, requires for its full realization a life of uninterrupted tranquillity or freedom from pain. For the moment we must accept this concept of happiness as a dogmatic assertion, for its full analysis belongs to the field of ethics. Epicurus' argument concerning the gods' indifference to the world picks up this concept of happiness, applies it to the gods and thereby removes from them any actions or feelings which take account of human affairs. Seneca summarizes this position: 'Hence god dispenses no benefits; he is impregnable, heedless of us; indifferent to the world . . . untouched by benefits and wrongs' (Us. 364).

The argument makes three assumptions. First, that there are gods. Secondly, that the gods are sublimely happy and immortal. Thirdly, that their happiness consists in uninterrupted tranquillity. We must now consider how Epicurus justified these assumptions.

Since he was disposed to combat all beliefs about divine control of the world it may seem surprising that Epicurus accepted even the existence of supernatural beings. For, if the gods could be shown to be fictions, all activities associated with them would necessarily also be ruled out. Epicurus argued however that the universal beliefs of mankind establish the fact that gods exist. 'What people or race is there which lacks an untaught conception of gods?' (Cic. *N.D.* i 43). The argument claims that *a* belief in gods exists independently of institution-

---

[1] It was clearly Epicurean practice to attack all theological views which differed from their own; cf. Cic. *N.D.* i *passim*. Epicurus must have found much to object to in the writings of Plato's successor, Xenocrates, whose theology contained 'daimons' as well as celestial divinities and who foreshadowed the Stoics in referring the names of certain gods to natural substances.

alized religion or custom. It is therefore something *natural*. Of course the belief might be natural and false. But Epicurus uses a basically Aristotelian premise (*E.N.* 1172b35) to reject this objection: 'That about which all agree must be true.'

The same principle, *consensus omnium*, is used to establish the properties of the gods. All men are also said to have a natural belief that the gods are immortal, sublimely happy and of human shape.[1] Epicurus held that these common beliefs are 'preconceptions' derived from experience—visions which people have when awake and all the more when asleep. He argued that these visions must, like all sensations, be caused by something real, that is to say atomic configurations or images (effluences) which come from the gods themselves and which penetrate to our minds. The theory is naïve and fails to take account of other factors which might have led men to believe in gods. If as a matter of fact human beliefs about gods were as consistent with each other and as similar as Epicurus claims, the hypothesis of mental perception of divine images would offer a reason for the *consensus omnium*: we are all acted upon by the same kind of external images. But Epicurus assumes the *consensus omnium*, and then seeks to explain it in psychophysical terms.

According to Lucretius the properties of sublime happiness and immortality were inferred by men from their mental images of the gods:

They endowed the gods with eternal life, because images of the gods were constantly supplied with unchanging form, and also because they believed that beings possessed of such strength could not be vanquished by any chance force. And they supposed that the gods enjoyed supreme happiness because no fear of death troubled any of them, and because in dreams the gods were seen to do many remarkable things without any expenditure of effort (v 1175–82).

Lucretius proceeds to argue that early men, having acquired a belief in gods, supposed them to be the agents of astronomical and meteorological phenomena through ignorance of the real cause of these things. Elsewhere he argues at length that the gods cannot have had any desire or ability to create the universe, the imperfections of which are clear evidence that it is not under divine direction (v 156–94). The gods, like true Epicureans, dwell in *sedes quietae* ('tranquil resting-places') enjoying a life free of all trouble (iii 18–24).

[1] Cic. *N.D.* i 45–6; see also *Ep. Men.* 123–4 which refers to the false conceptions of the 'many' about gods.

Besides the natural conceptions of mankind Epicurus himself gave other reasons for justifying his account of the gods' nature. He defended their anthropomorphic appearance by the argument that this is the most beautiful of all shapes and therefore the shape which belongs to beings whose nature is best (Cic. *N.D.* i 46–9). Not all of his statements about the gods can be reduced to the supposed evidence of natural conceptions.[1] But while recognizing that the images which men receive from the gods are 'insubstantial' and difficult to perceive, he clearly hoped to show that primary knowledge of the gods is something similar in kind to the direct acquaintance with physical objects which we obtain through our sense organs.

How is the physical structure of the gods to be conceived of and what manner of life do they lead? The evidence which bears on these questions is difficult and must be dealt with summarily here. The basic problem is the everlasting existence of the gods. Atoms and void are imperishable, for atoms possess a solidity which is impervious to all 'blows' and void is unassailable by 'blows' (Lucret. iii 806–13). But the ordinary objects of experience, because they are compounded out of atoms and void, are not of a kind to resist destruction indefinitely. So Lucretius writes:

By (natural) law they perish, when all things have been made weak by outflow (of atoms) and give way to the blows which come from outside (ii 1139–40).

Epicurus sought to avoid this difficulty by introducing a mode of being which is not a compound body in any ordinary sense. Our main evidence is a difficult text of Cicero. After observing that the gods are perceived by the mind and not the senses, Cicero writes that they do not possess 'solidity' nor 'numerical identity', like the ordinary objects of perception, but 'an unlimited form of very similar images arises out of the innumerable atoms and flows towards the gods' (*N.D.* i 49, cf. 105). Elsewhere the gods are perhaps spoken of as 'likenesses' and some gods (or all of them from one point of view) are 'things which exist by similarity of form through the continuous

---

[1] See further, K. Kleve, *Symbolae Osloenses*, suppl. xix. Epicurus (Cic. *N.D.* i 50) also inferred that there must be divine beings equal in number to mortals by the principle of 'equal balance' or 'reciprocal distribution' (*isonomia*). 'From this,' we are told, 'it follows that if the number of mortals is so many there exists no less a number of immortals, and if the causes of destruction are uncountable the causes of conservation must also be infinite.'

onflow of similar images which are brought to fulfilment at the same place' (Us. 355).[1] Scholars have questioned the accuracy of these statements on the grounds that they make the atoms which flow *towards* the gods 'images'. But these doubts may be misplaced. 'Image' (or *eidôlon* in Epicurus' terminology) is distinguished from 'solid body'. There can be 'images' in this sense which are merely patterns of fine atoms lacking the density to constitute a solid body. We may perceive Centaurs in virtue of such 'images', but they are not images contrasted with a real Centaur; for there is no solid body corresponding to a Centaur. Similarly, there is no solid body which emits images of the gods. For the gods do not possess a solid body. They are called 'likenesses', in all probability, because their nature is continuously reconstituted by a moving stream of 'images', discrete arrangements of fine atoms which possess *similar* form.

The gods then have no numerical identity. If their substance were that of an ordinary compound body they would be subject to an irreplaceable loss of atoms and hence destructible by external 'blows'. Their identity is 'formal', a consequence of the constant arrival and departure of similar forms at the points in space occupied by the gods. It has sometimes been aptly compared with the nature of a waterfall the shape of which is determined by continuous flow. Epicurus does not explain why there should be a continuous supply of atoms patterned in the right way to constitute the form of the gods. If pressed he would probably have argued that in a universe which contains an infinite number of atoms this is not impossible in principle (see p. 46, n. 1); and that our experience of the gods—the fact that we can have more than momentary visions of them—proves the continuity of their form, and therefore the supply of appropriate atoms. Moreover we think of them as immortal.

Does this strange notion of the gods' physical structure imply that they themselves make no contribution to their own unceasing existence? The evidence discussed so far could imply that the gods are simply happy beneficiaries of a constant supply of atoms which replace those they have lost. Some scholars have adopted such a view. But Philodemus, who wrote a work *On the gods* (as did Epicurus himself), parts of which are preserved on a Herculaneum papyrus,

---

[1] The word 'brought to fulfilment' (*apotetelesmenôn*) should not be emended with Kühn and Usener to *apotetelesmenous*: it is the 'images' not the gods which are brought to fulfilment; cf. *Ep. Pyth.* 115, 'by the meeting of atoms productive of fire'.

seems to have argued that the gods' own excellence and powers of reason secure them from destructive forces in the environment.[1] It should not be supposed that this is a laborious activity for the gods. On the contrary, all our sources stress the fact that the gods enjoy an existence completely free of toil. They are able, in virtue of their nature, to appropriate the atoms which preserve their existence and to ward off atoms of the wrong kind. This seems to have been Philodemus' view, and we may reasonably credit it to Epicurus himself.

The gods' tenuity of structure is explained by the 'images' which form their bodies, a theory ridiculed by ancient critics (*N.D.* i 105). We may now see why the gods are not said to have body but quasi body, not blood but quasi blood (Cic. *N.D.* i 49). They are seen above all in dreams and are themselves dreamlike in substance, insubstantial like the 'images' which make up their being. It may seem strange that Epicurus should have credited such creatures with perfect happiness, but this becomes less odd when we study what their happiness consists in. It is something negative rather than positive. The gods have no occupations, they can be affected by no pain, they are liable to no change. They dwell in no world but in the spaces which separate one world from another (*intermundia,* Cic. *N.D.* i 18). And since it is Epicurus' claim that absence of pain is the highest pleasure, and pleasure is the essence of happiness, the gods are perfectly happy. In the later Epicureanism of Philodemus more positive things are said about the gods, including the fact that they speak Greek! But Epicurus, so far as we know, did not go in for such crude anthropomorphism.

> . . . The Gods, who haunt
> The lucid interspace of world and world,
> Where never creeps a cloud, or moves a wind,
> Where never falls the least white star of snow,
> Nor ever lowest roll of thunder moans,
> Nor sound of human sorrow mounts to mar
> Their sacred everlasting calm![2]

Human affairs are no concern of the gods. But are the gods, or should they be, any concern of men? Epicurus seems to have held that certain forms of ritual and private devotion are appropriate because,

---

[1] *De dis* iii fr. 32a p. 52 Diels. For further discussion of Philodemus' evidence and theories based upon it, cf. W. Schmid, *Rheinisches Museum* 94 (1951) 97–156, K. Kleve, *Symbolae Osloenses* 35 (1959), who attributes the gods' self-preservation to the exercise of free will.

[2] Tennyson, *Lucretius,* based on Lucret. iii 18–23, itself a translation of Homer.

although the gods cannot be touched by prayers or sacrifices, they provide men with a model of beatitude. Whether or not a man is benefited by the gods depends upon his state of mind when he apprehends divine 'images'. If he himself is tranquil he will attain to the right view of the gods (Lucret. vi 71–8), and a passage in the *Letter to Menoeceus* (124) is perhaps to be interpreted along the same lines: those whose disposition is already akin to that of the gods can appropriate and gain benefit from divine 'images'. It is in the same spirit that Philodemus writes: 'He [*sc.* Epicurus] appeals to the completely happy in order to strengthen his own happiness' (Diels, *Sitz. Berl.* 1916, p. 895).

(vii) *The soul and mental processes*

Death is nothing to us; for that which has been dissolved lacks sensation; and that which lacks sensation is no concern to us (*K.D.* ii).

The first thing which Epicurus strove to establish in his psychological theory was the complete and permanent loss of consciousness at death. All his philosophy has the ultimate aim of removing human anxiety, and the therapeutic aspect of his psychology is a most conspicuous example of this. By denying any kind of survival to the personality after death, Epicurus hoped to show that beliefs in a system of rewards and punishments as recompense for life on earth were mere mythology. It is difficult to assess precisely the strength and prevalence of such beliefs in Epicurus' own time. But apart from his vehement desire to undermine them, which must be evidence that they were not uncommonly held, we find independent confirmation in literature and the popularity of 'mystery cults'.

Traces of such beliefs are already to be found in fifth-century writers. It is not likely that they declined during the fourth century. Plato, in the *Republic*, writes scathingly of those who provide books of Musaeus and Orpheus, and try to persuade 'whole cities as well as individuals' to absolve themselves from their crimes by performing certain rituals. Such men hoodwink people into believing that they will reap benefits in this world and the next, while those who fail to observe the rituals will be confronted with 'terrible things' (*Rep.* ii 364e). Cephalus, the old man who figures at the beginning of the *Republic*, is portrayed as someone who has been tormented by fears of having to expiate his offences in Hades. Plato himself condemns the quacks who try to exploit such fears by offering absolution at a fee.

But he ends the *Republic* with a myth which has judgment of the dead and rewards and punishments for earthly existence as its central feature. Similar myths are used by him in the *Phaedo* and the *Gorgias*. Both the pre-existence and the survival of the soul, after death, are central Platonic doctrines which he combines with the theory of metempsychosis.

The fear of death is common to all peoples at all times. Epicurus may have exaggerated the psychological disturbance he attributed to explicit beliefs in a destiny for the soul after death. But he did not confine his diagnosis of the fear of death to eschatological dogmas. As he himself writes (*Ep. Hdt.* 81), and as Lucretius writes at greater length, men also fear death who believe that it is the end of all sensation. Lucretius uses an argument to remove such fear which simply asserts that this is a true belief and *therefore* no grounds for anxiety: events which took place before we were born did not disturb us, for we did not *feel* them. By parity of reasoning, nothing can disturb us when we cease to be conscious of anything (iii 830–51). A little later he goes on:

> If there is to be any trouble and pain for a man he too must exist himself at that time in order that ill may affect him. Since death removes this and prevents the existence of him to whom a mass of misfortunes might accrue, we may be assured that there is nothing to be feared in death and that he who no longer exists cannot be troubled (iii 861–8).

For Epicurus birth and death are limits which contain the existence of a person. *I* have not existed in another body prior to this life, nor am *I* liable to experience a further incarnation following this life. There is such a thing as *psychê*, soul, the presence of which in a body causes that body to possess life. Here Epicurus agreed with philosophical and popular conceptions. But he also insisted against Plato and other dualists that the soul cannot exist independently of the body, and that a living being must be a union of the body and the soul. Disrupt this union and life ceases. His view bears comparison with that of Aristotle who defined soul as 'the first actuality of an organic natural body' (*De an.* ii 412b5). For Aristotle too, most functions of the soul are necessarily related to the body, though Aristotle made an exception of intellect. We should not however press this comparison. Aristotle's treatment of soul proceeds by very different steps from Epicurus'. It calls for distinctions between form and matter and between potentiality and actuality which are quite foreign to

Epicurus' way of thinking; in Aristotle soul is not a kind of physical substance, as it is for Epicurus. That on which they broadly agree is the mutual dependence of body and soul.

What then did Epicurus say about the soul? Or, to put the question another way, how did he explain life? The first point is that life must be accounted for by reference to something corporeal. For that which is not body is void, and void cannot *do* anything nor *be affected* by anything (*Ep. Hdt.* 67). The grounds for denying that soul is incorporeal show that Epicurus regards the capacity to act and to be acted upon as a necessary condition of that which animates a living being. More specifically, soul consists of atoms which act upon and are affected by the atoms constituting the body itself.

'Soul is a body, the parts of which are fine, distributed throughout the whole aggregate. It resembles most closely breath mixed with heat' (*Ep. Hdt.* 63). Lucretius enables us to amplify this description. The atoms which form the soul, he tells us, are very small and they are also round. Roundness is inferred from the speed of thought: the soul atoms can be stirred by the slightest impulse (iii 176ff.). Furthermore, breath and heat (Lucretius adds air as well) are not sufficient to account for soul. That soul is warm and airy is clear from the fact that warmth and breath are absent from a corpse. But breath, heat and air cannot create the movements which bring sensation (iii 238–40). Something else is needed—a 'fourth nature', consisting of atoms which are smaller and more mobile than anything else which exists. They have no name.

How are we to conceive of the relation between the different kinds of atoms which constitute soul? As I observed earlier when discussing compound bodies, fire, breath and so forth are things which can only arise when certain kinds of atoms are combined. We are probably therefore to suppose that the atoms which can, in appropriate combinations, create the substances specified by Lucretius are in the soul combined in such a way that they form a body which is analysable as a *mixture* of fire, breath, air and the unnamed element. But the soul will not be divisible into these things. Lucretius says explicitly that 'no single element [of the soul] can be separated, nor can their capacities be divided spatially; they are like the multiple powers of a single body' (iii 262–6).[1]

This body, in virtue of the unnamed element, can produce the movements necessary to sensation. It is the unnamed element which

[1] See further Kerferd, *Phronesis* 16 (1971) 89ff.

gives the soul its specific character. Life and vital functions in general are thus explained by reference to something which cannot be analysed fully into any known substances. Epicurus wants to avoid the objection that life has been simply reduced to an appropriate mixture of familiar substances. Life requires these and something else as well. Given the primitive notions which the Greeks had of chemistry, Epicurus was wise to refrain from attempting to explain life purely in terms of the traditional four elements.

The soul then, so constituted, is the 'primary cause of sensation'. But soul by itself cannot have or cause life. It must be contained within a body. That is to say, a living being can be constituted neither out of soul alone nor out of body alone. Placed within a body of the right kind, the soul's vital capacities can be realized. From the soul the body acquires a derivative share in sensation; there is physical contact, naturally, between the body and the soul, and the movements of atoms within the body affect and are affected by those of the soul. Epicurus illustrated the relation of body and soul by considering the case of amputation (*Ep. Hdt.* 65). Loss of a limb does not remove the power of sensation; but loss of the soul removes all vitality from the body, even if the body itself remains intact. By insisting that soul must be contained in the body, Epicurus denied any prospect of sensation and consciousness surviving death.

In Lucretius (iii 136ff.) and some other sources a spatial distinction is drawn between the *animus* (rational part) and the *anima* (irrational part). The *animus* is located in the chest; the rest of the soul, though united with the *animus*, is distributed throughout the other regions of the body. These two parts of the soul do not undermine its unity of substance; they are introduced to explain different functions. That in virtue of which we think and experience emotion is the *animus*, the mind. This governs the rest of the soul. Epicurus had no knowledge of the nervous system, and we may most easily think of the *anima* as fulfilling the function of nerves—reporting feelings and sensations to the *animus* and transmitting movement to the limbs. If Epicurus had known of the nerves and their connexion with the brain he would probably have been fully prepared to accept the notion that the brain is equivalent to the *animus*.[1]

Lucretius' account of the soul inspired some of his finest poetry. It also shows much acute observation of behaviour. Before considering

[1] The nervous system was discovered by the medical scientists, Herophilus and Erasistratus, during the first half of the third century B.C.

further aspects of Epicurean psychology, we may pause over one or two passages in which Lucretius calls attention to the relations between body and soul:

If the vibrant shock of a weapon, forced within and opening to view bones and sinews, falls short of destroying life itself, yet faintness follows and a gentle falling to the ground, and on the ground there ensues a storm of the mind, and moment by moment an unsteady desire to stand up. Therefore it must be the case that the mind is corporeal in substance, since it suffers under the blow of bodily weapons (iii 170–6).

Furthermore we perceive that the mind comes into being along with the body, develops with the body and grows old with it. Just as young children totter whose body is frail and soft, so too their powers of judgment are slight. Then, when maturity has developed bringing hardy strength, their judgment too is greater and their strength of mind increased. Later, after their body has been assailed by the tough force of age and their limbs have failed with their strength blunted, the intellect grows lame, the tongue raves, the mind stumbles, all things fail and decline at the same time. And so it is appropriate that all the substance of vitality should be dissolved like smoke into the lofty breezes of the air (iii 445–56).

Again, if the soul is immortal and can feel when separated from our body we must, I believe, cause it to be equipped with the five senses. There is no other way in which we can imagine to ourselves souls wandering below in the realm of Acheron. And so painters and former generations of writers have presented souls endowed with the senses. But neither eyes nor nostrils nor hand nor tongue nor ears can exist for the soul apart from the body. Therefore souls on their own cannot feel, nor even exist (iii 624–33).

The psychological function on which we have most copious information is sense-perception. This is due no doubt to its importance in Epicureanism as a whole. In discussing the theory of knowledge I have already described Epicurus' concept of effluences or images from external objects which enter the sense organs, or which penetrate directly to the mind, and thereby cause our awareness of something. Perception is thus ultimately reducible to a form of touch, physical contact between the atoms of the percipient and atoms which have proceeded from objects in the external world (cf. Lucret. ii 434f.). It will not be possible in this context to discuss the treatment of specific problems of optics and other matters which Lucretius deals with at great length in Book iv. But some more general aspects of the theory

need consideration.[1] In particular, it would be desirable to know how
we are to conceive of the 'sense-bearing movements' which the soul
bestows on the body. Lucretius states that it is not the mind which
sees through the eyes, but the eyes themselves (iii 359–69), and the
same holds good for the other sense organs. The eye is an organ of
the body. When it is struck by a stream of effluences which have the
appropriate size, we are probably to suppose that this sets up a movement of the adjoining soul atoms, which then cause sensation in the
eye itself. The same internal processes will account for feelings—
burns, itches and so forth. Lucretius traces a series of movements
beginning with 'the stirring of the unnamed element' which passes
via the other elements in the soul to the blood, the internal organs and
finally the bones and marrow (iii 245–9). These stages represent an
increasing disturbance of 'everything' and life cannot be maintained if
the movements or sensations penetrate beyond a certain point. But
'generally the movements come to an end on the surface of the body'
(252–7).

All of this still leaves the notion of sensation or consciousness very
obscure. Is it simply a kind of movement, or is it rather something
which supervenes as an epiphenomenon upon a kind of movement?
Epicurus and Lucretius leave us in the dark here, and no wonder!
For no one has yet succeeded in giving a purely mechanistic explanation of consciousness.

The treatment of thought raises further problems. In Epicurus'
Letter to Herodotus (49–50) and in Lucretius, thought is assimilated to
sense-perception so far as its objects and causes are concerned:

> Come now, learn what things stir the mind, and hear in a few words the
> source of those things which enter the understanding. First of all, I declare
> that many likenesses of things wander in many ways in all regions in all
> directions; they are fine in texture and easily become united with one another
> in the air when they meet. . . . They are much finer than those things which
> seize hold of the eyes and rouse vision, since they pass right through the
> vacant spaces of the body and stir the fine nature of the mind within and
> rouse its awareness (Lucret. iv 722–31).

Lucretius proceeds to illustrate these statements by reference to
the perception of monsters and the dead. From this we might suppose
that he is describing only certain kinds of mental perception. But he

---

[1] Epicurus himself writes about seeing, hearing and smell, *Ep. Hdt.* 49–53.
Lucretius also discusses taste, iv 615–72.

goes on to argue that the thought of a lion is also produced, like the sight of a lion, by *simulacra leonum* ('images of lions'). He also asks the question, 'How is that we are able to think of things at will?' The answer which he suggests is curious:

> In a single period of time which we perceive, that is, the time it takes to utter a single word, many times escape notice which reason discovers; and so it happens that in any time all the images are available, ready in every place. So great is their power of movement, so great the supply of them. . . . Because they are fine the mind can only distinguish sharply those on which it concentrates. Therefore all except those for which it has prepared itself pass away. The mind prepares itself and expects that it will see what follows on each thing; therefore this comes about (iv 794–806).

We should expect thought to be explained by reference to data, images, or what not which are somehow already present in or created by the mind. But that is not what Lucretius says. He clearly implies that the 'supply' of images is external, and that the mind apprehends just those images to which its attention is directed. Thinking, on this interpretation, is analogous to noticing something which falls within the scope of vision.

Many scholars have been reluctant to take this passage at its face value. They have presumed that Epicurus must have envisaged an internal store of images in terms of which some thought at least and memory are to be explained. It has been suggested that the effluences which are received by the sense organs or the mind cause a change in the movements of the soul atoms, and this new pattern of movement persists as a memory or thought-image. But if Epicurus held such a view no evidence about it has survived, and it is not presupposed in the theory recorded by Lucretius. According to this theory, thought is a kind of internal film-show in which the mind controls the images which it permits to enter the body. Not only thought but volition also requires the consciousness of appropriate images. Lucretius observes that we walk when 'images of walking fall upon the mind' (iv 881). Then the will rouses itself, and passes on movement to the rest of the soul so that finally the limbs are activated. In dreaming, too, passages are open in the mind through which images of things can enter (iv 976–7).

We must suppose that this is Epicurus' own theory, and it is quite consistent with the strange idea that images of the gods possess objective status. But if memory is not explicable by a storehouse of images how is it to be accounted for? The few texts which bear upon this question suggest that memory is a disposition, produced by repeated apprehension of images of a certain kind, to attend to such images as continue to exist after the previously experienced object which produced them may have perished or changed in other ways. Hence we can remember the dead.

Although Lucretius' account of thought should be given full weight as orthodox Epicurean doctrine, certain forms of thinking must have been explained in other ways. There are no images of atoms and void; there is no image of the principles of confirmation and non-contradiction. Yet these are things which cannot be grasped except by thought. Epicurus himself distinguished between what he called 'the theoretical part', and 'apprehension' whether by the senses or the mind.[1] I have already discussed 'apprehension', and rejected Bailey's claim that it guarantees the clarity of an image. What it does involve, I suggest, is the *direct* apprehension of some image. In other words, 'apprehension' covers awareness of all data, whether of the senses or the mind, which possess objective existence because they are in origin images which enter us from outside. 'The theoretical part' refers to thinking which may be presumed to function purely by internal processes. That is to say, it involves inference about things like atoms and void which are unable to be apprehended directly. How such thinking takes place in detail, and whether or not it involves images, are questions which we cannot answer categorically. It almost certainly must make use of 'preconceptions', general concepts arrived at by repeated observation of particular objects. Preconceptions however cannot be reduced to external images for there are no 'generic' images existing objectively. These must be constructions of the mind, which can be utilized in the formation of new non-empirical concepts. Epicurus may have explained them as patterns of movement in the soul, but his words on this subject, if he described it in detail, have not survived.

(viii) Freedom of action

Our next subject is one of the most interesting and controversial problems in Epicureanism. According to Lucretius and other later writers, the 'swerve' of atoms has a part to play in the explanation of 'free will' (*libera voluntas*). But what part? The answer must be sought,

[1] *De nat.* xxviii fr. 5 col. vi (sup.), col. vii (inf.), ed. A. Vogliano, *Epicuri et Epicureorum scripta in Herculanensibus papyris servata* (Berlin 1928).

if anywhere, from a difficult passage of Lucretius. It is the second argument which he uses to prove that atoms sometimes deviate from the linear direction of their downward movement through the void:

If every movement is always linked and the new movement arises from the old one in a fixed sequence, and if the primary bodies do not by swerving create a certain beginning of movement which can break the bonds of fate and prevent cause from following cause from infinity, how comes it about that living things all over the earth possess this free will, this will, I say, severed from fate, whereby we advance where pleasure leads each man and swerve in our movements at no fixed time and at no fixed place, but when and where our mind has borne us? For undoubtedly each man's will gives the beginning to these movements, and it is from the will that movements are spread through the limbs.

You see, do you not, that when the barriers are opened at an instant of time, the horses for all their strength and eagerness cannot burst forward as promptly as their mind desires. This is because the whole stock of matter throughout their whole body has to be set in motion, so that having been roused through all the frame it may make an effort and follow the desire of the mind. So you can see that a beginning of movement is engendered by the heart, and it comes forth first from the mind's volition and then is dispatched throughout the whole body and limbs.

It is not the same as when we move forward under the pressure of a blow from the mighty strength and strong constraint of another man. For then it is clear that the whole matter of the body in its entirety moves and is seized against our will, until the will restrains it throughout the limbs. So now you surely see that although an external force pushes many men and often compels them to go forward against their will and be driven headlong, yet there is something in our breast which can fight back and resist. At its direction too the stock of matter is at times compelled to change direction through all the limbs, and although pushed forward is checked and comes to rest again.

Therefore you must admit the same thing in the atoms too; that another cause of motion exists besides blows and weights which is the source of this power innate in us, since we see that nothing can arise out of nothing. For weight prevents all things happening by blows, by external force as it were. But a tiny swerve of the atoms at no fixed time or place brings it about that the mind itself has no internal necessity in doing all things and is not forced like a captive to accept and be acted upon (ii 251–93).

This is our only detailed evidence for the relation between the swerve and 'free' will in Epicurean literature.[1] No explicit word about the

---

[1] Cic. *De fato* 22 and *N.D.* i 69 also show that the swerve was supposed to save 'free will'. See also Diogenes of Oenoanda fr. 32 col. iii Chilton.

swerve from Epicurus himself has so far been discovered. We know however that he attacked 'the destiny of the natural philosophers' for its 'merciless necessity' (*Ep. Men.* 134). And he discussed the causes of human action in a book which is partially preserved on papyrus from Herculaneum.[1] The text contains so many gaps and defective lines that it is difficult to grasp a clear train of thought; more work may yield positive advances in our understanding of it. But Epicurus certainly distinguished sharply in this book between 'the cause in us' and two further factors, 'the initial constitution' and 'the automatic necessity of the environment and that which enters' (i.e. external 'images'). These distinctions should be borne in mind when one approaches Lucretius' text.

The first thing to notice is his context. Lucretius' main subject at this stage of his work is not psychology but the movement of atoms. He offers no formal argument to defend the 'freedom' of the will. Rather, he assumes it, exemplifies it by examples, and uses the assumption and examples to prove that atoms sometimes swerve.

The logical structure of the first paragraph might be expressed like this: (A) If all movements are so causally related to each other that no new movements are created by a swerve of atoms, then there could be no such thing as 'free will'. (B) For 'free will' entails the creation of a new movement at no fixed time and at no fixed place. (C) But there is such a thing as 'free will'. (D) Therefore the atoms sometimes create new beginnings by swerving.

In the next two paragraphs (as I have set out the text) Lucretius gives his examples to show that the will can create new beginnings of movement. First, he considers the case of the race-horses. When the barriers are raised they are free of any external constraint to move forward; and they do move forward (fulfil their desire to move) as soon as their will has had time to activate the limbs. This example is used to show that there is some faculty within the horses which enables them to initiate movement freely.

In his second example Lucretius considers a different case. Unlike the horses, which require a brief interval of time for their will's action to have an external effect, men may be pushed forward immediately by outside pressures; and such *involuntary* movements require no internal movements in the men before they occur. But men have something within them which can resist external pressures. This is a

---

[1] This is found in Arrighetti's edition, *Epicuro Opere* 31 [27] 3–9. It is just possible that the swerve is implied at 31 [22] 7–16.

power to cause atoms within the body to change their enforced direction of movement. In this case, the will initiates movement when the body is already undergoing compulsory movement. But the power which is exercised is the same as that faculty for initiating movement exemplified by the horses.

It seems clear to me that both examples are intended to illustrate 'free will', from different starting-points. And what are we to make of the 'blows' and 'weights' mentioned in the last paragraph? Lucretius does not exclude these as necessary conditions of a 'free' action. He denies only that they are sufficient to bring it about. We have already seen that the 'will' to walk requires 'images', that is, 'blows from outside' (p. 55), and nothing weightless could act or be acted upon in Epicurus' system. The weight of the mind's atoms affects its reaction to external blows. But an action caused solely by blows and weights could not be 'free'. The horses' movement and the men's resistance were 'free' in virtue of an additional third factor which Lucretius calls *voluntas*, 'will'. The will, it should be noted, is not treated as equivalent to desire. Desire is prompted by the awareness of some pleasurable object. Lucretius, I think, regards the will as that in virtue of which we seek to fulfil our desires (cf. ii 258, 265).

If we ask where the swerve features in all this, the answer seems to be that the swerve is a physical event which presents itself to consciousness as a 'free' will to initiate a new movement. Consciousness during waking states is normally continuous. But our external bodily movements are not wholly continuous. Nor are our intentions. Lucretius, I suggest, treats some animal actions as if they were relatively discontinuous events initiated by the 'will'. But they are not wholly discontinuous. Memory, reflection, habit, these and other dispositions are not ruled out as causal factors by anything which Lucretius says. A swerve among the soul atoms need not be supposed to disrupt all or even any character traits. The swerve is not treated in a context which enables us to place its precise function in the whole history of living things. But what does seem clear is its rôle as an initiator of new actions.

Once it is recognized that other causes besides the swerve are necessary to the performance of a voluntary act, certain difficulties observed by one recent writer become less acute. If the swerve, which by definition is something random and unpredictable, were sufficient by itself to explain voluntary actions, then the bonds of fate could seem to have been broken at the expense of making actions purposeless and wholly indeterminate. Sensing this difficulty, David Furley has suggested that the swerve need not be supposed to feature in the explanation of *every* voluntary action.[1] Its function, he argues, is rather to free the disposition from being wholly determined by heredity and environment. For this purpose he suggests that a single swerve of a single atom in an individual's *psyche* would be sufficient.

Furley's interesting arguments cannot be surveyed in detail here. But it is my own opinion that Lucretius' text is easier to interpret on the assumption that a swerve is at work in the freedom of particular actions. The theoretical single swerve which Furley postulates can hardly suffice to explain the 'beginnings of motion' which characterize each act of 'free' will. But Furley is right to object to interpretations which treat the swerve by itself as a sufficient condition. We know from Diogenes of Oenoanda that the swerve was held to be necessary by Epicureans if moral advice is to be effective (fr. 32 col. iii). But moral advice cannot be effective if it is to depend entirely on the possible occurrence of a swerve in the soul of the man being advised. I think we are to suppose that the swerve of a single atom is a relatively frequent event. It may occur when one is asleep or when one is awake, without having any observable or conscious effect. If however a man's natural disposition to seek pleasure or to avoid pain is roused by external or internal causes, and if at such times he is in a physical condition which makes it possible for him to act then, depending upon the kind of man he is, any swerve(s) among the atoms of his mind constitutes a free decision to act. If he is untrained in Epicurean philosophy he may decide to pursue objects which in the event cause more pain than pleasure. The true Epicurean's atoms may also swerve at a time when he walks down a Soho street, but having learnt that freedom from pain is more pleasurable than momentary sensations of pleasure he does not follow his companions into the night-club. Swerves help him to initiate new actions in the pursuit of tranquillity.

Before concluding this subject two general observations may be made. First, it may be asked whether the use of the swerve which I attribute to Epicurus is historically plausible. Furley believes not, but he omits one point which seems to me important. The so-called problem of 'free will' arises primarily out of two conceptions—

---

[1] 'Aristotle and Epicurus on Voluntary Action' in his *Two Studies in the Greek Atomists*. My brief remarks here cannot do justice to the importance of Furley's wide-ranging treatment. Much of his argument turns on similarities he has detected between Aristotle and Epicurus.

beliefs in God's omniscience and predetermination, and beliefs in the absolute continuity of physical causation. There is every reason to attribute the second of these to Zeno, the founder of Stoicism, and probably the first as well. Zeno and Epicurus were active in Athens together for thirty years, and I find it unlikely that Epicurus developed his opposition to determinism quite independently of Stoic theories. Those theories provide conditions which favour the emergence of a concept of volition which is not completely dependent upon the state of things at the preceding instant. I conjecture that Epicurus used the swerve to defend such a concept.

Secondly, the random nature of the swerve is a difficulty for Epicurus whatever its rôle in human psychology. But it seems to me logically possible to suppose that the swerve of a soul atom is not random so far as the consciousness of the soul's owner is concerned. And Epicurus attempted to solve that problem, so I think, by making the swerve a constituent of the 'will'. If it is not part of the will or cognitive faculty, but a random event which disrupts the soul's patterns of atoms from time to time, are not the consequences for morality which trouble Furley still more serious? He wants the swerve to free inherited movements of atoms and make character adaptable. But this raises new problems. A man of good Epicurean character will live in fear of an unpredictable event which may change him into a Stoic or something worse. I find it easier to posit some discontinuity between the antecedent conditions of an action and the decision to do it than discontinuity between movements on which character depends.

To conclude, Epicurus used the swerve of atoms in the soul to explain situations where men are conscious of doing what they want to do. Obscurities persist, and we cannot rule them out in order to make the theory more palatable or convincing. I pass now to a less controversial subject. Epicurus' theory of pleasure has already been referred to, and we must now consider its full ethical significance.

(ix) Pleasure and happiness

Epicurus was not the first Greek philosopher whose ethics can be called hedonist. In Chapter 1 I referred briefly to the earlier hedonism of Aristippus whose conception of the pleasant life differs sharply from Epicurus'. Unlike Aristippus, who regarded absence of pain as an intermediate condition, Epicurus claimed that the removal of all pain defines the magnitude of pleasure (*K.D.* iii), and his interest in specifying the conditions which establish a life free of trouble may well

have been roused by Democritus. The earlier atomist probably had
no systematic ethical theory, but he is credited with a conception of
happiness which consists above all in peace of mind (D.L. ix 45). It
was Epicurus' primary concern to show how this state can be attained.

Pleasure was also a topic which received considerable attention
from Plato, Aristotle and the Academy in general. It is highly probable
that Epicurus was familiar with ideas which Plato discusses in the
Philebus, and he may also have been influenced by some Aristotelian
notions, most notably the distinction between pleasure 'in movement'
and pleasure 'in rest' (*E.N.* 1154b28). The great difference between
Plato and Aristotle on the one hand and Epicurus on the other turns
on the relation they posit between happiness and pleasure. All three
philosophers are concerned in their ethics with specifying the necessary
conditions of happiness, but only Epicurus identifies happiness with
a life full of pleasure. Some pleasures for Plato and Aristotle are good,
and make a contribution to happiness; others are bad. For Epicurus
no pleasure in itself can be anything but good since the good means
that which is or causes pleasure. The fundamental constituent of
happiness for Plato and Aristotle is virtue, excellence of 'soul', which
manifests itself in the exercise of those activities appropriate to each
faculty of the personality and in moral action. (The differences between
Plato and Aristotle are less important for my present purpose than the
similarities.) But for Epicurus virtue is necessary to happiness not as
an essential ingredient but as a means to its attainment. This is the
most significant difference between Epicurus and his major predecessors:

> We say that pleasure is the starting-point and the end of living blissfully.
> For we recognize pleasure as a good which is primary and innate. We begin
> every act of choice and avoidance from pleasure, and it is to pleasure that we
> return using our experience of pleasure as the criterion of every good thing
> (*Ep. Men.* 128–9).

Subjective experience is a 'test of reality' for Epicurus, and it is on
this evidence that he based his doctrine of pleasure.

> All living creatures from the moment of birth take delight in pleasure and
> resist pain from natural causes independent of reason (D.L. x 137).

The goodness of pleasure needs no demonstration. Epicurus takes it as
an obvious fact that men, like all living things, pursue pleasure and
avoid pain. The attractiveness of pleasure is treated as an immediate
datum of experience comparable to the feeling that fire is hot (Cic.

Fin. i 30). We learn from Aristotle that his contemporary Eudoxus also inferred that pleasure is 'the good' from the allegedly empirical fact that all creatures pursue it (*E.N.* x 1172b9). Now it does not follow from the fact, if it is a fact, that men pursue pleasure that pleasure is what they ought to pursue. As G.E. Moore argued at great length in *Principia Ethica*, that which is desired is not equivalent to that which is desirable. Some scholars have indeed claimed that Epicurus is not concerned with what 'ought' to be or what is 'fitting', but only with what is.[1] But this claim is at best a half-truth. It would be a correct description of his view to say that we are genetically programmed to seek what will cause us pleasure and to avoid what will cause pain. And he probably held that no living creature whose natural constitution is unimpaired *can* have any other goals. But there is a place for 'ought' in his system because the sources of pleasure and pleasure itself are not uniform. What we ought to do is to pursue that which will cause us the greatest pleasure. 'Ought' here of course does not signify what we are obliged to do by any purely moral law. It signifies that which needs to be done if we are successfully to attain our goal, happiness or the greatest pleasure. It applies to means and not to ends:

Since pleasure is the good which is primary and innate we do not choose every pleasure, but there are times when we pass over many pleasures if greater pain is their consequence for us. And we regard many pains as superior to pleasures when a greater pleasure arises for us after we have put up with pains over a long time. Therefore although every pleasure on account of its natural affinity to us is good, not every pleasure is to be chosen; similarly, though every pain is bad, not every pain is naturally always to be avoided. It is proper to evaluate these things by a calculation and consideration of advantages and disadvantages. For sometimes we treat the good as bad and conversely the bad as good (*Ep. Men.* 129–30).

In order to grasp the implications of this important passage, we need to consider in more detail what Epicurus meant by pleasure and how he proposed to use pleasure as a guide to action. The most striking feature of his hedonism is the denial of any state or feeling intermediate between pleasure and pain. Pleasure and pain are related to one another not as contraries but as contradictories.[2] The absence

---

[1] So Bailey, *Greek Atomists*, p. 483, followed by Panichas, *Epicurus* (N.Y. 1967) p. 100.

[2] cf. Cic. *Fin.* ii 17, 'I assert that all those who are without pain are in a state of pleasure.'

of the one entails the presence of the other. If all pleasure is regarded as a sensation of some kind, this relationship between pleasure and pain makes no sense. For clearly most of us pass a large part of our waking lives without having either painful or pleasing sensations. But the periods of our waking life in which we could describe ourselves as neither happy nor unhappy, or neither enjoying nor not enjoying something, are much smaller. Epicurus' view of the relationship between pleasure and pain should be interpreted in this light. He has, as we shall see, a way of distinguishing the pleasures of bodily sensations and feelings of elation from pleasures which cannot be so described; absence of pain is not, he thinks, an adequate description of the former. Epicurus' mistake is a failure to see that indifference characterizes certain of our moods and attitudes towards things.

His analysis of pleasure rests on the assumption that the natural or normal condition of living things is one of bodily and mental well-being and that this condition is *ipso facto* gratifying. This is the meaning of the statement quoted above: 'Pleasure is the good which is primary and innate.' It is possible in English to speak of 'enjoying' good health, and we may also call this something gratifying, or something a man rejoices in. Epicurus' use of the word pleasure to describe the condition of those who enjoy good physical and mental health is not therefore purely arbitrary. In physical terms this pleasure is a concomitant of the *appropriate* movement and location of atoms within the body. If these are disturbed pain follows. In other words, pain is a disruption of the natural constitution. Pleasure is experienced when the atoms are restored to their appropriate position in the body (Lucret. ii 963–8).

The idea that pain is a disturbance of the natural state was not invented by Epicurus. We find it in Plato's *Philebus* along with the notion that pleasure is experienced when the natural state is 'replenished' (31e–32b). Plato however argued that pleasure is only experienced during the process of restoring the natural condition. According to his theory, pleasure and pain are movements or processes. There is also, however, a 'third' life in which any bodily processes produce no consciousness of pleasure or pain. This 'intermediate' condition cannot be regarded as pleasurable or painful (42c–44a).

It is interesting to find Plato attacking the theory that absence of pain can be identified with pleasure. Epicurus of course would not accept Plato's specification of an intermediate life. Like Plato, however, Epicurus holds that the process of removing pain results in pleasurable sensations. He calls this pleasure 'kinetic'. Suppose that a man is hungry: he desires to eat and the act of satisfying this desire produces 'kinetic' pleasure. If he succeeds in fully satisfying the desire for food he must have wholly allayed the pangs of hunger. From this complete satisfaction of desire, Epicurus argues, a second kind of pleasure arises. This is not an experience which accompanies a process, but a 'static' pleasure. It is characterized by complete absence of pain and enjoyment of this condition. Torquatus, the Epicurean spokesman in Cicero's *De finibus*, expresses the distinction between pleasures thus:

> The pleasure which we pursue is not merely that which excites our nature by some gratification and which is felt with delight by the senses. We regard that as the greatest pleasure which is felt when all pain has been removed (*Fin.* i 37).

'Static' pleasure follows the complete satisfaction of desire. Desire arises from a sense of need, the pain of lacking something. In order to remove this pain, desire must be satisfied, and the satisfaction of desire is pleasurable. 'Kinetic' pleasure is thus (or so I think) a necessary condition of at least some 'static' pleasure, but it is not regarded by Epicurus as equivalent in value to 'static' pleasure.[1] For if freedom from pain is the greatest pleasure, we should satisfy our desires not for the sake of the pleasurable sensations which accompany eating, drinking and so on, but for the sake of the state of well-being which results when all the pain due to want has been removed:

> When we say that pleasure is the goal we do not mean the pleasures of the dissipated and those which consist in the process of enjoyment . . . but freedom from pain in the body and from disturbance in the mind. For it is not drinking and continuous parties nor sexual pleasures nor the enjoyment of fish and other delicacies of a wealthy table which produce the pleasant life, but sober reasoning which searches out the causes of every act of choice and refusal and which banishes the opinions that give rise to the greatest mental confusion (*Ep. Men.* 131–2).

Epicurus, in this passage, is not denying that drink, eating good food, sex, and so on are sources of pleasure. He is asserting that the pleasures which such activities produce are to be rejected as goals because they

---

[1] This interpretation of the relation between 'kinetic' and 'static' pleasure seems to me to suit the evidence best and to make the best sense. It has also been argued that 'kinetic' pleasure serves only to 'vary' a previous 'static' pleasure; see most recently J. M. Rist, *Epicurus* (Cambridge 1972) ch. 6 and pp. 170ff.

do not constitute a calm and stable disposition of body and mind. It is freedom from pain which measures the relative merits of different activities. This is the basis of Epicurus' hedonist calculus. His criticism of luxury and sexual indulgence is not grounded in any puritanical disapproval:

> If the things which produce the pleasures of the dissipated released the fears of the mind concerning astronomical phenomena and death and pains ... we should never have any cause to blame them (*K.D.* x).

He holds that the greatest pain is mental disturbance produced by false beliefs about the nature of things, about the gods, about the soul's destiny. Any pleasure therefore which fails to remove the greatest pain is ruled out as an ultimate object of choice by application of the rule—absence of pain establishes the magnitude of pleasure. Furthermore, the pleasure which arises from gratifying the senses may have a greater pain as its consequence. A man may enjoy an evening's drinking or the thrill of betting, but the pleasure which he derives from satisfying his desires for drink and gambling must be set against the feeling of the morning after and the anxiety of losing money.

Epicurus' concept of pleasure is closely related to an analysis of desire:

> We must infer that some desires are natural, and others pointless; of natural desires some are necessary, others merely natural. Necessary desires include some which are necessary for happiness, others for the equilibrium of the body and others for life itself. The correct understanding of these things consists in knowing how to refer all choice and refusal to the health of the body and freedom from mental disturbance since this is the goal of living blissfully. For all our actions are aimed at avoiding pain and fear. Once we have acquired this, all the mind's turmoil is removed since a creature has no need to wander as if in search of something it lacks, nor to look for some other thing by means of which it can replenish the good of the mind and the body. For it is when we suffer pain from the absence of pleasure that we have need of pleasure (*Ep. Men.* 127–8).

Epicurus' analysis of desires is consistent with the principle that freedom from pain is the greatest pleasure. The desire for food and clothing is natural and necessary. Failure to satisfy this desire is a source of pain. But, Epicurus argues, it is neither necessary nor natural to desire this food or clothing rather than that, if the latter is sufficient to remove the pain felt by absence of food or clothing (Us. 456). Hence Epicurus becomes an advocate of the simple life, on the grounds that we cause ourselves unnecessary pain if we seek to satisfy desires by luxurious means. Necessary desires, he holds, can be satisfied simply, and the pleasure which we thus experience is no less in quantity even if it differs in kind. Moreover, those who seek pleasure in luxuries are likely to suffer pain unnecessarily either as a direct consequence of luxurious living or through an inability to satisfy a desire:

> We regard self-sufficiency as a great blessing, not that we may always enjoy only a few things but that if we do not have many things we can enjoy the few, in the conviction that they derive the greatest pleasure from luxury who need it least, and that everything natural is easy to obtain but that which is pointless is difficult. Simple tastes give us pleasure equal to a rich man's diet when all the pain of want has been removed; bread and water produce the highest pleasure when someone who needs them serves them to himself. And so familiarity with simple and not luxurious diet gives us perfect health and makes a man confident in his approach to the necessary business of living; it makes us better disposed to encounter luxuries at intervals and prepares us to face change without fear (*Ep. Men.* 130–1).

Time and again in his *Principal doctrines* Epicurus asserts that pleasure cannot be increased beyond a certain limit.[1] So far as sensual gratification is concerned, this limit is reached when the pain which prompted desire has ceased; thereafter pleasure can be 'varied'—by 'kinetic' pleasure—but not augmented. This is something which needs to be grasped by the intellect, since the flesh itself recognizes no limits to pleasure (*K.D.* xviii; xx). The mind has its own pleasures the 'limit' of which is reached with the ability to calculate correctly the pleasures of sensual gratification and to assess the feelings which cause mental disturbance. Ancient critics familiar with Plato's distinction between the soul and the body criticized Epicurus for failing to draw a sharp distinction between bodily pleasures and the 'good' of the soul (Us. 430, 431). But when Epicurus distinguishes body and soul in statements about pleasure he has nothing like Platonic dualism in mind. Body and mind are in physical contact with one another; pleasurable sensations are 'bodily' events but they also give rise to pleasure or joy in the mind (Us. 433, 439). Unlike the body however the mind is not confined for its objects of pleasure to the experience of the moment:

[1] e.g. *K.D.* iii, ix, xviii, xix, xx.

The body rejoices just so long as it feels a pleasure which is present. The mind perceives both the present pleasure along with the body and it foresees pleasure to come; and it does not allow past pleasure to flow away. Hence in the wise man there will always be present a constant supply of associated pleasures, since the anticipation of pleasures hoped for is united with the recollection of those already experienced (Us. 439).

The memory of past pleasures can 'mitigate' present sufferings (Us. 437), and the same holds for the anticipation of future pleasures. Unlike the Cyrenaics who regarded bodily pleasures of the moment as the greatest, Epicurus is reported by Diogenes Laertius to have argued that the mind's capacity to look forward and back entails that both its pleasures and its pains are greater than those of the body (x 137).

The distinction between 'kinetic' and 'static' pleasures applies to both body and mind (D.L. x 136). Corresponding to the 'kinetic' pleasure of satisfying a desire for food, drink and the like, the mind can experience 'joy' when, say, meeting a friend or solving a problem in philosophy. This pleasure, consisting in motion, is to be distinguished from the 'static' pleasure of 'mental repose' which corresponds to the body's pleasure in freedom from pain.

Since pleasure is the only thing which is good in itself, prudence, justice, moderation and courage, the traditional four 'moral virtues' of Greek philosophy, can have value only if they are constituents of or means to pleasure. Epicurus settled for the second alternative. Torquatus puts his position succinctly, opposing the Epicureans to the Stoics:

As for those splendid and beautiful virtues of yours, who would regard them as praiseworthy or desirable unless they produced pleasures? Just as we approve medical science not for the sake of the art itself but for the sake of good health . . . so prudence, which must be regarded as the 'art of living', would not be sought after if it achieved nothing. In fact is is sought after because it is the expert, so to speak, at discovering and securing pleasure. . . . Human life is harassed above all by an ignorance of good and bad things, and the same defect often causes us to be deprived of the greatest pleasures and to be tormented by the harshest mental anguish. Prudence must be applied to act as our most reliable guide to pleasure, by removing fears and desires and snatching away the vanity of all false opinions (Cic. *Fin.* i 42–3).

Moderation, on the same principle, is desirable because and only because 'it brings us peace of mind'. It is a means to attaining the greatest pleasure since it enables us to pass over those pleasures which involve greater pain. Similarly, Torquatus finds the value of courage in the fact that it enables us to live free of anxiety and to rid ourselves, as far as possible, of physical pain. Justice and social relationships are analysed in the same way, but I will say a little more about Epicurus' treatment of these at the conclusion of this chapter.

Although Epicurus regarded the virtues as means and not as ends, he held that they are necessary to happiness and inseparably bound up with the hedonist life:

> Of sources of pleasure the starting-point and the greatest good is prudence. Therefore prudence is something even more valuable than philosophy. From prudence the other virtues arise, and prudence teaches that it is not possible to live pleasurably without living prudently, nobly and justly, nor to live prudently, nobly and justly, without living pleasurably. For the virtues are naturally linked with living pleasurably, and living pleasurably is inseparable from them (*Ep. Men.* 132).

This association between virtue and pleasure is striking, but it should not be interpreted as giving an independent value to prudence and the other virtues. The necessary connexion between pleasure and the virtues is due to the notion that pleasure requires for its attainment a reasoned assessment of the relative advantages and disadvantages of a particular act or state of affairs, a capacity to control desires the satisfaction of which will involve pain for the agent, freedom from fear of punishment and the like. The pleasure which men should seek is not Bentham's 'greatest happiness of the greatest number'. Epicurus never suggests that the interests of others should be preferred to or evaluated independently of the interests of the agent. The orientation of his hedonism is wholly self-regarding.

(x) *Justice and friendship*

> Natural justice is a pledge of expediency with a view to men not harming one another and not being harmed by one another (*K.D.* xxxi).

> Of all the things which wisdom secures for the attainment of happiness throughout the whole of life, by far the greatest is the possession of friendship (*K.D.* xxvii).

Aristotle asserted that 'man is naturally a political animal', and Plato held that the true good of the individual is also the good of the community to which he belongs. Epicurus took a very different view, which, though less forcefully than the Cynics, challenged fundamental values of Greek society. In his opinion human beings have no 'natural' leanings towards community life (Us. 523). Civilization has developed by an evolutionary process of which the determinants have been external circumstances, the desire to secure pleasure and to avoid pain, and the human capacity to reason and to plan. Learning by trial and error under the pressure of events, men have developed skills and formed social organizations which were found to be mutually advantageous. The only details of this process which survive in Epicurus' own words concern the origin and development of language (*Ep. Hdt.* 75–6). But Lucretius treats the whole subject at some length in Book v. Following the invention of housing and clothing, the discovery of how to make fire, and the introduction of family life, he writes, 'neighbours began to form friendships desiring neither to do nor to suffer harm' (1019–20). From this supposed historical stage in human culture Epicurus traces the origins of justice.

He describes justice as 'a kind of compact not to harm or be harmed' (*K.D.* xxxiii), prefacing this statement with the words: 'It is not anything in itself', an implicit attack on Plato's theory of the autonomous existence of moral values. Several longer statements on justice are preserved in the *Principal doctrines*, and a selection of these will serve to illustrate Epicurus' position:

Injustice is a bad thing not in itself, but in respect of the fear and suspicion of not escaping the notice of those set in authority concerning such things (*K.D.* xxxiv).

It is not possible for one who secretly acts against the terms of the compact 'not to harm or be harmed', to be confident that he will not be apprehended. . . . . (*K.D.* xxxv).

Evidence that something considered to be just is a source of advantage to men, in their necessary dealings with one another, is a guarantee of its justice, whether or not it is the same for all. But if a man makes a law which does not prove to be a source of advantage in human relationships, this no longer is really just. . . . (*K.D.* xxxvii).

The just man is most free from trouble, but the unjust man abounds in trouble (*K.D.* xvii).

This concept of justice, which recalls Glaucon's analysis in Plato (*Rep.* ii), is not the 'social contract' of Rousseau. Epicurus is not saying that people have an obligation to act justly because of an agreement entered into by their remote or mythical ancestors. The 'contractual' element in his concept of justice is not advanced as a basis of moral or social obligation. Epicurus' justice requires us to respect the 'rights' of others if and only if this is advantageous to all parties concerned. Justice, as he conceives of it, does imply recognition of the interests of others besides oneself. But the basis of this recognition is self-interest. The 'compact' of which he speaks has self-protection as its basis. It is an agreement to refrain from injuring others if they will refrain from injuring oneself.

Epicurus' comments on the fears of apprehension which beset the unjust man show clearly that justice is desirable for the freedom which it brings from mental distress as well as physical retaliation. This is wholly consistent with his calculus of pleasures and pains. Injustice is bad not in itself but because of the painful consequences which it involves for the unjust man. In a book of *Problems* Epicurus raised the question: 'Will the wise man do anything forbidden by the laws, if he knows that he will escape notice?'; and he replied, 'The simple answer is not easy to find' (Us. 18). Epicurus' comments in *K.D.* xxxv imply that the problem is a purely academic one. No one in practice *can* be confident that his injustice will be unnoticed; as Lucretius puts it, 'fear of punishment for crimes during life' is the real hell, and not the Acheron of myth (iii 1013–23). Realizing this the wise man acts justly in order to secure tranquillity of mind.

In Epicurus' eyes political life is a rat-race or 'prison' from which the wise man will keep well clear (*Sent. Vat.* lviii).[1] He diagnoses political ambition as a 'desire for protection from men', and argues that this in fact can only be secured by a quiet life in retirement from public affairs (*K.D.* vii, xiv). But Epicurus' rejection of political life as a context for the attainment of happiness was not based upon misanthropy. On the contrary, he held that friendship is 'an immortal good' (*Sent. Vat.* lxxviii). So today, 'opting out' *and* communal life are practised by many who find society at large 'alienated'. Torquatus, in Cicero's *De finibus*, asserts that 'Epicurus says that of all the things which prudence has provided for living happily, none is greater or more productive or more delightful than friendship' (i 65). Once again we notice that the value of something other than pleasure or happiness is referred to this end. But Epicurus, when writing of friendship, uses almost lyrical language at times, as when he says:

[1] See also D.L. x 119 and Lucretius' brilliant denunciation of *ambitio*, iii 59–77, related to the fear of death.

'Friendship dances round the world, announcing to us all that we should bestir ourselves for the enjoyment of happiness' (*Sent. Vat.* lii).

There is no doubt that Epicurus practised what he preached. The Garden was a community of friends, and Epicurus clearly derived intense happiness from friendship. We are told that he was famous for his 'philanthropy' to all (D.L. x 10), and on the day of his death, when racked by pain, he wrote to Idomeneus that he was happy, with the joyous memories of their conversations (Us. 138). Some of Epicurus' remarks about friendship might imply that it is compatible with altruism and self-sacrifice. But the basis of friendship, like justice, is self-interest, though Epicurus in the same breath says that it is 'desirable for its own sake' (*Sent. Vat.* xxiii). There is probably no inconsistency here. 'He is not a friend who is always seeking help, nor he who never associates friendship with assistance' (*Sent. Vat.* xxxix). One can enjoy or derive pleasure from helping a friend independently of any tangible benefit which this brings. When Epicurus writes of the 'benefits' of friendship he does not mean the pleasure which may come from helping others but the actual practical help which friends provide for each other. Apart from this, however, friendship is desirable because 'it is more pleasant to confer a benefit than to receive it' (Us. 544). One again we are brought back to pleasure as the sole criterion of value.

There is an elegant simplicity to Epicurus' ethics, a refreshing absence of cant, and also much humanity. He was born into a society which, like most societies, rated wealth, status, physical attributes and political power among the greatest human goods. It was also a slave-based society which reckoned men as superior to women and Greeks as superior to all other peoples. The good for man which Epicurus prescribes ignores or rejects these values and distinctions. Freedom from pain and tranquillity of mind are things which any sane man values and Epicurus dedicated his life to showing that they are in our power and how we may attain them. His ethics is undeniably centred upon the interests of the individual, and some have, with justification, praised the nobility of Epicurus more highly than his moral code. Yet we must see it in its social and historical context. No Greek thinker was more sensitive to the anxieties bred by folly, superstition, prejudice and specious idealism. At a time of political instability and private disillusionment Epicurus saw that people like atoms are individuals and many of them wander in the void. He thought he could offer them directions signposted by evidence and reason to a way of being, a way of living, a way of relating to others, other individuals. Negative, self-centred, unstimulating we may regard it; we cannot say priggish or self-indulgent, and in antiquity many found liberation and enlightenment in Epicureanism. For a modern reader too there is much philosophical interest in the consistency with which Epicurus applies his basic principles. What he has to say about family life and sexual love is entirely based on the proposition that the greatest good is freedom from pain in body and mind. But consistency can be purchased too dearly; a few criticisms of Epicurus' hedonism will show this.

First, it may be objected that Epicurus misapplies the factual observations with which he starts. Unless pleasure is used analytically to mean merely that which is desired, it is difficult to agree that pleasure is the object of every desire. But such a usage of pleasure tells us nothing about what is desired or desirable, and Epicurus does not use pleasure in this empty way. He is claiming that the desire to attain a state of consciousness which we find gratifying is sufficient to explain all human action. And this seems to be patently false. Secondly, Epicurus can fairly be charged with failure to grasp the complexity of the concept of pleasure. As we say, one man's meat is another man's poison, but Epicurus seems to think that he can classify by reference to absence of pain the magnitude of any man's pleasure. This may often be good advice, but many will argue from their own experience that Epicurus' claims have no basis in fact. They will also reject his assertion that sharp pains are short and long pains mild.

Ancient critics complained that Epicurus has united under the term pleasure two quite different *desiderata*, positive enjoyment and the absence of pain (Cic. *Fin.* ii 20), and there is some grounds for the complaint. Such remarks as 'The beginning and root of all good is the pleasure of the stomach' (Us. 409) are much more naturally interpreted in the former sense, even if Epicurus did not intend this. In particular, it is difficult to make sense of the notion that absence of pain entails that pleasure can only be varied and not increased. If I derive pleasure from smelling a rose at a time when I am suffering no pain, it seems perverse to say that my pleasure is merely varied. For what I experience is something *sui generis*, a new sense of gratification which is more than a variation of my previous state of consciousness. Even if it is reasonable to call tranquillity of mind a kind of pleasure it is straining language and common sense to call it the greatest pleasure. That procedure leaves us no way to take account of experiences which cannot be assimilated to tranquillity and which do cause us intense gratification without pain.

Thirdly, under 'static' pleasure Epicurus seems to have classified two quite different things. The pleasure which follows from the satisfaction of desire is normally related closely in time to the desire. When I leave hospital, restored to health, it makes sense to say 'You must be pleased to be better'. But it makes much less sense to say this a long time later. The mental equilibrium enjoyed by an Epicurean of ten years' standing seems to be something quite different.

These and other observations could be prolonged. I have confined my comments to Epicurus' own theories, and it is hardly necessary to dwell on some of the obvious objections to egoistic hedonism as a 'moral' theory. But in this book Epicurus should have the last word, and it is eloquently expressed by his great disciple and admirer, Lucretius:

When the winds are troubling the waters on a mighty sea it is sweet to view from the land the great struggles of another man; not because it is pleasant or delightful that anyone should be distressed, but because it is sweet to see the misfortunes from which you are yourself free. It is sweet too to watch great battles which cover the plains if you yourself have no share in the danger. But nothing is more pleasing than to be master of those tranquil places which have been strongly fortified aloft by the teaching of wise men. From there you can look down upon other men and see them wandering purposelessly and straying as they search for a way of life—competing with their abilities, trying to outdo one another in social status, striving night and day with the utmost effort to rise to the heights of wealth and become masters of everything. Unhappy minds of men, blind hearts! How great the darkness, and how great the dangers in which this little life is spent. Do you not see that nature shouts out for nothing but the removal of pain from the body and the enjoyment in mind of the sense of joy when anxiety and fear have been taken away. Therefore we see that for the body few things only are needed, which are sufficient to remove pain and can also provide many delights. Nor does our nature itself at different times seek for anything more pleasing, if there are no golden statues of youths in the entrance halls holding in their right hands fiery torches so that evening banquets may be provided with light, or if the house does not gleam with silver and shine with gold and a carved and gilded ceiling does not resound to the lute, when, in spite of this, men lie on the soft grass together near a stream of water beneath the branches of a lofty tree refreshing their bodies with joy and at no great cost, particularly when the weather smiles and the time of the year spreads flowers all over the green grass (ii 1–35).

CHAPTER THREE

Scepticism

(i) Pyrrho and Timon—early Pyrrhonism

Scepticism is an ability which sets up antitheses among appearances and judgments in any way whatever: by scepticism, on account of the 'equal weight' which characterizes opposing states of affairs and arguments, we arrive first at 'suspension of judgment', and second at 'freedom from disturbance' (Sextus, *P.H.* i 8).

IN the first book of his *Outlines of Pyrrhonism*, Sextus Empiricus gives this definition of 'scepticism' (*skepsis* means speculation or investigation in its non-technical use). The starting-point of scepticism, he continues, is 'the hope of attaining freedom from disturbance' (ibid. 12). We are to suppose that this motive led certain men to search for a *criterion* by reference to which 'truth' and 'falsity' might be established. They failed in this quest but achieved their long-term aim, 'discovering freedom from disturbance, as if by chance, as a consequence of suspending judgment (about the inconsistency which belongs to appearances and judgments')' (ibid. 29).

Sextus was a Greek physician who flourished at the end of the second century A.D. His medical writings have perished, but he also wrote a lengthy account of Greek Scepticism, and a series of books in which he attacks the doctrines of the 'Dogmatists' from the Sceptic point of view. These works, in the form they have come down to us, occupy four volumes of the Loeb Classical Library. Sextus Empiricus' chief source is Aenesidemus, a Greek philosopher of uncertain date, whose works have not survived independently. Aenesidemus is an important figure. He was probably the first to establish in formal terms the 'modes' of judgment as we find them in Sextus and elsewhere.[1]

[1] The 'modes' are a series of arguments designed to show that 'suspension of judgment' should be our attitude towards all things claimed to be real or true in any objective sense. Ten of these arguments are recorded by Sextus (*P.H.* i 31–163) and Diogenes Laertius (ix 79–88); and a further set of five, probably intended to replace them, was introduced by Agrippa, a Sceptic later than Aenesidemus (Sextus, ibid. 164–86; D.L. ibid. 88–9). On Aenesidemus' date I

Aenesidemus almost certainly drew heavily upon the Academic sceptics whom I discuss later in this chapter, but in name at least his scepticism is something which has its roots in the fourth century B.C. Pyrrho of Elis, an older contemporary of Epicurus, was the founder of Greek Scepticism in its technical sense. The revival and detailed working-out of Pyrrhonist principles by Aenesidemus and his followers falls outside the scope of this book. Here I shall be concerned largely with those characteristics of Pyrrhonism which can reasonably be supposed to have developed in the Hellenistic period.

I say 'reasonably' because there is no denying the fact that reliable evidence about early Pyrrhonism is scanty and problematical. The problem, which has been much discussed, is to judge how much impetus towards the kind of scepticism documented in our late sources can be credited to Pyrrho himself. Some have said virtually none, but this certainly goes too far.[1] We should be cautious about ascribing much of the theoretical detail in Sextus and Diogenes Laertius to Pyrrho, and I do not maintain that my outline of Pyrrhonism in this chapter is a wholly accurate account of the historical Pyrrho. I have deliberately incorporated some evidence from what is probably later Pyrrhonism in order to fill out the presentation of attitudes adopted by Pyrrho. But, as we shall see, Timon of Phlius, Pyrrho's publicist and younger contemporary, provides some means of controlling later evidence, and when the sources called upon are of philosophical rather than historical significance I try to indicate the fact. The term 'Pyrrhonist' is also used, rather than 'Pyrrho' or 'Timon', in these latter contexts.

Those who are doubtful about the extent of Pyrrho's scepticism have often pointed to the fact that Cicero refers to him as a strict, dogmatic moralist (e.g. *Fin.* iv 43) but does not mention him more than once in the *Academica,* a work devoted to arguments for and against scepticism. In just one passage Cicero states that Pyrrho denied perception of 'indifferent' things by the wise man (*Acad.* ii 130). Leaving that passage aside for the moment, we may next observe that in Diogenes Laertius Pyrrho is said to have denied anything to be

am inclined to think with Brochard, *Les Sceptiques grecs* (Paris 1923) p. 246, that the first century B.C. fits the evidence best. This point has been well argued by J. M. Rist who offers an interesting interpretation of Aenesidemus' so-called Heracliteanism, *Phoenix* xxiv (1970) 309–19.

[1] The accounts of Pyrrho by Zeller and Brochard are much better balanced than the books by L. Robin, *Pyrrhon et le scepticisme grec* (Paris 1944) and most recently A. Weische, *Cicero und die neue Akademie* (Münster 1961).

morally good or bad; human behaviour is governed by convention (ix 61). This seems to chime very oddly with Cicero's Pyrrho, who asserted that 'virtue is the only good' (*Fin.* iii 12). Are we then to conclude that Pyrrho held quite contradictory positions, or alternatively that scepticism was improperly fathered upon him by later Pyrrhonists? Is Cicero quite wrong about Pyrrho?

Cicero's evidence should not be lightly discarded; he was much closer in date to Pyrrho then Sextus or Diogenes, both of whom wrote after Pyrrhonism had been revived by Aenesidemus. But if Pyrrho was not a sceptic in any recognizably philosophical sense, why did Aenesidemus and his followers call themselves Pyrrhonists?[1] A number of considerations raise doubts about Cicero's Pyrrho. For one thing, Cicero seems to know nothing of Timon's writings. Cicero's sources for scepticism were Academic writers, notably Clitomachus, Philo of Larisa and his pupil Antiochus, who reverted to dogmatism (see pp. 222ff.). The Academic sceptics did not acknowledge indebtedness to Pyrrho. They claimed Socrates and Plato as the founders of their methodology. Yet Arcesilaus, the founder of Academic scepticism, was lampooned by Timon and by the Stoic Ariston in verses which explicitly indicate a close similarity between his position and that of Pyrrho (D.L. iv 33).

I have just referred to Ariston, and mention of his name by Cicero also casts doubt upon the latter's knowledge of Pyrrho. Cicero regularly names Pyrrho alongside Ariston. We know that Ariston's most notable doctrine was the impossibility of drawing any distinction of value between 'indifferent' things, that is, things which in a moral sense are neither good nor bad. The orthodox Stoic view was that some 'indifferent' things are to be 'preferred' to others (see p. 193). It is likely that Cicero knew far more about Ariston than he knew about Pyrrho, who wrote nothing, and that he mistakenly assimilated Pyrrho's 'indifference' to externals, which was based upon problems about criteria of perception, to Ariston's advocacy of total indifference to anything apart from virtue and vice.

Cicero's evidence certainly raises problems. But perhaps it can be squared with other reports more satisfactorily than is apparent at first glance. Cicero does not say what Pyrrho meant by 'virtue' or *honestum*. We do not know whether Pyrrho thought that the word *aretê* ('virtue')

---

[1] The argument that Aenesidemus did so because he was dissatisfied with the Academy's move back to dogmatism under Antiochus of Ascalon begs the question.

had a valid usage; but suppose that he did think so, and suppose that he used it to designate the tranquillity of mind which Pyrrhonists regarded as the consequence of a disposition to suspend judgment. Then, Cicero's evidence might be regarded as curiously defective rather than totally anomalous. Pyrrho could consistently claim to be a sceptic concerning knowledge of the external world or objective moral standards, and at the same time maintain that 'indifference' does not extend to tranquillity and mental disturbance. About the respective goodness and badness of these states of mind he could claim to be subjectively certain (so too perhaps Timon ap. Sext. *Adv. math*, xi 20). Pyrrho's motive in advocating suspension of judgment may well have been the practical one of freeing people from the disturbance caused by certain beliefs, especially beliefs which conflict with each other. But this was also the professed goal of later Pyrrhonism, and the practical orientation of Pyrrho's philosophy does not speak against his competence in arguments (cf. D.L. ix 64). The little that is known about his life tells strongly in favour of his having, what we may call, a professional philosophical background.

As the name of a philosophical method or particular school Scepticism originates with Pyrrho. But long before Pyrrho of course we can find philosophers expressing sceptical attitudes. The fallibility of sense-perception as a source of knowledge was emphasized in different ways by Heraclitus, Parmenides, Empedocles and Democritus in the Presocratic period. Earlier than all of these Xenophanes had written:

That which is wholly clear no man has seen, nor will there ever be a man who has intuitive knowledge about the gods and about everything of which I speak. For even if he should chance to speak the complete truth, yet he himself does not know it; what occurs concerning all things is seeming (DK 21B34).

Plato in the fourth century replied that 'seeming' is only the ontological condition of phenomena. We can know that which is fully real—the Forms—but these changeless and eternal entities are not objects of sense-perception. Plato's distinctions between seeming and being and between belief and knowledge can be traced to a desire to establish a set of objects (the Forms) which are not liable to the unstable and uncertain judgments made about phenomena. Some earlier philosophers had already faced the problem of knowledge in a different way. Protagoras, instead of looking like Parmenides for some unchanging noumenal subject of the verb 'exists', argued that the senses must be accepted for what they are—sources of subjective awareness. Truth can only be relative; what is true for me—that the wind feels cold—is true; but this says nothing about the temperature of the wind in itself or how it feels to you. Protagoras did not, in my judgment, deny the existence of a world external to the percipient. He denied the validity of statements which seek to go beyond the experience of individuals.

Plato's answer to Protagorean relativism is a large and complex subject. The important point for this chapter is that certain problems of knowledge to which Pyrrho drew attention had already been recognized by earlier philosophers, who put forward different kinds of answers for resolving them. Pyrrho's scepticism has its closest conceptual connexion with Protagoras among his predecessors. But it looks forward rather than back. Both the Epicureans and the Stoics argued that objective knowlege of the world is possible. In Epicureanism the 'clear view' and its derivative, 'preconception', in Stoicism the 'cognitive impression', are laid down as valid criteria for true perceptual statements. Pyrrho's scepticism provides the basis for a penetrating criticism of such theories of knowledge, though there is no evidence that Pyrrho himself attacked Epicurus and Zeno specifically; indeed Epicurus is said to have admired Pyrrho (D.L. ix 64). The second feature of Pyrrhonism which marks its contemporary character is the ethical goal, 'freedom from disturbance'. No one had previously suggested that scepticism might be made the basis of a moral theory. This was Pyrrho's innovation, but in seeking for a means to attain tranquillity of mind he is at one with Epicurus and the Stoics.

Pyrrho was born at Elis in the north-west of the Peloponnese about 365 B.C. We know little about his life and philosophical background. He is said to have been a pupil of Bryson son of Stilpo (D.L. ix 61). This is probably a corruption for 'Bryson or Stilpo' who were both adherents of the Megarian school. There is no reason to question the likelihood of some early connexion between Pyrrho and the Megarians. From them Pyrrho would have acquired a training in dialectic and reasons for distrusting the evidence of the senses. He did not however espouse the positive aspects of Megarian teaching, which drew upon Eleatic monism and Parmenides' prescription 'judge by reason'. Stilpo also incorporated features of Cynic doctrine into his own philosophy. Anecdotes about Pyrrho suggest that he was sympathetic to the Cynic advocacy of a simple life in withdrawal from civic affairs (D.L. ix 62–9).

A second source of Pyrrho's scepticism may be found in an association he had with Anaxarchus. This obscure figure is said 'to have abolished the criterion' by Sextus (*Adv. math.* vii 48; 87f.), and if he was a Democritean (D.L. ix 58) he may also have adopted the early atomist subjectivism concerning perceptual judgments. Anaxarchus was a citizen of Abdera, Democritus' home town. Most of our information about him comes from Plutarch and Arrian's accounts of Alexander the Great.[1] Anaxarchus became a court philosopher, and accompanied Alexander on his eastern expedition. Pyrrho was also a member of the party, and Diogenes Laertius says that both philosophers consorted with the Indian 'Gymnosophists' (naked philosophers) and the Magi (ix 61). But it is impossible to know whether oriental influences played any significant part in Pyrrho's philosophical development. The evidence does not require such a hypothesis.

Pyrrho himself wrote nothing, possibly to avoid giving the impression of dogmatizing. Fortunately he had a follower, Timon of Phlius, who was less scrupulous, and some fragments of Timon's writings survive as quotations in later writers.[2] They provide the most reliable evidence of Pyrrho's own views. Timon is a colourful figure who defended the Pyrrhonist position in verse as well as prose. The majority of his fragments belong to the *silloi*, 'lampoons', in which he attacks the dogmatic philosophers. Diogenes Laertius' *Life of Pyrrho* also draws upon Timon's work; but the best starting-point for a discussion of Pyrrho's scepticism is a text from Aristocles' *On philosophy*, a Peripatetic treatise written in the second century A.D. and quoted by Eusebius, bishop of Caesaria (*Pr. Ev.* xiv 18, 758c–d). It is unlikely that this late summary preserves Timon's precise words, but the position attributed to Pyrrho seems entirely credible.

After observing that Pyrrho left nothing in writing, Aristocles continues:

His pupil Timon says that the man who means to be happy must consider these three questions: 1. what things are really like; 2. what attitude we should adopt towards them; 3. what the consequence of such an attitude will be. According to Timon Pyrrho declared that things are equally indistinguishable, unmeasurable and indeterminable.[3] For this reason neither our

[1] Testimonia in Diels-Kranz, *Vorsokratiker* ii 59.

[2] The evidence has been collected by Diels, *Poetarum philosophorum fragmenta* 9.

[3] These three adjectives have sometimes been interpreted in a descriptive rather than a modal sense, 'undistinguished' not 'undistinguishable' etc. But the second

acts of perception nor our judgments are true or false. Therefore we should not rely upon them but be without judgments, inclining neither this way nor that, but be steadfast saying concerning each individual thing that it no more is than is not, or that it both is and is not, or that it neither is nor is not. For those who adopt this attitude the consequence will be first a refusal to make assertions and second, freedom from disturbance.

Pyrrho's first question is one that had been asked and answered for the past two hundred years and more. Indeed, it might well be called the basic question of Greek philosophy.[1] The assumption that the 'nature' of things, or what the world is 'really' like, can be investigated and disclosed is basic to Presocratic philosophy as it is to Plato and Aristotle. Pyrrho, with his answer to this question, is rejecting the assumption and thereby denying legitimacy to philosophical speculation. All philosophy must start from certain assumptions, at least if it is to offer any account of reality. And one of the first assumptions which a philosopher must make is that something true can be said about the world; otherwise there can be no knowledge of external reality. Pyrrho, however, claims that truth and falsehood can characterize neither our perception of things nor the (other) judgments which we make; from which it follows that what we perceive or judge cannot be an object of knowledge. Pyrrho's claim is grounded in his answer to the question: 'What are things really like?' By answering 'Unknowable' Pyrrho removes the external world as a subject of philosophical discourse. If the real nature of things cannot be known either to the senses or to reason, then there is nothing by reference to which the truth or falsehood of statements about it can be tested.

The assertion that 'things are equally indistinguishable, unmeasurable and indeterminable' is not supported by any argument in the text quoted from Aristocles. But Pyrrho's own reasoning can be reconstructed with a fair degree of certainty from the fragments of Timon and from other Sceptic sources. Pyrrho is attacking all theories of knowledge which seek, as the Stoics and Epicureans sought, to show that certain perceptual experiences provide wholly accurate information about the real nature of (external) objects. The basis of his critique is that we cannot get at objects independently of sense-perception, and

---

and third have a termination (-*tos*) which most frequently signifies possibility or necessity, and this interpretation suits the argument better, cf. C. L. Stough, *Greek Skepticism* (Berkeley and Los Angeles 1969) pp. 18f.
[1] 'On what things are really like', literally 'On Nature', is the standard book title among early Greek philosophers. It was also the title of Epicurus' basic work (see p. 18).

sense-perception provides no guarantee that we apprehend things as they really are. Objects in themselves are therefore not available to test our sense-perception. Sense-perception reveals 'what appears' to the percipient; but 'what appears' cannot be used as sound evidence from which to infer 'what is'.

Let us consider the last statement more closely. Pyrrho is arguing that our perceptual experience can never be sufficient to warrant indubitable statements or beliefs about the external world. He does not deny that something, say, yellow, sweet and sticky *appears* to me; and he will admit that I may be justified in saying 'This looks like honey'. But he holds that my sense-perception is quite compatible with the proposition 'This is not honey' as well as the proposition 'This does not look like honey to Pyrrho'. In the 'modes' formulated by the later Pyrrhonists we find ten types of consideration for doubting the possibility of knowledge. They concentrate upon the fact that how we perceive anything is relative to the nature of the percipient and external circumstances. Thus the Pyrrhonist adopts certain everyday assumptions for the purpose of argument, for instance that the sun is a source of heat and the shade of cold, and then refers to someone who became warm in the shade and shivered in the sun (D.L. ix 80; Sextus, *P.H.* i 82). We cannot say that he was mistaken in *feeling* hot and cold as he did. But his feelings conflict with those of other men. The Pyrrhonist concludes that the same thing may 'appear' in contradictory ways to different people, and therefore nothing which 'appears' to any man is sufficient to found a belief on what anything is really like.[1]

With regard to the contradictions in their sceptical procedures they would first demonstrate the ways in which things induce belief and then use the same grounds to undermine their credibility. They argue that those things induce belief which are agreed upon by reference to sense-perception, and things which never or only rarely change—customs, things determined by laws, objects of pleasure and wonder. Then they showed that the probabilities are equal by means of things contrary to those which induce belief (D.L. ix 78–9).

Timon, and probably Pyrrho himself, distinguished sharply between statements of the form (1) '*x* appears to me to be *y*', and (2)

[1] A. J. Ayer writes: 'It would be hard for [the sceptic] to get a hearing if the procedures which he questions never led us astray. But it is not essential to his position that this should be so. All that he requires is that errors should be possible not that they should actually occur' *The Problem of Knowledge* (Harmondsworth 1965) p. 40.

'*x* is *y*', where *x* and *y* refer to the same object. Only the second statement is banned. The first statement is perfectly acceptable to the Pyrrhonists, since it does not commit the speaker to any claim about the relationship between what he perceives and what is the case independently of his perception. There is no wish or attempt to deny that we have genuine perceptual experiences:

We admit the fact that we do see, we recognize the fact that we do have this particular thought; but we do not know how we see or how we think. We say by way of description that 'this appears white', without confirming that it really is white (D.L. ix 103).

That honey is sweet I do not postulate, but I admit that it appears sweet (Timon, *On the senses*, D.L. ix 105).

It is important to observe that the subject of the type of statement acceptable to the Pyrrhonists is not what later philosophers have sometimes called a sense-datum. The subject of Timon's statement 'It appears sweet' is honey, a thing or material object. There would be no point to the distinction between '*x* appears to me to be *y*' and '*x* is *y*' if *x* were merely a sense-datum. Suppose that on eating something yellow and sticky I get a sweet taste. If *what* I taste is only a sense-datum then there could be no reason to deny that *it is* sweet. What is open to question is whether the sweetness which I actually taste is a real property of the yellow, sticky object. But this is not Timon's way of proceeding. He is not suggesting that we only see, hear, taste, touch or smell sense-data; but rather, that we perceive objects—honey, coffee, dogs, chairs—as our ordinary language suggests. The problem in the form which he raises it is not the relation between sense-data and objects, but the relation between the object as perceived and the same object independently of its being perceived. In brief, he is saying that the conditions of perception are such that they introduce a relationship between the object and the percipient which cannot be assumed to hold between the object and its own properties.

That this is Timon's procedure is shown clearly by the use of the words 'the apparent' (*to phainomenon*), or as I should prefer to paraphrase it, 'the object as perceived'.[1] Thus he writes: 'But the object

[1] The Pyrrhonists use the term 'the apparent' in preference to the term *phantasia* (presentation, impression, image); in Diogenes Laertius' *Life of Pyrrho* the latter term does occur in a section (107) concerning disagreement between Sceptics and dogmatists (*phantasia* is the word used by Epicureans and Stoics). The term *phantasia* means roughly what has been called a sense-datum in modern

as perceived prevails on every side, wherever it goes' (D.L. ix 105). What Timon means with these rather cryptic words can be inferred from a passage of Sextus:

> We say that the criterion of the Sceptic school is 'the object as perceived', using this term for what is in effect its impression on the senses. For since the impression is a matter of our being acted upon and involuntary feeling, it is not open to question. Hence no one, it may be, disagrees concerning the fact that the underlying object appears to be of this or that kind; the question is whether it really is such as it appears to be (*P.H.* i 22).

(Strictly, Sextus should have pointed out that what is perceived may have no 'underlying object'.)

The Pyrrhonists are denying that perception is something intentional. I cannot help seeing this as a printed sheet of paper; for that is the content of my present visual sensation. On the basis of this evidence I am entitled to make a type (1) statement. If I go further and say 'This is a sheet of printed paper' I utter a type (2) statement. The Pyrrhonist will now object that I have postulated a relation between subject and predicate for which I have no valid evidence. I have used my experience of 'the object as perceived' to infer a definite characteristic of the object in itself. The validity of this inference cannot be proved, and my type (2) statement is therefore neither true nor false.

Since sense-perception, in the view of the Pyrrhonists, provides no grounds for judgments about things-in-themselves, we should not make such judgments. This brings us to Pyrrho's answer to the second question in Aristocles' text. Our attitude to the world should be one of suspended judgment, which is summed up by the Pyrrhonists in the expression 'no more' (this than that).[1] The effect of this formula is to leave it entirely an open question whether the subject of an objective

---

philosophy. Pyrrho, on the evidence of Timon and Diogenes, preferred to use the language of 'appearance', i.e. to speak of 'the same thing appearing different to different people', but from a philosophical point of view there is little reason to choose one form of expression rather than the other, cf. R. M. Chisholm's excellent article, 'The theory of appearing' (*Philosophical Analysis* ed. Max Black, Ithaca, N.Y. 1950).

[1] See Sextus *P.H.* i 188–91. In the following chapters of this book Sextus gives a further glossary of Sceptic technical terms. The terms 'no more', 'I determine nothing' etc. are not themselves to be interpreted as positive assertions. They are merely a linguistic device for expressing the refusal to make any assertions (D.L. ix 76 reporting Timon), and are said to cancel themselves in being asserted: i.e. 'I determine nothing' is taken to entail that I do not determine that I determine nothing, cf. Sextus *P.H.* i 14ff. Sometimes these slogans were interpreted descriptively as indications of the Pyrrhonist's own state of mind (Sextus ibid. 201; D.L. ix 74).

judgment is what it is said to be, or whether it has the property attributed to it. Hence, if I say 'Snow is no more white than it is not white', I am to be taken as offering no positive description or determination of any material object. The Sceptic 'determines nothing', on the grounds that determining anything entails 'assenting to something non-evident', that is, what things are like in themselves.

The judgments which the Pyrrhonist outlaws are exclusively claims to know about things-in-themselves. We might with good reason call the statement 'This appears to be honey' a judgment. Our perceptual experience typically takes such a form. We see, or there appears to us, a cat or a rose not a black shape or a red shape, though there are times when the latter expressions do describe correctly what we see. But if 'A cat appears to me' is a judgment, it is a judgment which does not, at least normally, involve any conscious inference. And though such statements can be false, either deliberately or mistakenly, we normally treat a person's claims to see, hear and so forth as authoritative. The Pyrrhonists seem to have regarded these as mere reports of perceptual experience which are to be distinguished from 'judgments'. 'The Pyrrhonist procedure is a manner of reporting on objects as perceived' (D.L. ix 78). There is no indication that the Pyrrhonists regarded such statements as amenable to truth or falsity, and every reason to think that they are excluded from the condemnation of 'asserting'. To assert, for Pyrrho, is to make a statement of the type (2) form 'x is y'—this is white; by refusing to say 'x is no more y than it is not' etc. the Pyrrhonist repudiates the possibility of being right or wrong about this kind of assertion.

Pyrrho's suspension of judgment concerning the nature of material objects applies equally to moral concepts. Diogenes Laertius tells us that he 'denied that anything was morally good or bad' and that custom and convention govern human actions (ix 61). An extract later from the *Life* illustrates the Pyrrhonist style of argument about the relativity of moral judgments:

Either all that is held to be good by anyone must be said to be good or not all. But all cannot be said to be good since the same thing is held to be good by one person, for instance pleasure by Epicurus; and bad by another, Antisthenes. The consequence will be that the same thing is both good and bad. But if we do not admit that everything judged to be good by anyone is good, we shall have to distinguish between different opinions. This is impossible owing to the equal weight of arguments on both sides. Therefore that which is really good is unknowable (ix 101).

In the passage of Aristocles with which this discussion began, reason as well as sense-perception is ruled out as a possible criterion of truth. Once again there is no direct evidence for Pyrrho's own arguments about this, but both Diogenes Laertius and Sextus supply arguments which were used by later Pyrrhonists. We have already seen that Epicurus, like Aristotle, based his epistemology on empirical evidence and the same is true of the Stoics. The Pyrrhonists adopted this position for their own critical purposes, and used the unreliability of sense-perception as the ground for denying reason's claims to any knowledge of the real nature of things:

> If every intelligible thing has its source and basis of confirmation in sense-perception, and the things apprehended through sense-perception are inconsistent (with each other), as we have argued, the same must be true of the intelligibles; so that the premises of the proof, of whatever kind they are, must be unreliable and insecure. Therefore demonstrative reasoning is not trustworthy (Sextus, *Adv. math.* viii 356).

The practical outcome of this attitude to reality is said to be 'freedom from confusion'. Various anecdotes are told about Pyrrho's suspension of judgment: he would have fallen into pits or would have been attacked by dogs if it had not been for the help of his friends (D.L. ix 62). Such stories should be taken with more than a grain of salt. Pyrrho's scepticism entails nothing unpractical so far as everyday life is concerned. If it did, life would be full of confusion. The Pyrrhonists do have a criterion for practical purposes, 'the object as perceived'.[1] But it is not a criterion of truth in the sense required by them. They deny that seeing is believing, that is, believing that we can see or apprehend things as they are in themselves. The object of the Pyrrhonist's attack is not common-sense attitudes to the world but philosophical claims to knowledge. Knowledge makes a claim to certainty whether it be about the nature of material objects, the structure of the universe, moral values or the existence of God. In Pyrrho's scepticism we are not debarred from saying that we see cats and dogs, or, as his language would put it, that cats and dogs 'appear' to us. But the perceptual experiences which we have do not, he argues, entitle us to say anything about the entities which we assume to exist independently of such experiences. By suspending judgment we are freed from the confusion which may arise if we hear contradictory accounts of the gods, the nature of goodness, and so forth. The Pyrrhonist

---

[1] D.L. ix 106; Sextus, *P.H.* i 21–4.

accepts the conventions of everyday life as a practical criterion without troubling himself over questions about their rational justification. At a time when philosophers were competing with each other in logic, or natural and moral philosophy, Pyrrho took the step of criticizing all philosophers by questioning the basis of their claims to knowledge. At the same time his critique can be given a wider ambience, taking in religion and all dogmatic prescriptions for society and the individual. Like the Stoic and Epicurean insistence on the validity of their rational explanations of phenomena, Pyrrho's antithetical scepticism is an alternative answer for men dissatisfied with the traditional values and beliefs of a society in a state of transition.

Old Pyrrho, Pyrrho, how and whence did you discover release from servitude to the beliefs and empty theorizing of sophists? How did you unloose the shackles of every deception and inducement to belief? You did not trouble to inquire into the winds which prevail over Greece, whence each comes and whither it blows (Timon ap. D.L. ix 65).

It is of course an evasive answer, especially at a time when conventions and social values were changing. What did it mean at the end of the fourth century B.C. to 'follow convention'? Pyrrho's scepticism however has the great merit of underlining the fact that our perception of objects is relative to all manner of circumstances. Knowledge of the external world is not incorrigible. There are no necessary truths about empirical objects, and David Hume was probably right to argue that no sufficient reasons can be given for inferring the nature of physical objects from sense-perception. Most philosophers today are probably content to concede that the world as perceived may not be the world as it exists in some other relation. If that lands us in dualism it is not perhaps the philosopher's task to resolve the problem. We employ physicists to tell us about the structure of matter. But matter has nothing obviously to do with the world as we perceive it. Nevertheless, there is a most important rôle for truth and falsehood in judgments about the objects of perception. We are, as a matter of fact, remarkably successful in judging distance, shape, colour and size; the mistakes we sometimes make, or may be induced to make under certain perceptual conditions, do not do much to undermine this fact. Leaving aside things-in-themselves, we have criteria for identifying and distinguishing between objects of perception with a consistency and accuracy which the Pyrrhonists overlook. If we adopt the strict Pyrrhonist requirement of matching

objects as perceived with things-in-themselves, we may not succeed
in giving any rational justification for objective statements. Pyrrho
was quite right to see a difficulty here. But the Pyrrhonist is prepared
to say 'This appears to be white', without appreciating the significance
of the fact that such a sentence, as Epicurus recognized, presupposes
some similar previous experience also shared by others. The Academic
Sceptics under Carneades realized that conditions of truth can be laid
down which need not commit a philosopher to any claims to have
knowledge of things-in-themselves.

(ii) Academic Scepticism—Arcesilaus

Pyrrho died about 270 B.C. He founded no school in any formal sense,
and such dissemination as his views acquired was chiefly due to hearsay
and the writings of Timon. The next stage in the history of Greek
scepticism is marked not by Pyrrhonists but by the Academy. The
last half of Pyrrho's life overlaps the youth and middle years of
Arcesilaus, who became head of the Academy about 265 B.C. Arcesilaus,
like Pyrrho, is said to have denied the possibility of knowledge (Cic.
Acad. i 45), and to a late Sceptic like Sextus Empiricus Arcesilaus'
philosophical position seemed almost identical to Pyrrhonism (*P.H.*
i 232).[1] It is highly probable that Arcesilaus was influenced by Pyrrho,
but the intellectual background of the two Sceptics was very different.
Unlike Pyrrho, Arcesilaus is a figure of the Athenian philosophical
establishment, though he was to initiate radical changes in the character
of contemporary Platonism.

Arcesilaus was not an Athenian by birth. He came from Pitane in
Aetolia, and first studied there under a mathematician, Autolycus
(D.L. iv 29). At Athens he was a pupil of a musical theorist, Xanthus,
and Theophrastus.[2] But he left the Lyceum for the Academy, at a
time when Polemo was its head and Crantor and Crates were prominent members. As I have mentioned in the first chapter, the Academy
in the last part of the fourth century and the beginning of the third, seems
to have given increasing emphasis to practical moral teaching. Crantor,
for instance, wrote a 'little' book *On grief*, which is highly praised in
Cicero's *Academica* (ii 135). There is no reason to think that Arcesilaus

---

[1] Ariston, the heretical Stoic contemporary of Arcesilaus, described him in a
parody of a Homeric line as 'Plato in front, Pyrrho behind, Diodorus in the
middle' (Sextus, *P.H.* i 234); Diodorus Cronus, the Megarian philosopher, is
meant. Cf. Timon's remarks, D.L. iv 33.
[2] A. Weische, *Cicero und die neue Akademie* has attempted to find in the
Peripatos a source of Arcesilaus' scepticism; but his argument is not compelling.

disapproved of practical moral teaching. Had he done so the Academy under Polemo could hardly have attracted him in the first place. But Arcesilaus was not content to maintain this tradition. On the contrary, he seems to have felt that the Academy had lost the original incentive, which it derived through Plato from Socrates, towards dispassionate and undogmatic inquiry. It was not as a moral teacher that Arcesilaus made his name, but as a dialectician. According to Cicero 'what he chiefly derived from various books by Plato and from Socratic discourses was that neither the senses nor the mind can perceive anything certain' (*De orat.* iii 67). This is hardly a conclusion which someone who had studied Plato's writings as a whole would be entitled to draw, and it is not clear that Arcesilaus actually claimed Plato's authority as the support for his own scepticism. He doubtless admired Plato's dialectical methodology, but we are also told that he was the first Academic to disturb the system handed down by Plato, and that by means of question and answer he made it more disputatious (D.L. iv 28). It was the Socratic method rather than Plato's positive philosophy which influenced Arcesilaus.

In such early dialogues of Plato as the *Euthyphro, Ion, Laches* and *Lysis*, the discussion concerns itself with attempts to answer a 'What is *x*?' question, e.g. piety or courage. Socrates' interlocutor claims to be able to answer this question at the outset of the dialogue, but under examination his suggestion is found to be unsatisfactory and alternative answers are put forward. Socrates himself makes positive contributions, but subjects them along with those proffered by others to criticism. By the end of the dialogue various candidates have been considered, but none is accepted as satisfactory. Hence Socrates concludes the *Euthyphro* by saying: 'See what you've done, my friend! You are going away having destroyed all my hopes of learning from you about piety and impiety'; or the *Lysis*: 'We have become a laughing-stock, you two, and I, an old man. As they leave, all these people will say that we regard ourselves—for I class myself as one of you—as friends, but we have not as yet been able to discover what a friend is.' Socrates' procedure in these dialogues is consistent with the portrait painted of him by Plato in the *Apology*. There Socrates disclaims the possession of knowledge, but he also asserts that recognition of one's own ignorance is better than thinking that one knows something when one doesn't. Arcesilaus' philosophical method is the Socratic procedure updated to take account of the state of philosophy in the third century B.C.

The essence of this methodology consists in taking the position of one's opponents and showing it to be self-contradictory. The most detailed argument by Arcesilaus which survives exemplifies the technique very clearly.[1]

The Stoics distinguished three epistemological states: knowledge, apprehension, and belief. They held that knowledge was peculiar to the wise man and belief peculiar to the foolish (all other men). By 'apprehension' or 'grasping' (*katalêpsis*) the Stoics meant what we would call accurate or true perception. They maintained that through the senses we receive information about the external world, some of which is absolutely accurate, and it is this absolutely accurate information which we can *apprehend*. To apprehend something is therefore to grasp it as it really is. The details of this theory will require further discussion in the next chapter. But for the present, it is enough to observe that the Stoic theory of knowledge was based on the ground that certain sense-impressions—those which can be apprehended—are 'cognitive' or self-evidently 'true'.

The Stoics did not distinguish the wise from the foolish by reference to 'apprehension'. All men, they held, are capable of apprehending things, but only the wise man's apprehension is 'secure and unshakeable by argument'. This is the mark of knowledge—not mere apprehension but apprehension which is proof against any attempt that might be made to overturn it.

To this theory Arcesilaus made the following objections. First, apprehension is not, in fact, an independent test of truth since in practice it is either knowledge (in the wise man) or belief (in the fool). This point, we may note, is based upon the Stoics' own thesis: all men are either wise or foolish. In other words, Arcesilaus is arguing that the Stoics, by their exclusive disjunction between wise and foolish, make any intermediate cognitive state redundant. 'Apprehension' is *either* knowledge *or* belief; it is not something over and above one of these, and it cannot therefore serve as the criterion of truth.

Further, Arcesilaus took the definition of apprehension, 'assent to a cognitive impression', and argued that this was vitiated on two grounds: first, what we assent to is a proposition and not a (sense-)impression (the Stoics, and other philosophers, used 'true' in a much looser sense than would be acceptable today); secondly, and more important, 'no true impression is found which is of such a kind that it

---

[1] The evidence for the next four paragraphs is drawn from Sextus, *Adv. math.* vii 150–7; cf. also Cic. *Acad.* ii 77. For the Stoic theory in detail see pp. 123–31.

could not be false'. Later Academics set out detailed arguments in support of this point (see p. 96). It forms a direct contradiction of the Stoic thesis; for the Stoics argued that the characteristic of a cognitive impression is just the fact that it is true and cannot be false.

The Stoics held that the wise man will only suspend judgment in cases where apprehension is not possible. Arcesilaus' argument leads to the conclusion that the wise man must always suspend judgment. For if apprehension is ruled out, then all things must be non-apprehensible. Only a fool would assent to what is non-apprehensible, and this amounts to holding opinions. But the wise man, according to the Stoics, does not hold opinions, for that would equate him with fools. Therefore, Arcesilaus argues, the Stoic wise man will not assent to anything but will suspend judgment.

In this argument, Arcesilaus accepts the Stoic distinction between the wise and the foolish; he also accepts their distinction between giving and withholding assent. He attacks the Stoic claim that assent can ever be well-grounded by raising objections to the notion of apprehension. And thereby he turns the Stoics' own argument into a defence of the Sceptic position.

Arcesilaus was undoubtedly concerned to attack dogmatic claims to knowledge. Stoicism, with its postulate that sense-perception can provide grounds for statements which are certainly true, offered him a ready target. But it is not entirely clear that we should take Arcesilaus to be *positively* advocating scepticism.[1] Cicero reports that he 'denied that anything could be known, not even that which Socrates had left himself' (*Acad.* i 45). By this reference to Socrates, Arcesilaus means 'knowledge that we do not know anything'. If we take Arcesilaus' statement seriously, it entails that neither the validity of knowledge nor that of scepticism can be positively established. That is to say, Arcesilaus leaves it an open question whether true or false are legitimate predicates to apply to certain statements. He denies knowledge of any criteria which are adequate to sanction the use of true and false. But it does not follow from this that some statements are not true and others not false. Arcesilaus' open-mindedness on this question emerges in Cicero's next remarks:

[1] Sextus asserts that Arcesilaus put forward 'suspension of judgment' as the goal of life, *P.H.* i 232. But von Arnim, *R.E.* sv Arkesilaos, gives reasons for thinking that 'the discovery of truth' would be a better description of Arcesilaus' goal, cf. Cic. *Acad.* ii 60, *veri inveniendi causa*: ibid. 76, *verum invenire voluisse sic intelligitur.*

He believed that everything lies hidden in obscurity, and that there is nothing which can be perceived or understood; therefore it is improper for any-one to make any assertion or declaration or to give anything approval by an act of assent; a man must restrain himself and check his rashness from every slip, for one's rashness would be conspicuous if something false or unknown were approved of, and there is nothing worse than assent and approval running ahead of knowledge and perception.

If nothing can be perceived or understood there are no grounds for saying that such and such is certainly the case; but it may be the case. Arcesilaus' recommendation to refrain from assent is based here on the need to avoid error. In order to assent to or approve of something we require knowledge; otherwise we may assent to what is false. But nothing can be known. Therefore we should not assent to anything, and thus we avoid the possibility of error. As von Arnim says, for Arcesilaus 'the essential mark of wisdom is not possession of knowledge but freedom from error'.[1]

The positive feature of Arcesilaus' philosophical method is the desire to discover what is true. For this purpose 'it is necessary to argue *pro* and *contra* everything' (Cic. *Acad.* ii 60).[2] An important example of this will be discussed when we come to Carneades, but the metho-dology goes back to Arcesilaus. Cicero, generalizing about the New Academy (i.e. the Academy from Arcesilaus to Philo of Larisa), writes as follows:

> The only object of the Academics' discussions is by arguing both sides of a question to draw out and fashion something which is either true or which comes as close as possible to truth. Nor is there any difference between our-selves and those who think that they know except that they do not doubt that their doctrines are true, whereas we hold many things to be probable which we can easily adhere to but hardly affirm as certain (*Acad.* ii 8).

As we have seen, Arcesilaus rejected the Stoics' defence of an empiricist theory of knowledge based upon 'cognitive sense-impres-sions'. There is no evidence that he regarded this as a doctrine with respect to which reasons of equal cogency could be advanced on both sides. His Academic successors followed up Arcesilaus' criticism of sense-perception as a source of knowledge by developing rules for assent on the basis of 'probability'. No doubt the inspiration for this stems from Arcesilaus himself, but the detailed working out of the theory is credited in our sources to Carneades. Sextus tells us that

---

[1] op. cit. col. 1166. [2] cf. D.L. iv 28; Cic. *Acad.* ii 7f.

Arcesilaus 'says that the man who suspends judgment about every-thing will regulate his actions by "that which is reasonable" ' (*Adv. math.* vii 158). By this criterion Arcesilaus may have meant that for which good, as distinct from infallible, reasons can be given. It is not certain however that Arcesilaus put this forward as his own view.[1] Sextus refers to 'the reasonable' at the end of Arcesilaus' criticism of the Stoics, and his phraseology here is for the most part Stoic. Arcesi-laus may be simply applying to the Stoics the consequences of his own critique. It will not be possible for them, if knowledge has been undermined, to define a right act, as they did, in terms of knowledge. They will have to say simply that it is one for which good but not infallible reasons can be given.

Our information about Arcesilaus is too scanty to make it profitable to speculate further about his views. But he is an important figure in the history of philosophy. By challenging the Stoics and other dog-matists, he restored to philosophy a critical function which it was in serious danger of losing. Neither the successors of Plato nor the contemporary Peripatos could consistently cast doubt upon the foundations of knowledge while defending positivist views of their own. Arcesilaus sharpened awareness of the problems which surround empiricist theories of knowledge, and there are no strong reasons for thinking that he was more sympathetic towards a metaphysical theory such as Plato's Forms provided. It has sometimes been supposed, on the basis of statements in St. Augustine, Sextus and Cicero, that Arcesilaus confined his scepticism to criticism of the Stoics and other schools, while adhering to orthodox Platonism within the Academy itself.[2] But most scholars have rightly rejected this view.[3] Cicero, our best evidence for Arcesilaus, presents him as a wholly honest and consistent philosopher who regarded suspension of assent as an honourable attitude and one worthy of a wise man (*Acad.* ii 77). Since Arcesilaus, like Socrates, wrote nothing, it was easy for mis-conceptions about him to arise. It is unfortunate that we have so few examples of his famous powers as a dialectician. Under his leadership

---

[1] Here too von Arnim seems to me to be correct, *R.E.* sv Arkesilaos col. 1167 in pointing out the Stoic context of Arcesilaus' remarks about 'the reasonable'. Brochard, *Les Sceptiques grecs*, p. 112, sees a concession to Stoicism, inappro-priately in my view. It is characteristic of Arcesilaus' method to draw a conclusion from his opponents' premises.

[2] Augustine, *Cont. Ac.* i 38; Sextus, *P.H.* i 232; Cic. *Acad.* ii 60.

[3] e.g. Zeller, Brochard, Weische. An exception is O. Gigon, 'Zur Geschichte der sogennanten Neuen Akademie', *Museum Helveticum* i (1944).

the Academy seems to have recovered some of its former prestige, and we may presume that Arcesilaus lectured on a variety of subjects. He saw his rôle as a philosopher to consist in criticism and the stimulation of argument. His epistemological doubts are only one, though a very important one, of his contributions to philosophy. Happily we know rather more about the greatest of his successors, Carneades.

(iii) Academic Scepticism—Carneades

The immediate successors of Arcesilaus in the Academy are little more than names to us. The next important phase in the history of Greek scepticism begins with Carneades who flourished about a hundred years later. A key date in Carneades' career is 155 B.C. when he was one of three philosophers chosen to represent Athens as an ambassador at Rome; the others were Diogenes of Babylon, a Stoic, and the Peripatetic, Critolaus.[1] It was on this occasion that Carneades gave his famous lectures for and against justice on consecutive days, which Cicero summarized in the *De republica* (see p. 94). By this time Carneades was about fifty-eight years old, and he died in 129 B.C.

Just as Arcesilaus devoted his attention to a sharp criticism of early Stoicism, so Carneades made it his special task to combat vigorously the theories of Chrysippus. Chrysippus' enormous contribution to Stoicism was neatly expressed in the tag: 'If Chrysippus had not lived there would have been no Stoa.' Carneades parodied this with the quip: 'Without Chrysippus there would have been no Carneades' (D.L. iv 62). On theory of knowledge, ethics, theology and causality Carneades argued at length against the Stoics, and we shall see in the next chapter that his criticism prompted some amendments to Stoic doctrine. Since Carneades' arguments are so closely tied to Stoicism, it will be necessary to anticipate over the next few pages certain subjects treated more fully later. But our chief concern here is Carneades' own philosophical position, and in particular his epistemology.

Carneades followed the fashion set by Pyrrho and Arcesilaus of not writing philosophy (D.L. iv 65). But thanks above all to Cicero Carneades is relatively well documented. His arguments were recorded and expounded by pupils the most notable of whom, Clitomachus, is reputed to have written more than four hundred treatises (D.L. iv 67). Cicero's *Academica* refers explicitly to Clitomachus for some reports of Carneades' views (cf. *Acad.* ii 98ff.), and Clitomachus is probably

[1] Cic. *Tusc.* iv 5; Plutarch, *Cato Maior* 22.

the ultimate source of most detailed evidence on Carneades. As Carneades' close and devoted associate, Clitomachus may be regarded as a most scrupulous witness to his master's views, and he succeeded to the headship of the Academy on Carneades' death.

Many ancient writers comment upon Carneades' personal qualities. He emerges as a most formidable character, renowned for his dedication to philosophy and ability in argument. He became so absorbed in his work, says Diogenes Laertius, that his hair and his nails grew long (iv 62)!

Arcesilaus' sole alternative to knowledge was suspension of judgment. He did not work out in any detail the grounds on which someone might be justified in assenting to some proposition even if its truth could never be firmly established. Carneades agreed with Arcesilaus that no proposition can be certainly established as true or false. But he also developed with considerable care a theory of 'probability', and this may be called an epistemological theory provided that we recognize it makes no claim to, indeed specifically disclaims, certainty.

Carneades developed this theory after a consideration and rejection of Stoic epistemology. An objective criterion of truth, he argued, must satisfy the conditions laid down by the Stoics. No judgment about the world can be certainly true unless (a) it is based upon impressions which report the facts correctly, and (b) the reliability of such impressions is itself correctly recognized by the percipient (Sextus, *Adv. math.* vii 161, 402ff.). The Stoics held that both of these conditions are satisfied by the 'cognitive impression' (*kataleptikê phantasia*). The characteristic of such an impression is 'complete conformity with the object' (or fact), and in assenting to it we (supposedly) recognize this characteristic. Carneades admitted the existence of sense-impressions, and he also accepted that some of them will satisfy the first condition of the criterion.[1] But this, he pointed out, is of no use unless the second condition is also met; and it cannot be met. No sense-impression, he argued, can guarantee its own correspondence with the facts. Sense-impressions do not possess characteristics which mark off one that is certainly reliable from another that is not. In no particular case is any sense-impression *self-evidently* true to the object it

---

[1] It should be noted that Carneades cannot deny (a) if scepticism is to be derived by help of the premise 'There do occur false impressions' (Cic. *Acad.* ii 83). The essence of his position is not 'There are no true impressions' (*contra* Brochard, p. 128). If that were the case Carneades could not establish his conclusion: 'No true impression can be distinguished *as true* from a second identical impression which is false.' Similarly Arcesilaus, Cic. ibid. 77.

purports to represent. It may and often will be true, but it cannot be known to be true.

Carneades' arguments against the Stoic criterion need not be rehearsed at greater length here. They largely turn on the impossibility of specifying that *nota*, 'distinguishing mark', supposedly indicative of the 'cognitive impression'. By reference to particular circumstances in which apparently true impressions have subsequently proved false; by posing problems about distinguishing between identical twins or eggs; by calling in dreams and hallucinations, Carneades built up his general case against the so-called cognitive impression.[1] It is sufficient for his purpose to be able to show that a single impression which seems to be entirely trustworthy may in fact be false (Cic. *Acad.* ii 84). For the cognitive impression is by definition something which seems to be entirely trustworthy, yet the possibility must always remain that an impression's character does not correspond with the object it purports to represent.

Like Arcesilaus therefore Carneades regarded knowledge in the Stoics' sense as unattainable. He was not however content to recommend suspension of judgment as the attitude to be adopted towards everything. By considering the conditions of sense-perception, Carneades arrived at a theory of knowledge which anticipates in many respects modern types of empiricism.

He divided sense-impressions into two categories: (*a*) those which can be perceived as 'true' (i.e. corresponding to some fact or object) and (*b*) those which cannot be so perceived (Cic. *Acad.* ii 99–104). It follows from our previous summary that for Carneades all sense-impressions must fall under category (*b*). To these categories also correspond two further distinctions which he adopted: (1) true and false; (2) probable and non-probable, or apparently true and apparently false. (*a*) and (1) go together, and (*b*) and (2) go together. Carneades argued that the denial of (*a*) and therefore (1) as practical possibilities, entails nothing about (*b*) and (2). Even though nothing can be perceived as true or false, some sense-impressions can be distinguished as probable or apparently true from others which are non-probable or apparently false. The justification for this admission is founded on the important observation that sense-impressions can be considered either in relation to their (external) object or in relation to the person to whom they appear. Let us call these the objective and the subjective relation

---

[1] See Cic. *Acad.* ii 49–60 in which Antiochus attempts to counter such reasoning; Sextus, *Adv. math.* vii 403–11.

respectively. Then, Carneades is arguing that, in their subjective relation, certain distinctions can be drawn between sense-impressions which cannot be drawn in their objective relation.

The basic distinction is that between probable and non-probable. What did Carneades mean by this? The Greek term which he used ('probable' (*'probabile'*) is Cicero's Latin translation) literally means 'persuasive' or 'trustworthy'. Cicero describes it as 'the sense-impression which the wise man will use if nothing arises which is contrary to that probability' (*Acad.* ii 99). This however is not very informative, and it is to Sextus Empiricus that we must go for more precise information (*Adv. math.* vii 166–89).

Carneades' problem is to establish a criterion which will decide between one statement and its contradictory in the absence of anything admitting of certainty. His starting-point here is everyday assumptions. We do as a matter of fact distinguish between things that appear to us clearly and things which do not. In other words, we operate in practice with a criterion of degrees of trustworthiness. If the light is poor, or if we are tired, or if our vision is confused, we are less inclined to trust our eyes than at times when different conditions are satisfied. Thus the conditions under which we receive our sense-impressions provide some means of distinguishing between sense-impressions as a whole. The first requirement of a probable sense-impression is clarity or distinctness (*perspicuitas*).

If Carneades had stopped here however he would be liable to the criticism he levelled against the Stoics and Epicureans; for, on his own terms, an isolated sense-experience can never provide sufficient grounds for our accepting it as 'true' or even probable. Carneades therefore added to the condition of 'credibility and clarity' first, the concurrence of other sense-impressions and secondly the 'testing' of each of these in turn by careful scrutiny (*Adv. math.* vii 176–83). In order to be justified in saying 'This is Socrates', we need to consider all the circumstances which characterize our sense-impression or series of impressions—the man's physical appearance, his gait, his speech, clothes, where he is situated, who he is with etc. If none of these things arouses in us a doubt of our probably seeing Socrates we are fully justified in forming this judgment.

As this example shows, the questions which the Academic sceptic is required to ask himself are going to depend on circumstances. No specific principles can be laid down in advance, but the general rule can be formulated that a judgment will be the sounder the more rigorously all the circumstances attending it are examined. Carneades compared this procedure with the Athenian practice of publicly examining the credentials of would-be magistrates and judges:

> Just as at the place of judgment there are both the one who judges and that which is being judged, and the medium through which the judgment takes place and the spatial dimensions, place, time . . . we judge the particular character of each of these things in turn: e.g. we examine whether that which is judging has sharp vision or not, whether that which is being judged is sufficiently large to be judged, whether the medium, for instance the atmosphere, is dark. . . . (Sextus, *Adv. math.* vii 183).

It is not always necessary or indeed possible to appraise all the perceptual conditions in such a systematic way. Carneades proposed that in relatively trivial matters probability can and should be established simply and quickly. Where it is a case of human well-being, however, the test of probability should be as rigorous as possible (ibid. 184).

The significant feature of Carneades' theory is his recognition that the reliance which we place upon our senses cannot be reduced to the simple terms approved by Epicurus and the Stoics. In practice we do not consciously often need to perform all the tests of probability which Carneades laid down. But that does not undermine the validity of his recommendations. He too accepted the fact that when we trust our senses, our acceptance of their evidence is generally immediate and not something which requires detailed examination. But if challenged to justify the assertion 'That is Socrates', Carneades would not appeal merely to the vividness of his visual sensations. He would point out that this apparently simple judgment is something highly complex: it involves a recognition that all the conditions which would need to be satisfied if the judgment were true are satisfied, *as far as we can observe*. We cannot, he argued, match our sense-impressions against physical objects as such; and for this reason no empirical judgment can ever be proved true or false. But we can compare one sense-impression with another; we can take account of our own previous experience and that of others; we can consider many of the factors which are involved in every perceptual experience. And on the basis of these considerations we can form some judgments about the world which, though they might in fact be false, we have every reason to accept as credit-worthy, or apparently true.

A passage from Cicero exemplifies the practical application of Carneades' doctrine:

When a wise man is boarding a ship surely he does not have it already grasped in his mind and perceived that he will sail just as he intends? How could he? But if at this moment he were setting out from here [Bauli] to Puteoli four miles away, with a good crew and an expert navigator and in these fine weather conditions, it would seem to him probable that he would arrive there safely (Cic. *Acad.* ii 100).

As we look back at such statements after two thousand years of philosophy they may strike us as somewhat pedantic, if not banal. That would be too hasty a judgment. There is no reason to think that Carneades' scepticism was intended as a recommendation to behave with exaggerated caution in everyday judgments. The scepticism of the Academics is not focused upon everyday judgments but upon philosophical theories which seek a criterion of certainty in sense-perception. In more modern terminology, Carneades is saying that the truth of empirical judgments is always contingent and never necessary. The world might, as a matter of fact, be quite different from our perception of it; but our empirical judgments can be true or false, provided that we refer truth or falsity to the world as we observe it and do not claim that our statements are true or false about the world in itself.[1]

Carneades' name, like that of Arcesilaus, is associated above all with his criticism of dogmatic claims to certainty. But whereas we know virtually nothing about Arcesilaus' arguments on any subject except theory of knowledge, there is a fair amount of evidence for Carneades' treatment of ethical doctrines, theology, and causality. On the first two topics at least, Carneades' contribution was destructive rather than constructive. This point needs stressing, for it has sometimes been maintained that Carneades had certain positive views of his own concerning ethics and theology. This would be quite inconsistent, if it were true, with his avowedly sceptical approach to problems, and there is ample evidence to refute such an interpretation. Let me take one example, from ethics.[2] In Cicero's *Academica* (ii 131) Carneades is said to have put forward the following definition of the *summum bonum*: 'to enjoy those things which nature has made primarily our own'. As Cicero observes, Carneades advanced this view 'not because he accepted it himself but in order to attack the Stoics'. The same

[1] On this point and on attempts to answer Carneades see Stough, *Greek Skepticism*, pp. 44–50.
[2] For a more detailed discussion see my article, 'Carneades and the Stoic Telos', *Phronesis* xii (1967) 59–90.

definition is ascribed to Carneades elsewhere by Cicero (*Fin.* v 20) 'for the purpose of disputation' (*disserendi causa*). It is a statement peculiarly suited to an attack on the Stoics since they claimed that the first human impulse is to desire 'the primary natural advantages' (i.e. a healthy body etc.), but they excluded this from the goal of mature men (see p. 187). Carneades therefore deployed against the Stoics one of their own concepts, arguing that it was inconsistent of them to accord natural advantages some value and yet to exclude them from constituents of the *summum bonum*. In another context Cicero writes that Carneades so zealously defended the statement that the *summum bonum* is a combination of virtue and pleasure that 'he seemed even to accept it' (*Acad.* ii 139). But Cicero adds the revealing comment: 'Clitomachus [Carneades' successor] declared that he could never grasp Carneades' own views' on this topic. Carneades' technique here, and in general, is the standard Academic one of exposing contradictions in the position of his opponents or adopting a contrary standpoint for purely critical purposes.[1]

A further instance of a similar kind is Carneades' criticism of Stoic theological doctrines. One technique which he used here is the *sôritês*. It takes its name from a 'heap', a term used to illustrate the difficulties of indicating precise differentiating characteristics. Suppose that someone is prepared to call a collection of thirty things a heap; subtract one thing and then another; when does the heap cease to be a heap? Clearly it is impossible to lay down precise quantitative criteria for designing a heap, yet 'heap' is a quantitative term. Carneades used this mode of argument to show the impossibility of drawing any firm distinction between that which is supposedly divine and that which is not. 'If gods exist, are the nymphs also goddesses? If the nymphs are, then Pans and Satyrs are also gods; but the latter are not gods; therefore the nymphs too are not. But the nymphs have temples vowed and dedicated to them by the state. Are the other gods then not gods who have temples dedicated to them?' (Cic. *N.D.* iii 43). If the opponent declines to accept a link in the chain then the sceptic can ask what it is, say, about nymphs which marks them off as divine from Pans and Satyrs; or what it is about nymphs that marks them off from the other gods, given that both sets of things have temples set

---

[1] It is of course possible that Carneades defended as 'more probable' one set of moral principles, cf. Brochard, pp. 160–2, who opts for 'striving to attain that which is primarily in accordance with nature'. But I find no evidence that Carneades, whatever he may have done in practice, had any positivist moral theory.

up in their honour. In the course of this discussion Cicero notes that Carneades used such arguments not to overturn religion but to show the unconvincing nature of Stoic polytheism (ibid. 44).

Like other Sceptics Carneades exploited differences of opinion between the dogmatic schools. Epicurus, as we have seen, argued that the world's obvious imperfections give clear evidence against its being under the control of the gods. The Stoics argued in quite the opposite way: the world is manifestly the work of providence, the supreme example of which is man himself, a rational being designed by the gods to live a virtuous life. Carneades held that the sufferings of the virtuous and the flourishing of malefactors prove that the gods are quite indifferent to human affairs (Cic. *N.D.* iii 79–85). Here as before Carneades is picking out a Stoic tenet, the gods' providential care for mankind, and citing evidence which seems to be wholly inconsistent with it. Man's possession of reason, he argues, cannot be used as proof of the gods' providential interest in mankind (ibid. 66–79). For reason is only a good thing, that is, something which might establish providential intentions in the giver, if it is used well; but whether reason is used well or badly by men depends on us, on how we choose to use it. The mere bestowal of reason, if in fact it is the gift of the gods, speaks rather against their providence than for it.[1]

Carneades' philosophical acumen is demonstrated particularly well in his treatment of free will. Here Cicero's *De fato* provides our main evidence. In the last chapter I discussed Epicurus' theory that the capacity of living things to initiate new movements or actions is proof of the fact that individual atoms swerve at no fixed time or place. This theory was interpreted by the Stoics at least as an admission that such movements are uncaused; and they attacked it on the ground that every movement or effect must have an antecedent cause. The Stoics were led to this notion of a necessary connexion between cause and effect by a variety of reasons. But for the present it is necessary to consider only one of these. Chrysippus argued as follows:

If there is an uncaused movement not every proposition . . . will be true or false; for that which will not have efficient causes will be neither true nor false; but every proposition is either true or false; therefore there is no uncaused movement. But if this is so, then everything which happens happens as the result of antecedent causes; and if that is the case, then everything

---

[1] Traces of an attack by Carneades against the Stoic acceptance of divination are probably incorporated by Cicero in Book ii of *De divinatione*.

happens as the result of destiny; it follows therefore that whatever happens happens as the result of destiny (*Fat.* x 20–1).

Two points about this argument are to be noted. First, Chrysippus treats the proposition 'Everything happens as the result of antecedent causes' as logically equivalent to 'Everything happens as the result of destiny'. Secondly, he seeks to prove his thesis by means of the premise: 'Every proposition is either true or false.'

Carneades attacked this argument from two points of view (ibid. xi 23–8). First, he considered the statement 'No movement happens without a cause'. 'Without an antecedent cause,' he argued, does not necessarily mean 'without any cause at all.' We can say that a vase is empty without implying, as a physicist might use the word 'empty', that it contains absolutely nothing—void. We mean that the vase lacks water or wine etc. Similarly, if we say that the mind is not moved by any antecedent cause, we should not be taken to imply that the mind's movement is wholly uncaused. The notion of a voluntary movement *means* a movement which is in our power. This does not entail that such a movement is uncaused. Its cause is just the fact that it is in our power.

Secondly, Carneades argued that Chrysippus' inference of determinism from the premise 'Every proposition is true or false' is an invalid one. Chrysippus' grounds for this inference are recorded by Cicero as follows:

> True future events cannot be such as do not possess causes on account of which they will happen; therefore that which is true must possess causes; and so, when they (*sc.* true future events) happen they will have happened as a result of destiny.

Here Chrysippus is continuing to use 'cause' in the sense of 'antecedent cause'. Carneades replies to Chrysippus in a most interesting way. He argues that if a prediction proves to be true, for instance, 'Scipio will capture Numantia', this tells us nothing about determinism. It is simply a logical fact about propositions that if some event *E* takes place, then it was true before the event that *E* would take place.

> We call those past events true of which at an earlier time this proposition was true: 'They are present (or actual) now'; similarly, we shall call those future events true of which at some future time this proposition will be true: 'They are present (or actual) now.'

In these acute observations about truth and tenses, Carneades is making a point which has been admirably expressed by Gilbert Ryle:

Why does the fact that a posterior truth about an occurrence requires that occurrence not worry us in the way in which the fact that an anterior truth about an occurrence requires that occurrence does worry us? . . . A large part of the reason is that in thinking of a predecessor making its successor necessary we unwittingly assimilate the necessitation to causal necessitation. . . . We slide, that is, into thinking of the anterior truths as *causes* of the happenings about which they were true, where the mere matter of their relative dates saves us from thinking of happenings as the effects of those truths about them which are posterior to them. Events cannot be the effects of their successors, any more than we can be the offspring of our posterity.[1]

The 'slide' from facts about truth into beliefs about causality was made by Chrysippus and other Stoics. Chrysippus' mistake emerges with complete clarity through his attempt to establish determinism by a premise about the truth of propositions. From the proposition 'E will take place is true' it follows that E must take place. But 'must' here refers to logical not causal necessity. It was a considerable achievement on Carneades' part to have distinguished these two senses of necessity and something which neither Aristotle nor the Stoics succeeded in doing.[2] From his distinction Carneades concludes that there are, to be sure, causes of such events as Cato's entering the senate at some future date. But they are not causes 'which are contained in the nature of the universe'. 'Contingent' (*fortuitae*) is his term to describe them and likewise the facts described by propositions about such things. Thus he argues that prediction can only be reliable concerning events the occurrence of which is necessary (*Fat.* xiv 32–3). It is not clear that Carneades thought that there were any such events.

Did Carneades himself accept in practice a belief in the freedom of the will? There are good reasons for thinking that his own views on this subject were positive and yet consistent with his scepticism concerning the external world. Cicero attributes to him this argument:

If all events are the results of antecedent causes they are all bound and fastened together by a natural chain. But if this is so, all things are brought about by necessity; if that is the case, nothing is in our power. Now something is in our power; but if everything happens as a result of destiny all things happen as a result of antecedent causes; therefore whatever happens does not happen as a result of destiny (*Fat.* xiv 31).

This argument relies on the premise 'something is in our power'.

[1] *Dilemmas* (Cambridge 1960) p. 21.
[2] On Aristotle's treatment of necessity in the context of determinism cf. J. L. Ackrill, *Aristotle's Categories and De Interpretatione* (Oxford 1963) pp. 132ff.

Carneades assumes the truth of this premise, and he might be merely advancing it for the purpose of refuting the Stoics. But if the premise means 'We are conscious of having something in our power', Carneades is quite entitled to assert this as a valid datum of subjective experience. It is not a claim about the nature of the external world.

Carneades, as I have mentioned, represented Athens as an ambassador to Rome along with other philosophers in 156–155 B.C. In the *De republica* Cicero used Carneades' arguments for and against justice as material in his third book. This work has reached us in a badly fragmentary condition, but fortunately Lactantius in his *Institutiones divinae* has preserved a summary of Carneades' argument against justice:

> When Carneades had been sent by the Athenians as an ambassador to Rome, he discoursed at length on justice in the hearing of Galba and Cato the censor, the greatest orators of the time. On the next day he overturned his own discourse with a speech putting the opposite position, and undermined justice which he had praised on the previous day, not with a philosopher's seriousness, whose judgment should be firm and consistent, but in the style of a rhetorical exercise arguing on both sides. This he made a practice of doing in order that he might refute those with any positive opinion (Cic. *Rep.* iii 9 [Lact. *Inst.* 5, 14, 3–5]).

Lactantius then reports certain arguments about the excellence of justice which Carneades put forward for the purpose of refuting them. The essence of this case in favour of justice was that justice is something which benefits all men; it gives to each his due and maintains fairness among everyone. Carneades, we are told, now set out to refute this position 'not because he thought that justice deserved to be censured, but to show that its defendants put up a case for justice which was quite insecure and unstable' (ibid. 11):

> This [says Lactantius] was the basis of Carneades' argument: men have ratified laws for themselves for the sake of utility . . . and among the same people laws are often changed according to circumstances; there is no *natural* law. All human beings and other creatures are directed by their own natures to that which is advantageous to themselves. Therefore either there is no such thing as justice or, if there is, it is the height of folly, since a man injures himself in taking thought for the advantage of others (*Rep.* iii 21 [Lact. *Inst.* 5, 16, 2–4]).

In this argument Carneades is attacking the claim that justice can benefit those who act justly. This of course was the position which

Plato sought to demonstrate in the *Republic*, and Carneades' argument recalls the sophistic theories about justice which Plato explicitly aimed to combat. It adds however an interesting contemporary note. By 'advantage of others' Carneades does not mean 'specific individuals within a state', but other states or peoples. He is arguing that the Romans do have justice in the form of laws and constitutional practices, but that these laws and practices work wholly in the interests of Rome and against those of non-Romans: 'What are the advantages of one's native land save the disadvantages of another state or nation? That is, to increase one's territory by property violently seized from others.' Carneades pointed out that according to imperialist ideologies those who augment the state are praised to the skies. So far as the state is concerned their behaviour is perfectly just, but it is not 'justice' in the sense laid down by the defendants of the universal beneficence of justice: it is entirely self-interest.

Carneades proceeded to develop his case by considering the behaviour of the individual:

Suppose that a good man has a run-away slave or an unhealthy and plague-ridden house; that he alone knows these faults and puts the things up for sale accordingly. Will he admit the faults or will he conceal them from the buyer? If he admits them, he is certainly a good man, since he does not cheat; but he will be judged a fool since he will be selling for a song or not selling at all. If he conceals the facts he will be a wise man because he will consult his own interests but also bad, because he cheats (ibid. 29).

In interpreting this argument we need to remember that Plato, Aristotle and the Stoics were at one in holding that both justice and practical wisdom, or prudence, are characteristic of the good man. Carneades forces his opponents to distinguish between justice and prudence. A man who deliberately allows himself to make a bad bargain cannot be called prudent: this is the essence of Carneades' argument. The argument clearly has weight only if both parties agree on the same criteria for establishing prudence. We saw in the last chapter that by Epicurus justice was commended on the ground that it is never in one's interests to run the risk of being exposed as a criminal. Plato, Aristotle and the Stoics on the other hand would reply that happiness depends on a certain condition of the soul or moral character; justice does benefit the practitioner because justice is an integral constituent of his happiness.

Carneades must have known perfectly well that his opponents

would not accept his own use of the term 'prudence' in this argument. But he could reply that everyday usage fully supported the notion of prudence which he was using. Thus his argument is a challenge to any moral philosopher who seeks to show that justice and self-interest can be combined in a coherent ethical system. In basing his arguments on ordinary language and on empirical observations which the majority of men would accept, Carneades is closer to the spirit of modern British philosophy than perhaps any other ancient thinker. Refusing to dogmatize himself, he criticized with great rigour those who were prepared to erect theories on the basis of what he regarded, sometimes with justification, as shaky and often slipshod arguments. The Stoics themselves, as we shall see, modified some of their theories in the light of his criticism, and by his follower, Clitomachus, Carneades was praised for his 'Herculean labour in ridding our minds of rash and hasty thinking' (Cic. *Acad.* ii 108). The distinctions which Carneades drew between certitude and probability, necessity and contingency, and causal and logical relations are sufficient on their own to establish his achievement as an outstanding philosopher. Had he been followed by men of comparable stature the history of philosophy might have been very different in the next hundred years.

But this was not to be. Clitomachus made it his main business to systematize and publicize Carneades' own philosophical method. The tradition was continued in the Academy by Philo of Larisa (*c.* 148–77 B.C.) with some modifications (see p. 223), but his most famous pupil, Antiochus of Ascalon, rejected the sceptical methodo-logy of the Academy in favour of an eclectic assimilation of Stoicism to certain features of Platonic and Aristotelian philosophy. Antiochus was an influential figure about whom more must be said later in this book, and his views are discussed at length by Cicero who declared his own allegiance to the New Academy of Arcesilaus, Carneades and Philo. Under Antiochus the Academy abandoned the tradition first formally established by Arcesilaus two hundred years previously. But scepticism, if it languished temporarily, was to be revived in Alexandria under the name of Pyrrhonism by Aenesidemus, and it has been perpetuated in the writings of Sextus Empiricus.

CHAPTER FOUR

Stoicism

The remarkable coherence of the system and the extraordinary orderliness of the subject-matter have made me prolix. Don't you find it amazing, in heaven's name? . . . What is there which is not so linked to something else that all would collapse if you moved a single letter? But there is nothing at all which can be moved (spoken by 'Cato' in Cicero, *Fin.* iii 74).

STOICISM was the most important and influential development in Hellenistic philosophy. For more than four centuries it claimed the allegiance of a large number of educated men in the Graeco-Roman world, and its impact was not confined to Classical antiquity. Many of the Christian fathers were more deeply affected by Stoicism than they themselves recognized, and from the Renaissance up to modern times the effect of Stoic moral teaching on Western culture has been pervasive. Sometimes Stoic doctrines have reappeared in the work of major philosophers. Spinoza, Bishop Butler and Kant were all indebted to the Stoics. But the influence of Stoicism has not been confined to professional philosophers. Cicero, Seneca, and Marcus Aurelius were read and re-read by those who had time to read in the sixteenth, seventeenth and eighteenth centuries. These Roman writers helped to disseminate the basic principles of Stoicism to priests, scholars, politicians and others. Of course, Stoicism was pagan and Christendom abhorred the pagan. But it was easy enough to abstract from Stoicism those precepts on duty and manliness which Christianity was far from wishing to deny. In the deism and naturalism so fashionable in the eighteenth century Stoicism found a welcoming climate of opinion. Even today, the influence persists at the most mundane level. Not only the words stoic (uncapitalized) and stoical recall it. In popular language to be 'philosophical' means to show that fortitude in the face of adversity recommended by Stoic writers. This is a small, but highly significant example, of Stoicism's influence.

In modern academic circles the study of ancient Stoicism has been curiously uneven. In Europe, especially in France and Germany, major contributions have been made since the nineteenth-century revival of

Classical scholarship. In Britain and the United States Stoicism has suffered greater neglect. Until about twenty years ago, it is probably fair to say that Stoicism attracted less scholarly attention in this part of the world than any other important aspect of ancient philosophy. Now things have begun to change. The Stoics present those who are willing to take them seriously with a fascinating series of philosophical problems. But this is still not widely appreciated. The habit of thinking in terms of a Classical period of Greek culture which was extinguished by Alexander's conquests dies hard. Early Stoicism like Hellenistic culture in general has suffered in modern estimation because our detailed knowledge of its achievements is so defective.

A general characterization of the system may help to set the scene. The Stoics, as the quotation at the head of this chapter indicates, prided themselves on the coherence of their philosophy. They were convinced that the universe is amenable to rational explanation, and is itself a rationally organized structure. The faculty in man which enables him to think, to plan and to speak—which the Stoics called *logos*—is literally embodied in the universe at large. The individual human being at the essence of his nature shares a property which belongs to Nature in the cosmic sense. And because cosmic Nature embraces all that there is, the human individual is a part of the world in a precise and integral sense. Cosmic events and human actions are therefore not happenings of two quite different orders: in the last analysis they are both alike consequences of one thing—*logos*. To put it another way, cosmic Nature or God (the terms refer to the same thing in Stoicism) and man are related to each other at the heart of their being as rational agents. If a man fully recognizes the implications of this relationship, he will act in a manner which wholly accords with human rationality at its best, the excellence of which is guaranteed by its willing agreement with Nature. This is what it is to be wise, a step beyond mere rationality, and the goal of human existence is complete harmony between a man's own attitudes and actions and the actual course of events. Natural philosophy and logic are fundamental and intimately related to this goal. In order to live in accordance with Nature a man must know what facts are true, what their truth consists in and how one true proposition is related to another. The coherence of Stoicism is based upon the belief that natural events are so causally related to one another that on them a set of propositions can be supported which will enable a man to plan a life wholly at one with Nature or God.

This very briefly is the basis of Stoicism. But now we must pass from such generalities to details, beginning with a short treatment of the history of the school and our sources.

I. THE STOA, PERSONALITIES AND SOURCES

About 301/300 B.C. Zeno of Citium began, in the words of Diogenes Laertius (vii 5), to pace up and down in the Painted Colonnade (*Stoa*) at Athens, and to engage in philosophical discourse there. The Stoa bordered one side of the great piazza of ancient Athens, and from it, as one can see today, those who promenaded there looked directly at the main public buildings, with the Acropolis and its temples towering in the background. Unlike Epicurus, Zeno began his teaching at Athens in a central public place, which came to stand as the name of his followers and their philosophical system. From a decree inscribed on stone in his honour it appears that Zeno like Socrates numbered young men particularly among his adherents, and provided them with a paradigm of virtue in the life which he led (D.L. vii 10). At the time when he founded the school Zeno was in his early thirties. He was born at Citium in Cyprus about 333/2 B.C. His age on coming to Athens, like the date of his birth, is disputed by ancient sources; but the testimony of his younger follower, Persaeus (D.L. vii 28), probably gives the most reliable evidence: he arrived in Athens at the age of twenty-two (i.e. about 311 B.C.) and died in 262/1, aged seventy-two.

Such a chronology allows Zeno a decade or so in Athens before he set up as a philosopher in his own right. In other words, he came to Athens some ten years after the deaths of Aristotle, Diogenes of Sinope and Alexander, shortly before Epicurus established the Garden as his centre. What brought Zeno to Athens in the first place is not entirely clear. According to one account he began life as a merchant; was shipwrecked on a journey from Phoenicia to Piraeus; arrived somehow or other at Athens, and encountered philosophy through reading about Socrates in Xenophon (D.L. vii 2). The story continues that he was so delighted by his reading that he asked where he might find men like Socrates. At that moment Crates, the Cynic, passed by and the bookseller, in whose shop Zeno had found his Xenophon, said: 'Follow that man.' This romantic tale may be more fiction than fact. But the mention of Crates rings true. The first major influence on Zeno's philosophical development is likely to have been a Cynic one, although his aquaintance with Socratic doctrines, which the Cynics would have encouraged, may have begun before he left Cyprus (D.L. vii 31). Fragments of Zeno's *Republic* survive and they show marked Cynic elements such as the abolition of coinage, temples, marriages, and the notion that the true community must be one consisting of good and virtuous men.[1] Zeno is said to have written his *Republic* while still a young associate of Crates (D.L. vii 4), and it may have been intended as a direct attack on Plato.

The main interest of the Cynics lay in ethics (see pp. 3–4). From them Zeno inherited the notion, fundamental to all Stoicism, that the real nature or *physis* of a man consists in his rationality (*SVF* i 179, 202). Expressed in such general terms this notion was hardly revolutionary. Plato and Aristotle would agree; indeed it is ultimately Socratic in inspiration. But Diogenes, and perhaps Antisthenes before him (see pp. 7–8), gave it a particularly extreme and rigorous interpretation, an ascetic twist, which was not accepted by Plato and Aristotle. For Diogenes, a man needs nothing but physical and mental self-discipline to fulfil himself, to live according to nature (D.L. vi 24–70). Things conventionally regarded as good—property, a fine appearance, social status—all these are irrelevant if not actually inimical to human well-being (D.L. vi 72). True happiness can have no truck with anything that fails to meet the test: 'Does it accord with my nature as a rational being?' It is difficult to know precisely what Diogenes meant by reason, *logos*, but I think we can understand him to have had *phronêsis*, 'practical wisdom', in mind. He advocated a way of life in which a man so acts that what is truly valuable to him, his inner well-being, cannot be affected by conventional social and moral judgments or changes of fortune; only thus is real freedom attainable (D.L. vii 71). Such a life would be *natural* in the sense that it required nothing except minimal physical requirements from the external world. We find the Cynics appealing to the habits of primitive men and animals. This life would also be *natural* in the sense that reason is an innate human endowment which transcends cultural and geographical boundaries. Diogenes rejected all theories of human well-being which cannot pertain to all wise men whatever their ethnic and social status.

The connexion between these principles and certain Stoic ideas will appear in due course. Later Stoics were sometimes embarrassed by some of the more extreme Cynic positions which their predecessors

[1] H. C. Baldry gives a good discussion in 'Zeno's Ideal State', *Journal of Hellenic Studies* lxxix (1959) 3–15.

took over—I refer for instance to the claims that incest and cannibalism may be justifiable in certain circumstances (*SVF* ii 743–56)—
but throughout the history of the Stoa we find an emphasis on *indifference* to externals (with an important qualification to be treated later),
on rationality as the sole source of human happiness, on 'cosmo-
politanism' and moral idealism, which all reflect Zeno's allegiance to
Cynic doctrines.

Some of these attitudes are of course Socratic, and the influence of
Socrates on Zeno, either through the Cynics or through books and
oral tradition, is of great importance. The following basic Socratic
propositions were all embraced by Zeno: knowledge and goodness go
hand in hand, or the good man is wise and the bad man ignorant; from
knowledge right action follows necessarily; and the greatest evil is a
bad condition of the soul.

Undoubtedly Zeno's basic goal was a practical one—to demonstrate
the good for man as he conceived it. But that was no novel enterprise.
What Zeno may have begun to defend in the proselytizing manner of
Diogenes and Crates he proceeded to develop into a coherent philo-
sophical system. Diogenes had no sympathy for the Academy, even
though he appealed to Socrates as a model.[1] But Zeno passed on from
Crates to study both with Megarian philosophers, Stilpo and Diodorus
Cronus, and with the Academic, Polemo (D.L. vii 2; 25).

From the Megarians Zeno is likely to have acquired a facility at
logic and a general interest in linguistic theory. It is improbable that he
himself developed Stoic logic in much detail; this was rather the
achievement of Chrysippus. But the titles of Zeno's works include
logical subjects—*Solutions, Disputatious arguments, On signs,* and
Modes of speech (D.L. vii 4)—and he certainly used formal arguments
for the presentation of some doctrines. Epictetus reports on Zeno's
authority that the philosopher's speculative activity consists in 'know-
ing the elements of *logos,* what each of them is like, how they fit
together and what follows from them' (iv 8, 12 = *SVF* i 51). One
cannot be certain that these are Zeno's own words, but their sense is
wholly appropriate. A further trace of Megarian influence may be seen
in Stoic monism (see earlier, p. 8). That the cosmos is 'one' was
asserted by Zeno (D.L. vii 143 = *SVF* i 97), and the 'unity of being',
defended by the Stoics, goes back through the Megarians to Parmenides.

---

[1] Diogenes Laertius' *Life of Diogenes* contains many polemical and amusing
encounters between Plato and the Cynic. Their authenticity is doubtful.

Platonic influences, apart from those which come from Socrates, can be identified more easily, but I will not enumerate them in detail here. It is sufficient to note the clear links between 'creative reason', Zeno's cosmic principle, and the divine craftsman, or soul of the world, in Plato. The theology of Plato's *Laws* with its eloquent defence of providence has affinities with Stoicism which cannot be accidental. These points of common ground, and others which will be mentioned later, exist alongside some profound differences between the Platonic and the Stoic world-picture. No doubt much of Zeno's acquaintance with Platonic doctrines was gained through his association with Polemo. But too little about Polemo's own teaching is known to make a clear assessment of his personal influence possible (see further p. 225). The influence of the Peripatetics raises further problems, though for quite different reasons. Polemo's name is linked with Zeno's, but there is no ancient evidence concerning Zeno's relationship with Theophrastus or other Peripatetics. It is probable however that Zeno knew individual members of the Lyceum, and virtually certain that he had read some of their works. I have already discussed the question of Aristotle's writings in the early Hellenistic period (pp. 9–10), and it is very difficult to believe that Zeno did not know some of them. We find Aristotelian terminology in early Stoicism and also a number of doctrines which seem to betray clear indications of Aristotelian thought.[1]

Add to all this the acknowledged indebtedness to Heraclitus (see p. 145), and we may confidently say that Stoicism from its outset drew readily upon contemporary and earlier philosophy. This is not to deny originality to Zeno. Both he and his successors advanced new theories on a variety of subjects, and the Stoic synthesis to which borrowings from existing systems contributed has a character which is entirely its own. But the Stoics' attitude to other philosophers and to Greek culture in general differentiates them sharply from Epicurus. By the time of Chrysippus at least, Stoicism had become a learned and highly technical philosophy. The view that Epicurus was only interested in a rough-and-ready philosophical methodology is mistaken, but there is no denying his unintellectual posture. The Stoics were keenly interested in literature, they established grammar for the first time on a rigorous basis, and they had a general influence on intellectual as

[1] See further J. M. Rist, *Stoic Philosophy* (Cambridge 1969) pp. 1–21 and my article, 'Aristotle's Legacy to Stoic Ethics', *Bulletin of the Institute of Classical Studies* 15 (1968) 72–85.

well as moral thinking. It was a Stoic maxim that the wise man will normally take part in politics, and Sphaerus who was a pupil of Zeno and Cleanthes acted as tutor and adviser to Cleomenes, the king who sought to reform Spartan society (*SVF* i 622–3). Cato the Younger, Seneca and Marcus Aurelius are three examples of Stoics eminent in public life. To this extent, Stoicism is much closer than Epicureanism to the spirit of classical Greek philosophy, and it can be considered as continuing rather than diverging from the Platonic and Aristotelian tradition (see p. 226).

Zeno died about 261 B.C., leaving a set of works with such titles as *Life according to nature, Emotions, That which is appropriate, Greek culture, Universals, Homeric problems* (five books), *Disputatious arguments* (two books), D.L. vii 4. He also left a reputation the significance of which is indicated by the award of a golden crown from the Athenian people, a tomb built at public expense in the Kerameikos, funeral reliefs in the Academy and Lyceum, and the high regard of Antigonus, the Macedonian Regent.[1] Of his immediate successors the most important are Cleanthes and Chrysippus. How these men whose origins were in Asia Minor came to Athens we do not know. But the old theory that Stoicism incorporates Semitic ideas cannot be defended, as it has been, merely on the provenance of its three great authorities. And there seems to be nothing in Stoicism which requires the hypothesis of Semitic influences.[2] Owing to the state of our evidence it is difficult to attain an entirely clear grasp of the innovations by Cleanthes and Chrysippus. But it is probable that Cleanthes' interests centred upon natural philosophy and theology. Chrysippus, who was head of the Stoa from about 232 up to his death in 208/4, won immense renown in antiquity as a dialectician, and reference was made in the last chapter to the saying, 'Without Chrysippus there would have been no Stoa.' This tag probably does less than justice to Zeno and Cleanthes, and Chrysippus did not claim to be the real founder of Stoicism. Rather, we are to see him as Stoicism's great scholar, a man who refined and clarified Zeno's teaching.[3] He must have made many innovations himself, particularly in Stoic

[1] D.L. vii 6; 10, see W.S. Ferguson, *Hellenistic Athens* (London 1911) pp. 185–7.
[2] Such points as Pohlenz alludes to—fatalism, the concept of moral obligation, the absolute distinction between good and bad (*Die Stoa* ed. 2, Göttingen 1959, vol. i pp. 164f.) do not establish Semitic influences.
[3] For a survey of modern views on Chrysippus' contribution cf. Josiah B. Gould, *The Philosophy of Chrysippus* (Leiden 1970) pp. 14–17.

logic (Cic. *Fin.* iv 9). In this field his energy was prodigious, and he wrote three hundred and eleven treatises (D.L. vii 198). For later Stoics, Chrysippus became the general canon of orthodoxy, and it is reasonable to assume that the majority of ancient summaries which begin with the words, 'The Stoics say that', report his views or views which he would have approved. Unfortunately the majority of surviving fragments are only a few lines in length, and since many of them are cited for polemical purposes by opponents of Stoicism we probably have too little evidence to form an opinion on Chrysippus' style and quality of argument at its best. But he was undoubtedly a philosopher of immense versatility.

Throughout the later part of the third century B.C. the Stoics were engaged in controversy with the Academic Sceptics and the Epicureans, but apart from Arcesilaus' arguments against Zeno's theory of knowledge (see pp. 90f.) little is known about the details of such disputes. For the second century our evidence is much better. This was the period of Carneades who debated so vigorously with the Stoics on many fronts. Chrysippus himself did not live to answer Carneades' criticism, but as a result of it Antipater of Tarsus, who was head of the Stoa after Diogenes of Babylon, Chrysippus' successor, modified the ethical theory (see p. 196) and other anonymous changes were also made. The object of these was to protect Stoicism against Carneades' objections. In fact, Antipater achieved an uneasy compromise which involved both an apparent weakening of the earlier idealism of Stoic ethics and which also failed to satisfy common sense. Early Stoicism offered a ready target to charges of setting up a goal beyond human attainment, and it is no accident to find the next important Stoic, Panaetius of Rhodes (*c.* 185–109 B.C.), developing the practical side of Stoicism in perhaps an original manner. Cicero's *De officiis* is based upon the work of Panaetius, and it provides a set of rules for conduct which are categorically stated to be a 'second-best' system of ethics, designed for the guidance of men who are not yet sages and competent to be good in the ideal Stoic sense. Panaetius spent much of his middle life in Rome. He was an intimate acquaintance of Scipio Africanus, and the spread of Stoicism among Romans of the late Republic probably owed much to his influence.

From the second half of the second century onwards Stoicism became well established at Rome. In Athens the Stoa continued to flourish as a school, and Panaetius succeeded Antipater as its head in 129. By this time however Stoicism had a number of other centres throughout the Mediterranean world. Posidonius (*c.* 135–50 B.C.) who came from Apamea, an ancient city on the Orontes in Syria, set up a school in Rhodes after studying under Panaetius in Athens; and Cicero, who visited Rhodes between 79 and 77, formed a lasting admiration for him. Posidonius is the last Stoic philosopher who is known to have shown any great inclination for original thinking. A polymath who did important work in history and geography, Posidonius remains for us a somewhat shadowy figure. He certainly rejected Chrysippus' psychology in favour of a Platonic tripartite division of the soul, and won Galen's approval for doing so (*De placitis Hippocratis et Platonis* iv and v). Following this, Posidonius modified Stoic ethics in an interesting way. We are not well informed about any other major deviations from orthodoxy. As I shall explain later, Posidonius' general conception of philosophy and his attachment to science have closer connexions with Aristotle than earlier Stoics professed. But Chrysippus' authority continued to be the strongest influence on late Stoicism.

One of the great difficulties, which has contributed to the neglect of Stoicism in modern times, is the state of our evidence. The history of the Stoa is often divided into three phases—Early, Middle, and Late—and it is the last of these, represented above all in the writings of Seneca, Epictetus and Marcus Aurelius, which is the best documented. For Early Stoicism (Zeno-Antipater) and Middle Stoicism (Panaetius and Posidonius) we must make do with quotations and summaries in later writers. No complete work by any Stoic philosopher survives from these two phases. The unfortunate fact is that our evidence is best from a period when Stoicism had become an authorized doctrine rather than a developing philosophical system. What matters above all to Epictetus and Marcus Aurelius in the second century A.D. is moral exhortation within the framework of the Stoic universe. On details of physics, logic, or theory of knowledge they have little to say. But if Epictetus and Marcus confirm rather than add to our general knowledge of Stoic theories, they do something else which is immensely valuable. Through them we learn what it meant in practice to be a committed Stoic. Thus the theory comes alive, and the dry summaries of early Stoic doctrine take on flesh and blood. None of these writers however is setting out to give an historically accurate account of early Stoicism, and in certain instances, for example their treatment of the faculties of the soul, all three diverge from Chrysippus' methodology.[1]

[1] They all tend to oppose body and soul in a manner which is Platonic rather

But if their evidence is used with care and compared with texts which undoubtedly report early Stoic views it can provide a most useful supplement to explicit reports of Zeno and Chrysippus.

Our evidence for the first two phases of Stoicism can be arranged under four categories. First, Herculaneum papyri: a few badly damaged fragments of Chrysippus have been recovered, and it is possible that further work on such material may yield new evidence, though not too much can be expected from this quarter (cf. especially *SVF* ii 131: 298a). There is also a fascinating papyrus text which preserves substantial fragments of the *Foundations of ethics* by an Alexandrian Stoic called Hierocles, a contemporary of Epictetus.[1] This illuminates the relation between ethics and psychology, and it is wholly consistent with evidence of early Stoicism.

Secondly, we have quotations. Many of these are attributed to individuals, a most important example being Cleanthes' *Hymn to Zeus* (*SVF* i 557), written in hexameter verse. The Stoic most frequently quoted is Chrysippus, and the widest selection of quotations comes from Plutarch who in his *De Stoicorum repugnantiis* and *De Communibus notitiis* repeatedly sets one passage from Chrysippus against another in order to expose apparent inconsistencies in Stoicism. By Galen too the actual words of Chrysippus and Posidonius are often cited in his discussion of the faculties of the soul (*SVF* iii 456–82). Cicero, Diogenes Laertius, John of Stobi (Stobaeus) and a number of other writers also preserve some quotations, but most of their evidence is in the form of doxography. We also find quotations which are not attributed to any individual. In his treatise *On Destiny*, Alexander of Aphrodisias, the Aristotelian commentator who flourished at the end of the second century A.D., records a number of passages, some of them quite lengthy, which are wholly Stoic in style and content. But Alexander does not identify the authors, and never refers to 'The Stoics' explicitly throughout his treatise.[2]

Thirdly, we have a copious supply of second-hand reports, the form of which may be illustrated by this passage from Aulus Gellius: 'Zeno held that pleasure is indifferent, that is, something neither good nor bad, a point which he expressed in Greek with the word *adiaphoron*'

---

than Chrysippean, cf. Sen. *Ep.* 24, 17; 65, 16; *Cons. Helv.* 11, 7; Epictet. ii, 12. 21ff.; Marcus x 11.

[1] The text has been published and discussed by H. von Arnim, *Hierokles, Ethische Elementarlehre* (Berlin 1906).

[2] I have discussed Alexander's methodology in *Archiv für Geschichte der Philosophie* 52 (1970) 247–68.

(ix 5, 5 = *SVF* i 195). Such statements are to be found in all the sources already mentioned, and other important sources of this kind are Sextus Empiricus, Clement of Alexandria, and Simplicius. Fourthly we have a class of reports often combined with one or both of the two previous categories, which are either attributed to 'The Stoics' or are inferred to be Stoic from their content and from characteristics of the authors. Cicero's *De finibus* provides a most important general statement of the main principles of Stoic ethics, without, in many cases, referring to individual Stoic philosophers. The same is true of Diogenes Laertius and Stobaeus. But such authorities, who are explicitly recording Stoic doctrines, cause less difficulties than writers who incorporate material for their own purposes without acknowledgment. The problem in the case of, say, Cicero or Stobaeus, is to decide whether some general statement should be fathered on Chrysippus or on another individual Stoic philosopher. In such cases we know that some Stoic held this view, and it will normally be a fair presumption that it belongs to Chrysippus. But from writers such as Plotinus and Philo of Alexandria it is much more difficult to dissect what is or may be Stoic material. Philo in particular is an important Stoic source, but in attempting to reconcile doctrines of Judaism with Greek thought he drew upon Plato and Aristotle as well as the Stoics; and the Stoic who may have influenced him most deeply was probably Posidonius.

At least as early as the first century B.C. handbooks were available giving summaries of philosophical doctrines. Arius Didymus, who taught the emperor Augustus, was the author of a compendium of Stoic and Peripatetic ethics which was used by Stobaeus about the fifth century A.D. The summary of Stoicism by Diogenes Laertius probably drew upon Arius Didymus and other similar collections. So too perhaps did Cicero, though he certainly went direct to some Stoic writers (e.g. Panaetius for the *De officiis*) as well. Cicero in fact is our oldest indirect evidence for Stoicism. The problem of discriminating between sources is a large one, and it may be best if I conclude this section by explaining the methodology which I shall adopt rather than treat the subject itself at greater length.

The phase of Stoicism most central to the purpose of this book begins with Zeno and ends with Antipater. It would be desirable to chart the contributions of individuals, but in many cases this cannot be done; we are in a better position to say, 'This was the general Stoic view of virtue', than 'Zeno put it thus' and 'Chrysippus' view was this'. In some cases where an innovation or divergent opinion is well documented I will indicate the fact. But my primary aim is to give an analysis of the basic Stoic doctrines. Within each section the material will be presented historically if that seems to be appropriate, and in this way some sense of the development within Stoicism during its first phase should emerge. Proper names will be used whenever this is justified by the evidence; otherwise I shall refer to 'The Stoics' meaning either a point of view which there is every reason to regard as common ground in early Stoicism or, what will usually come to the same thing, evidence attributed to the Stoics in general. In the fifth chapter the Middle Stoics, Panaetius and Posidonius, will be discussed, and that will also be the place to say something about the eclectic synthesis between Stoicism and certain doctrines of Platonism and the Peripatetics which was attempted by Antiochus of Ascalon.

II. STOIC PHILOSOPHY: SCOPE AND PRESENTATION

No part of philosophy is separate from another part; they all combine as a mixture (D.L. vii 40).

The Stoics followed the Platonist Xenocrates in treating philosophy under three broad headings: logic, physics and ethics (D.L. vii 39). These English terms, though each is derived from the Greek word which it conventionally translates, are all relatively misleading. By 'logic' the Stoics meant something which includes theory of knowledge, semantics, grammar, and stylistics as well as formal logic. In Stoicism these elements of 'logic' are all associated with each other because they have *logos* as their subject-matter. *Logos* means both speech and reason; and speech can be considered both from a phonetic and from a semantic aspect. Or again, a Stoic will discuss under 'logic' both the rules of thought and valid argument—logic in the strict sense—and also parts of speech, by which thoughts and arguments are expressed. To know something in Stoicism is to be able to assert a proposition which is demonstrably true, and thus epistemology becomes a branch of 'logic' in the generous sense given to that term by the Stoics.

The subject-matter of 'physics' is *physis*, nature, and this too must be interpreted broadly enough to take in both the physical world and living things including divine beings as well as men and other animals. Thus 'physics' embraces theology in addition to subjects which might be loosely classified under natural science, and in no case is the approach to these subjects scientific in an exact sense. The early Stoics left it to men like Strato the Peripatetic and Archimedes to make advances which are more recognizably scientific. Stoic 'science' is speculative—philosophy of nature—though much of it is also rooted in the observation of particular phenomena.

Finally, ethics. Like Epicurus and other Greek philosophers the Stoics were practical and not merely theoretical moralists. They did offer an analysis of moral concepts; but this was preparatory to showing why such concepts are valid and what is as a matter of fact the foundation of human well-being, the best life which a man can lead.

These three subject headings, logic, physics and ethics, were adopted by the Stoics for the purpose of expounding their system, and I will adhere to their methodology in the following pages. But this division of philosophy must be interpreted purely as a methodological principle. It is not an affirmation of three discrete subjects of study. On the contrary, the subject-matter of logic, physics and ethics is *one* thing, the rational universe, considered from three different but mutually consistent points of view. Philosophy, for the Stoics, is 'the practice of wisdom' or 'the practice of appropriate science' (*SVF* ii 35, 36), and they explained the relationship of philosophy to its parts in a number of similes: 'Philosophy is like an animal in which the analogue of bones and sinews is logic, that of the fleshy parts ethics, and that of the soul physics.' In a second simile philosophy is compared to an egg which has logic as its shell, ethics as its white and physics as the yolk. And according to a third simile, philosophy resembles a fertile field in which logic corresponds to the surrounding wall, ethics to the fruit and physics to the soil or vegetation (D.L. vii 40).

Clearly the chief object of these curious analogies is to show that philosophy is something organic to which each of its so-called parts makes an integral and necessary contribution. They need not, and I would argue should not, be interpreted as illustrating a hierarchy of subjects. Logic and physics have fundamental ethical implications, and ethics itself is wholly integrated with physics and logic. In one sense of course the practical goal of 'living well' may be said to make physics and logic subordinate in Stoicism to ethics. But the Stoic view is that these latter subjects cannot be practised adequately unless one is a good or wise man, and conversely, being a good or wise man requires supreme competence at physics and logic. In its broadest sense ethics

informs all the parts of Stoic philosophy. But as a sub-division of
philosophy in Stoicism ethics refers to a series of subjects such as
virtue, impulse and appropriate acts, which require an understanding
of physics and logic as their basis (D.L. vii 84ff.).

This necessary relation between physics, logic and ethics has been
admirably expressed by Émile Bréhier:

> They are indissolubly linked together since it is one and the same reason
> (*logos*) which in dialectic binds consequential propositions to antecedents,
> which in nature establishes a causal nexus and which in conduct provides
> the basis for perfect harmony between actions . . . it is impossible to realize
> rationality independently in these three spheres.[1]

The two fundamental concepts in Stoicism are *logos* (reason) and
physis (nature). It is because nature as a whole is informed by reason
that Stoicism seeks to unify all aspects of philosophy. Stoic philosophy,
we might say, is designed to make for complete correspondence
between language and conduct on the one hand and the occurrence of
natural events on the other hand.[2]

Diogenes Laertius asserts that it was customary to combine the
teaching of logic, physics and ethics (vii 40), and it must have been
necessary to stress the interconnexions of subject-matter which I have
just described. But he also says that Zeno and Chrysippus used to
begin with logic, then pass to physics and end with ethics. This is
probably too sharp a division to correspond precisely with early
Stoic practice. Chrysippus is reported by Plutarch to have advocated
logic as the subject which the young should study first, followed by
ethics and finally physics (*Stoic. rep.* 1035a = *SVF* ii 42). The contradiction may be only apparent. Chrysippus made it absolutely clear
that ethics depends upon an understanding of nature in the widest
sense. He may then, in his lectures and written courses of study, have
prefaced his treatment of ethics with some general consideration of
natural philosophy, leaving to the last detailed problems which only
advanced students may have been encouraged to pursue.

The scope of Stoic philosophy must have varied considerably
according to the interests and abilities of its exponents. The moral
goal of the system and the emphasis on exhortation and casuistry
among later Stoics should not be taken to imply that early Stoic

---

[1] *Histoire de la philosophie* (Paris 1931) I p. 299.
[2] Chrysippus declared that the goal of man is 'to live in accordance with
experience of natural events', D.L. vii 87.

philosophers devoted all their energies to inculcating practical morality. Chrysippus and Posidonius like Aristotle were deeply interested in theoretical problems. And there is no real discrepancy between theory and practice. Aristotle regarded the contemplative life as the activity in man of that which is best and most divine (*E.N.* xii 1177b24–1178a8). For a true Stoic the study of nature in any of its aspects cannot fail to contribute to the harmonious relationship between his own disposition and cosmic reason (D.L.vii 88).

III. STOIC LOGIC

The essential unity of Stoic philosophy creates considerable difficulties for anyone trying to write about it. If the general significance of details is continuously pointed out there is a danger of confusing the reader and boring him by repetition. Yet, if details are treated as if they were wholly self-contained a one-dimensional presentation of Stoicism will emerge which cannot be entirely satisfactory. This dilemma has been faced in different ways by modern scholars. Benson Mates and Martha Kneale have discussed the formal aspects of Stoic logic in an illuminating way.[1] But neither writer offers a comprehensive account of the subjects which constituted 'logic' for the Stoics, nor do they show the place of 'logic' in the system as a whole. I propose here to take a wider conspectus of the subject and to concentrate upon those topics which seem to throw most light upon the general character of Stoicism. Inevitably some things will be treated cursorily, and others not at all. But the notes to this section, with their references to further reading, are intended to make good some of its omissions.

The Stoics, probably from Chrysippus onwards, divided the subject-matter of 'logic' under two headings, rhetoric and dialectic (D.L. vii 41). To understand the significance of this subdivision a few historical comments are necessary. What has come to be called logic was determined for the philosophers of later antiquity by a group of Aristotle's works which they named *Organon*, 'instrument'. Aristotle did not classify these writings under a single title, but his commentators were proceeding quite sensibly when they did so. The *Organon* comprises the *Categories*, the *Topics*, the *De sophisticis elenchis*, the *De interpretatione*, and most importantly, the *Prior* and *Posterior analytics*. What unites all these works is Aristotle's concern with language, but

---

[1] Benson Mates, *Stoic Logic* (Berkeley and Los Angeles 1953); Martha Kneale in W. and M. Kneale, *The Development of Logic* (Oxford 1962) pp. 113–76.

this is also an important theme in the *Metaphysics* and more specifically, in the *Rhetoric* and the *Poetics*; likewise, metaphysics enters into the logical works, especially *Categories*. Logic, in our formal sense, is treated most fully in the *Analytics* where Aristotle sets out the principles of syllogistic reasoning. The *Topics* and the *De sophisticis elenchis* have 'dialectical reasoning' as their subject-matter. This is distinguished from 'demonstrative reasoning' (the subject of the *Analytics*) by reference to the premises from which it starts: dialectic for Aristotle means reasoning which takes men's convictions for its premises; the premises of the demonstrative syllogism are 'true and primary'. Semantics and problems about positive and negative statements are two subjects discussed in the *De interpretatione*, while the *Rhetoric* deals with the real or apparent means of persuasion. Aristotle posits a very close and un-Platonic connexion between dialectic and rhetoric. He asserts that both of these have to do with subjects that belong to human knowledge in general; hence neither of them is a science (*epistêmê*) which has any specific subject matter. Each is within its own province, a faculty for furnishing arguments (*Rhet.* i 1, 1–14).

If we think of all this as Aristotle's contribution to logic, then 'logic' is being used in a loose and extremely wide sense. But the problem is largely terminological. Language and reasoning are two fundamental properties of rhetoric, though the goal of rhetoric unlike that of demonstrative science is a practical one. The Stoics were therefore not aberrant when they classified rhetoric under 'logic'. On the contrary, in asserting 'logic' to be a *part* of philosophy they were proceeding more systematically than Aristotle himself. 'Logic' in Stoicism may perhaps be best described as 'the science of rational discourse'.

There are a number of extremely interesting differences between the Stoics' conception of dialectic and that of Aristotle. The essential point is that in Stoicism, as in Plato, dialectic is a science which has the real nature of things as its field of study. Not that dialectic means the same procedure in both systems. For Plato the dialectician is someone who arrives by a process of question and answer at true definitions, and who discovers in this way what things are. The Stoics recognized question and answer as one of the methods which dialectic uses, but for them this procedure seems to have been an educational device rather than the only proper way of doing philosophy. Dialectic in Stoicism is defined as 'knowledge of what is true, false and neither true nor false' (D.L. vii 42). As such it is the faculty which a philosopher must possess, and the Stoics claimed that the dialectician must be a wise man. Diogenes Laertius gives a brief statement of why this is so, and it forms the conclusion to his compendium of the logical doctrines.

After reporting that only the sage is a dialectician, Diogenes writes:

> For all things are intuited by means of investigation in language, both the subject-matter of natural science and that of ethics. . . . Of the two kinds of linguistic study which fall under virtue, the one considers what each thing is, the other what it is called (vii 83).

Words, things, and the relations which hold between them—that in a nutshell is the subject of Stoic dialectic. We must not forget that rhetoric, 'knowledge of how to speak well' (*SVF* i 491), was also treated as a subject of 'logic' in its broader sense. But the Stoic theories on figures of speech and the arrangement of an oratorical discourse will not be discussed here.[1] They are only of marginal philosophical interest from our point of view, though an ancient reader would have formed a different judgment.

(i) *Theory of knowledge*

Stoic 'dialectic' embraces two large topics, 'things which are signified', and 'things which signify' (D.L. vii 62). A most important class of things signified is the meaning of a term, phrase or sentence, what 'is said' by language, and we shall consider this in some detail shortly. But the Stoics did not confine the scope of 'things signified' to statements and the meaning of isolated words. They also treated under this heading sense-impressions and concepts, which may not be initially presented or signified by words. Indeed we are told that the Stoics gave the first place in their treatment of dialectic to 'impressions' (D.L. vii 49).

But what have 'impressions' to do with dialectic? The Stoic answer is that language and thought are not endowed with content *a priori*. The ability to speak and to think is something which develops over a long period in any individual man. At birth the mind is like a blank sheet of paper (*SVF* ii 83), well fashioned for becoming imprinted. The first imprinting is a consequence of sense-perception. External objects act upon the sense-organs (see p. 126) and cause an impression to occur in the mind. If this impression is 'cognitive', a condition which

---

[1] For a penetrating study cf. the last chapter of Karl Barwick's excellent monograph, *Probleme der stoischen Sprachlehre und Rhetorik* (Berlin 1957).

I will explain later, its occurrence constitutes perception, awareness of something that is real or actual. Impressions leave a record of their occurrence in the mind, and repeated records of the same thing or type of thing give rise to general concepts.[1] The Stoic theory at this point is virtually identical to the Epicurean 'preconception'. Some general concepts, however, are not direct derivatives of sense-perception. By various mental processes, 'resemblance', 'analogy', 'transposition', 'composition' and 'contrariety', other concepts may be formed (e.g. the concepts of a Centaur, of death, of space) and the Stoics, as this makes clear, did not confine the term 'impression' to awareness of sensible objects. In order to be aware of anything a man's mind must have something presented to it. His capacity to form general concepts is innate, but the realization of this capacity calls for experience, experience of the external world and self-consciousness, awareness of his own states of mind.[2] Intelligence is shaped and developed by the general concepts which a man 'naturally' builds up from his primary sense-experiences.

This seems to be a coherent and generally acceptable account of mental development, and to it must now be added a linguistic dimension which gives Stoicism a very modern ring in the light of transformational grammar.[3] Every living creature, they held, has its own governing-principle (*hêgemonikon*), and in man, when he is mature, the governing-principle is 'rational'. The full psychological implications of human 'rationality' need not be considered at this stage (see p. 175). What I wish to stress is that in Stoicism being 'rational' connotes the ability to speak articulately, to use language. This is not its only connotation: rationality is an extremely broad concept in Stoicism. But, in our present context, the important point is the notion that thinking and speaking are two descriptions or aspects of a unitary process (similarly, Plato, *Soph.* 263e). We may call this process articulate thought.

The relation of the doctrine of impressions to articulate thought is expressed very clearly as follows:

[1] On the ontological status of universals see p. 141.

[2] Cf. F. H. Sandbach, 'Ennoia and Prolepsis in the Stoic Theory of Knowledge' (*Class. Quart.* xxiv 1930, 45–51 =ch. 2 of *Problems in Stoicism* ed. A. A. Long, London 1971) for further discussion of concept-formation.

[3] The Stoics would be happy to agree with Noam Chomsky that 'the person who has acquired knowledge of a language has internalized a system of rules that relate sound and meaning in a particular way', *Language and Mind* (N.Y. 1968) p. 23.

Impression leads the way; then thought, which is able to speak, expresses in discourse what it experiences as a result of the impression (D.L. vii 49).

In this satement a sharp distinction appears to be drawn between a passive state, the awareness of something, and an active state, the interpretation of this impression by articulate thought. Certainly the impression is conceived as prior to articulate thought. But we should not suppose that this need always imply temporal priority. The Stoics would agree with other empiricist philosophers that in some sense there is nothing in the mind which was not previously in the senses. But it does not follow from this that every act of articulate thought is directly preceded by the occurrence of an impression. The priority referred to in our passage only implies that we cannot think articulately of something which is not present either as a sense-impression or as a memory-image or as something based upon prior experience. Impressions and articulate thought will normally be two aspects of a single mental process.

It will be well to dwell a little longer on this notion of articulate thought. The Stoics are arguing that the rational interpretation of experience requires language. A passage from Sextus Empiricus focuses upon this in a most illuminating way:

The Stoics say that man differs from irrational animals because of internal speech not uttered speech, for crows and parrots and jays utter articulate sounds. Nor does he differ from other creatures in virtue of simple impressions—for they too receive these—but in virtue of impressions created by inference and combination. This amounts to man's possessing an idea of 'connexion', and he grasps the concept of signal because of this. For signal itself is of the following form: 'If this, then that'. Therefore the existence of signal follows from the nature and constitution of man' (*Adv. math.* viii 275f.).

Here the relationship between impressions and articulate thought is set in a logical context. A man is a creature who possesses the capacity to see connexions (and to use language) as a natural endowment. To do this is to think articulately, to speak within oneself, to order the impressions of experience and to create new ideas from them. For the Stoics the whole world is the work of immanent *logos* or reason, and in his power of articulate thought a man is supposed to have the means to formulate statements which mirror cosmic events. Language is part of nature and provides man with the medium to express his relationship with the world.

We may pass next to the main question of this section: What is it in Stoicism to know something? According to Zeno (*SVF* i 68) to know something is to have grasped or apprehended it in such a way that one's grasp or apprehension cannot be dislodged by argument. The Greek term used by the Stoics to denote grasp is *katalêpsis*, and some aspects of this notion were considered in the last chapter with reference to criticism by the Academic Sceptics. Now it can be set in its proper Stoic context.

The Stoics analysed perception as a mental act in which we 'assent' to some impression. External objects cause disturbances to the material (air or water) which surrounds them, and under appropriate conditions these movements in the intervening material are conveyed to our sense-organs. They are then transmitted within the body to the governing-principle, which has its centre in the heart. The result of this process is an impression, which Chrysippus described as a 'modification' of the governing-principle (*SVF* ii 56). So far, perception is conceived as something in which the percipient himself is acted upon by external objects. Zeno illustrated this stage by the simile of an open hand. He then partly closed his hand, and so represented the response of the governing-principle to the impression: the mind assents to it. Having next made a fist he likened this to cognition ('grasping'). And finally, grasping his fist with the other hand he said: 'This is what knowledge is like' (Cic. *Acad.* ii 145).

It is the first two stages which concern us immediately. By distinguishing between the passive receipt of impressions and the mental act of assent the Stoics are drawing a distinction between mere awareness and noticing or perceiving or giving attention to something. Thanks to the stock of concepts which it has acquired through experience, the governing-principle is not normally limited in its reaction to registering awareness of the impression. It responds to the impression by interpreting and classifying it, seeing it as, say, a black dog and not merely as a shape of a certain colour and size.[1] Perception is rightly treated by the Stoics as a form of judgment: in assenting to the impression we are admitting that our sense-experience corresponds to some expressible fact, for instance, that what I see is a black dog.

But might I not be mistaken? The Stoics would concede this. The mere fact that I accept some impression as 'seeing a black dog' offers no guarantee that such an object actually exists outside my conscious-

---

[1] On this point and on the 'cognitive impression' in general cf. Sandbach, ch. 1 of *Problems in Stoicism*.

ness. Ill-health, hallucination, bad light, these and other conditions may distort my vision and make many perceptual judgments which I choose to make false. But the early Stoics claimed that there is one class of impressions on the basis of which I cannot form a false judgment (later Stoics qualified this claim, see below). The 'cognitive impression' is 'stamped and moulded out of the object from which it came with a character such as it could not have if it came from an object other than the one which it did come from' (Cic. *Acad.* ii 18, cf. Sextus, *Adv. math.* vii 402). Such impressions, as the careful definition asserts, are unmistakably trustworthy and in assenting to them we reach the third stage in Zeno's simile of the hand: we grasp something.

What is it that we grasp? Not merely the impression. The impression is something 'which reveals itself and its cause' (*SVF* ii 54). And its cause, in the case of a cognitive impression, is 'the real object'. So, in assenting to such impressions we also grasp the object which prompts them.[1] That is one way of expressing the Stoic theory, but in putting it thus we raise a difficulty which must now be faced. The words 'real object' are only an approximate translation of the original Greek. The Greek phrase is most literally rendered, 'that which is', and the word for 'is' (*hyparchei*) can be used with the sense 'exists' or 'is real' or 'is the case'.[2] We talk in English about objects existing or being real, and therefore since the cause of a cognitive impression is a physical object, it is reasonable to say that cognitive impressions enable us to grasp what exists or what is real (cf. Sextus, *Adv. math.* viii 85). But what we grasp is also 'that something is the case', for instance 'that I see a black dog'; indeed only in a metaphorical sense can we be said to 'grasp the object', for we do not physically take hold of it. We might put the Stoic position by saying: 'We assent to the impression *that* there really is a black dog' which we see.

The special characteristic of the cognitive presentation is that 'it can be grasped'. We are supposed to recognize this intuitively. Not that the cognitive impression by itself can provide all the information that we need to say 'This is a black dog'. Any statement of such a form also requires the prior acquisition of certain concepts. The cognitive impression guarantees that there is some actual object which corresponds precisely to itself. Our general concepts enable the assent

---

[1] cf. Sandbach, ibid.
[2] For a more detailed treatment of this point and what follows see my discussion in ch. 5 of *Problems in Stoicism*.

to a cognitive impression to be a recognition of *what* its corresponding object is.[1]

As we have seen, the Academic Sceptics attacked this representational theory of knowledge strongly. No impression, they argued, can guarantee its own reliability. The Stoics replied that unless some impressions are immediately trustworthy there can be no firm basis of knowledge. And they continued, some impressions just are of this kind. But how can we be absolutely certain that any particular impression necessarily corresponds to one particular fact or object? If the Stoics had stopped short of claiming 'necessary correspondence' they would have been able to fend off the main fire of the Sceptics. As it is, they defended a position which was always open to the rejoinder, 'How do you know this cognitive impression is cognitive?' Later Stoics, faced with such objections, conceded that even a cognitive impression might be misinterpreted owing to external circumstances; and they added to their specification of this criterion, 'provided that it has no obstacle' (Sextus, *Adv. math.* vii 253). When this extra condition is satisfied, 'being clear and striking the cognitive impression all but seizes us by the hair and drags us to assent' (ibid. 257).

This modified doctrine implies that the assent to a cognitive impression is normally instantaneous and not something calling for deliberate choice on our part. The 'obstacles' which these later Stoics had in mind are referred to by Sextus as 'external circumstances' (ibid. 254ff.): Menelaus returning from Troy received a cognitive impression of Helen, but failed to assent to it owing to a belief that Helen was still on his ship; in fact the Helen on his ship was a phantom fashioned by the gods to look like the real Helen. Now this example raises an important point. If our beliefs about a situation are mistaken we may see what is not there, or fail to see what is there. But suppose we say, as later Stoics apparently did (cf. Sextus ibid. 258), that if a man wants to grasp something as it really is, then he must take every step to obtain a 'clear and striking impression'. If he is in Menelaus' position his judgment will still go astray. The requirement of a criterion of truth is its power to establish certainty. But unless we know in advance, as Menelaus did not, when there are obstacles to our recognition of a cognitive impression, the doctrine loses all its original force. We shall need a further criterion to establish the fact that our impression is cognitive no matter how improbable this may seem at the time.

[1] Hence general concepts are also said to be a criterion of truth, *SVF* ii 473. cf. Gerard Watson, *The Stoic Theory of Knowledge* (Belfast 1966) ch. 2.

This concession therefore plays into the hands of the Sceptics, since it robs the cognitive impression of unconditional reliability. The later Stoics were in effect making the wholly unhelpful statement: 'A cognitive impression is a test of what is real if and only if it is recognized to be such.'

In the previous chapter the Stoics' distinction between knowledge and belief was noted. Belief, in philosophy, is typically regarded as something which may be either true or false, and the Stoics recognized this. But they expressed it in an odd way. For 'true' in reference to belief they used the term 'weak', classifying beliefs as acts of assent to something, which are either weak or false.[1] The point of this terminology seems to be primarily logical. Knowledge in Stoicism must be 'secure', and any cognitive state which lacks this property cannot be knowledge. The absence of knowledge is belief or ignorance, but beliefs are not monolithic. Some of them are patently false; others are acts of assent to what is true. But these latter lack the grip—one hand clasping another—by which Zeno characterized knowledge. 'Weak assent' describes the cognitive state of someone who has 'grasped' the object or what is really the case. But for Zeno this is still so far from constituting knowledge that he assimilated 'weak assent' to ignorance (Cic. *Acad.* i 41–2). As Arcesilaus saw, there is really no intermediate stage in Stoicism between knowledge and lack of knowledge. Unless you know something, you don't *know* it. That is the strict Stoic doctrine. But, obviously, a man who has grasped something however weakly is in a better position to aspire to knowledge than the complete ignoramus. We shall see later that the Stoics posited an equally exclusive disjunction between virtue and vice; but they also admitted that one man might progress further towards virtue than another.

What is required to convert weak assent into knowledge? Zeno's definition of knowledge has already been mentioned (p. 126), and knowledge is also described as 'a disposition in the acceptance of impressions which cannot be shaken by argument' (D.L. vii 47). These passages imply that there is something systematic about knowledge which makes it proof against refutation. From the fact that a man has assented to a cognitive impression that p, it does not follow

---

[1] Sextus Empiricus co-ordinates the predicates weak and false (e.g. *Adv. math.* vii 151) but Stobaeus correctly distinguishes an opinion which is 'assent to a non-cognitive impression' that is a totally 'false' opinion, from 'weak supposition' (*SVF* iii 548).

that he could defend *p* against every argument. Like the young slave
in Plato's *Meno* he might assent correctly to all the steps of a geo-
metrical proof; but the true opinion which he ultimately reaches needs
to be 'tethered by reason' before it can count as knowledge. He must
be able to show why the argument is valid. In claiming that knowledge
must be irrefutable the Stoics were asserting that its possessor can
prove what he knows by means of propositions that are necessarily
true.

The Stoics drew a distinction which is curious at first sight between
'truth' and 'the true' (*Adv. math.* vii 38ff.).[1] It ties in however very
neatly with their distinction between knowledge and belief (='weak
assent'). 'The true' is said to be 'simple and uniform', and it is applied
to any proposition which states what is the case. But 'truth' is something compound and a collection of many things. Unlike 'the true',
'truth' is peculiar to the wise man, and it is corporeal whereas 'the true'
is incorporeal. The significance of the distinction between corporeal
and incorporeal will require further consideration. But it is notable
that 'truth' is cited alongside cause, nature, necessity and *logos* as
things which refer to the same 'substance' (*SVF* ii 913). Each of these
picks out an aspect of the universe. This cosmic 'truth' is also mentioned by Marcus Aurelius who calls it 'the first cause of all that is
true' (ix 2). It seems to refer to the chain of necessary causes and
effects. To know these is to know what must happen and therefore a
set of necessary truths. That is the condition of the Stoic wise man.
He never errs, never fails to grasp things with complete security. His
knowledge is logically equivalent to 'truth', since it is based upon the
causal nexus which controls cosmic events. Unlike the ordinary man
who utters some true statements which he cannot prove against
every attempt to overturn them, the wise man's judgments are infallible
since he knows why each of them must be true.

This concept of knowledge and the wise man should be borne in
mind throughout the chapter as further details of Stoicism are discussed. To the 'cognitive impression', which is its starting-point, the
Stoics seem to have traced back any true statement (Cic. *Acad.* i 42).
Most of our evidence places the cognitive impression in a treatment
of perceptual judgments, and, as we have seen, it is perception which
provides the foundation of all concepts. But the Stoics also recognized
a class of 'non-sensible' impressions to which no physical object or
single physical object would correspond. The impression that 'man

[1] See further *Problems in Stoicism*, ch. 5 pp. 98–101.

is a rational animal' or 'fifty is five times ten' falls under the category of rational or non-sensible impressions. From Sextus' criticism of the cognitive impression (*Adv. math.* vii 416–21, viii 85–7) it seems certain that the Stoics must have ultimately appealed to this doctrine to support such statements, and the same probably holds good for knowledge of moral concepts. That however is a problem which must be considered in the general context of Stoic ethics. For the present, further aspects of 'logic' require our attention.

(ii) Grammatical and linguistic theory

Although the Stoics treated 'impressions' as a species of 'things signified', this expression was also applied more narrowly to linguistic significance. What is language and what is it that language can be used to express? To these questions the Stoics devoted considerable attention. Unfortunately, the evidence which survives concerning their answers is seriously defective, and many obscurities might be removed if some of the linguistic books by Chrysippus and other Stoics had survived. But we know enough to see that their work in this field was of great interest and importance. The first ancient grammarian from whom a book is extant, Dionysius Thrax (second century B.C.), was strongly influenced by the Stoics, and the same is true for Varro, Priscian, and many others. In a loose sense language had been a subject of philosophical discussion since the Presocratics. Heraclitus' assumption that it is one and the same *logos* which determines patterns of thought and the structure of reality is perhaps the most important single influence upon Stoic philosophy. And we shall return to this point at the end of the section. The sophists, notably Protagoras and Prodicus, were interested in 'correctness of speech', and it was natural that the interpretation of poetry and the teaching of rhetoric, undertaken by the sophists, stimulated some discussion of semantics and grammatical forms.[1] Plato and Aristotle made a number of perceptive contributions, but their achievements in logic and the philosophical use of language are incomparably greater than their insights into its structure and form. In this latter subject the Stoics were pioneers. They helped to systematize much that was previously unsystematic, and they also established ways of analysing language some of which are still in use today.

[1] Much of the evidence on Greek language theory is now conveniently assembled and discussed by R. Pfeiffer, *History of Classical Scholarship* (Oxford 1968).

'The study of dialectic begins with the subject of voice' (D.L. vii 55). Distinguishing between human and animal utterances Diogenes of Babylon (a Stoic whose linguistic work was particularly influential) defined voice in its human sense as 'an articulate product of thought' (ibid.). From a physical point of view 'voice' is a 'vibration of air', and the Stoics regarded words in their phonetic aspect as material objects. This point is important because it marks a contrast with language in some of its semantic aspects: 'what is said' by a predicate or a sentence is 'incorporeal'.

The distinction between corporeal and incorporeal is a fundamental Stoic doctrine. It belongs to a metaphysical thesis that the only things which can be said strictly to exist are bodies. The test of something's existence, which they alone satisfy (see p. 153), is the capacity to act and to be acted upon. Air and voice meet this condition, but the meaning of a sentence does not. In order that something meaningful shall be said, certain material conditions must be satisfied: words of a particular kind must be uttered in a particular sequence, and this presupposes the existence of a rational being. In so far as he is thinking, and thinking or speaking in an articulate manner, something meaningful 'coexists' with his thought (Sextus, *Adv. math.* viii 70). But this meaning has no independent existence. In itself, it neither acts nor is it acted upon.

This notion of meaning as incorporeal will require further analysis, for I have given but the merest outline of its metaphysical implications. But a preliminary sketch must suffice until we have considered an apparently quite different dimension of Stoic phonetic and semantic theory. When philosophers first began to think seriously about language they were interested above all in the question, 'What is the relation between words and things—physical objects?' Or more strictly—for they had no word which corresponds precisely to 'word' —they formulated the question in terms of 'names': What is it that names stand for and why is, say, *anthrôpos*, the Greek name for man? Before problems about the meaning of phrases and sentences were properly formulated most thinkers would probably have adopted the naïve realist notion that the meaning of a name is the thing or physical object named; but there was no general agreement about how things come to have the names which men apply to them. In the fifth century B.C. the sophists raised important questions concerning the natural or conventional foundations of human social institutions. This debate focused particular attention upon the basis of moral values, but it was also extended to cover other matters including language. Plato's *Cratylus* introduces spokesmen for and against the view that names are natural in the sense that they represent in a linguistic form the actual properties of the things which they designate. Socrates in the dialogue shows some sympathy for the idea that the components of certain names have a natural appropriateness. But he also argues that convention as well as natural resemblance between name and name-bearer is an important principle in the constitution of names. Unlike Cratylus who wants to hold that to know the name is to know the thing named, and that names give the only valid form of instruction into the nature of things, Socrates argues that it is not from names but from things themselves that our learning should proceed (435d–439b).

The *Cratylus* makes a number of significant advances to the understanding of language. One of these, which was interpreted in different ways by Aristotle and the Stoics, is a distinction between 'names' and 'things said about them', a concept which in Plato adumbrates both the grammatical distinction between noun and verb and the logical distinction between subject and predicate. But Plato's most important legacy to the Stoics was the suggestion, about which he himself is equivocal, that some names and their components (letters and syllables) possess properties which are common to the things which they name. The longest section of the dialogue is a semi-serious demonstration by Socrates of onomatopoeia, which he backs up by a copious number of supposed etymologies: for instance, *anthrôpos* is explained as a transformation of an original sentence meaning 'that which looks up at what it sees' (399c). Socrates suggests that some names are 'primary' while others have been compounded out of these, and that 'representation' of things is the special function of the primary names (433d). He then raises objections to this theory, but the Stoics put it to positive use. Unlike Aristotle, who regarded all words as conventional signs, the Stoics held that 'the primary sounds imitate things' (*SVF* ii 146).

We have no Stoic list of these 'primary sounds', but it is clear from later grammarians that they comprised words for which an explanation by onomatopoeia is at least plausible. The writer of the *Principia dialecticae*, traditionally identified with St. Augustine, observes that the Stoics selected those words 'in which the object designated harmonizes with the sense of the sound'; and as Latin examples he cites *tinnitus*, 'jangling', *hinnitus*, 'neighing' etc. (ch. 6, *Patres latini* xxxii 1412). The analysis was extended to individual letters and syllables, and it may be these rather than the words compounded from them which the Stoics regarded as 'primary sounds' (cf. *SVF* ii 148). 'Some syllables', writes Varro (fr. 113 G), 'are harsh; others smooth . . . harsh ones include *trux, crux, trans*; smooth ones, *lana, luna*' (*crux* means 'cross' as signified in crucifixion, *lana* means 'wool'). This strict onomatopoeic interpretation of language was only held to apply to the 'primary sounds' or words. In the terminology of the *Principia dialecticae* this is the principle of *similitudo*, 'resemblance'. Other principles of word-formation are also asserted in this tract: *contrarium*, 'opposition', explains the word *bellum*, 'war', by opposition to *bellus*, 'beautiful'; *lucus*, a 'grove', is derived from *lux*, 'light', in the same way! The source of these etymologies is Stoic, and it was probably Diogenes of Babylon who first introduced the principles taken over by the grammarians. Fanciful and fantastic though some of them are they deserve notice for several reasons. In particular, some of the etymological principles noted in the *Principia dialecticae* correspond with Stoic ways of concept-formation which I have already described (p. 124). And this is no accident. If words and what they signify have a natural relationship to each other, it is reasonable to suppose that there is some correspondence between the ways in which words have been formed and the formation of concepts.

The attention which the Stoics paid to etymology proves that they regarded this as a key to understanding *things* as well as words. A bizarre example of this is Chrysippus' explanation of the first person singular pronoun, *egô*. In uttering the first syllable of this word the lower lip and chin point to the chest; Chrysippus, who held that the heart and not the brain is the centre of consciousness, used this 'etymology' of *egô* as an argument in support of this psychological doctrine (*SVF* ii 884). Such etymologies were not unnaturally treated with little respect by some ancient critics, but in smiling at them ourselves we should remember that the correct principles of morphology have only been grasped in modern times; and the etymology of many words is still obscure. Ancient critics of Stoic etymology were right to attack many of their efforts, but they had nothing positive to offer instead.

It is possible that Zeno and Cleanthes attempted to defend the natural relationship of language to things more rigidly and less self-critically than their successors. Zeno's general maxim was that a spade should be called a spade, a view which fits someone who holds that this is the naturally appropriate word to use (*SVF* i 77). Chrysippus however, like Plato, realized that language had changed in the course of time and that there can be no one to one relationship between a word and its meaning.' Every word', he argued, 'is naturally ambiguous since the same word can be taken in two or more senses' (*SVF* ii 152). He also drew attention to 'anomaly', the fact that two unlike words can be used with the same sense and that similar words can be used with unlike senses (*SVF* ii 151). From these observations it follows that we cannot establish what someone is saying merely by analysing the linguistic components of his utterance. And on the evidence of a papyrus fragment Chrysippus seems to have drawn a distinction between someone's thought or what he means to say, and the statement which a listener may take him to be making (*SVF* ii 298a p. 107 col. x).

In a recent study, 'Grammar and Metaphysics in the Stoa', A. C. Lloyd suggests that 'there is a latent and unacknowledged conflict between the Stoic theory of meaning and the Stoic theory of etymology'.[1] The conflict to which he refers is the apparent disparity between meaning as 'incorporeal', and the theory that the elements of language are naturally similar to things in the world. I too think that there is a conflict and indeed some confusion, but this is perhaps to be explained by two things: first, innovations by Chrysippus which were grafted on to earlier Stoic theories; secondly, a metaphysical analysis of objects and their properties to which language was required to conform.

The fundamental concept in Stoic semantic theory is something which they called the *lekton*. This term may be translated 'what is said' or 'what can be said', and 'meaning', 'fact', 'statement' or 'state of affairs' are English interpretations which fit many of its uses in Greek. I shall prefer here to leave it transliterated. Two kinds of *lekton* were distinguished: 'deficient', which are exemplified by the meaning of verbs lacking a subject, for instance 'writes' or 'loves', and 'complete' statements as expressed by a sentence such as 'Cato is walking' (D.L. vii 63). *Lekta* of the latter kind, and only they, are true or false. The complete *lekton* is compounded out of a predicate, say, 'is walking', and something termed *ptôsis* (D.L. vii 64). This latter term is often translated 'subject', but its literal meaning is 'grammatical case', nominative, accusative, etc.

Now, grammatical form and syntax are certainly necessary constituents of meaningful utterance, but they are not traditionally regarded as a part of what we mean. The Stoics postulate a very tight

[1] *Problems in Stoicism*, ch. 4.

relationship, which might even seem to be identity, between meaning and grammatical form. But we must remember their distinction between corporeal and incorporeal. As an arrangement of letters and syllables grammatical form is a material property, a property of the utterance. 'What is said' by a sentence is a *lekton,* something incorporeal, which requires for its expression words that are inflected and arranged in a definite way.

Words which have a *ptôsis* are nouns (and adjectives), and these are never said to signify 'deficient *lekta*'. They may be said to signify a *ptôsis*, a grammatical case, or to signify 'common or particular qualities', according as they are common nouns or proper names.[1] Qualities in Stoic theory are corporeal, arrangements or dispositions of matter. But *lekta*, as we have seen, are incorporeal. This confusing account can be clarified by the help of a passage from Seneca:

> There are material natures, such as this man, this horse, and they are accompanied by movements of thought which make affirmations about them. These movements contain something peculiar to themselves which is separate from material objects. For instance, I see Cato walking; the sense of sight reveals this to me and the mind believes it. What I see is a material object and it is to a material object that I direct my eyes and my mind. Then I say 'Cato is walking'. It is not a material object which I now state, but a certain affirmation about a material object. . . . Thus if we say 'wisdom' we take this to refer to something material; but if we say 'he is wise' we make an assertion about a material object. It makes a very great difference whether you *refer* to the person directly, or *speak about* him (*Ep.* 117, 13).

As I understand this passage, Seneca is saying that the meaning of the isolated term 'wisdom' *is* a material object (the corporeal nature of mental and moral properties is orthodox Stoicism). And this fits in with the idea that nouns signify qualities. *Lekta* only come into play in actual discourse when we say something with the intention of ascribing some predicate to the subject of a sentence. In the complete *lekton* or statement, 'Cato is walking', we are not merely denoting some object; we are saying something about it. In the real world there are not two things, Cato and Cato's walking. The meaning of the word 'Cato' is an individual man. But in the sentence 'Cato is walking' we abstract from the real man something which has no independent existence (his walking) and refer to it by using a term

[1] Cf. Sextus, *Adv. math.* xi 29, D.L. vii 58, and my discussion on pp. 104ff. of *Problems in Stoicism.*

which denotes (Cato) and a term which 'says something' (is walking). It is not entirely clear why the complete *lekton* as a whole is incorporeal, since it does and must contain a designating term. But I would conjecture that the Stoics thought of nouns as fulfilling different functions depending upon whether they are used as mere names or as the means of signifying the subject of a sentence. In the latter case, noun and verb combine to form a sentence the meaning of which is not a thing but an abstraction—not Cato the man plus something else, but the statement 'Cato is walking'.

It was probably the Stoics' very strong presumption that only bodies can exist which led them to distinguish between merely denoting something and the making of statements. Statements cannot be thought of as having corporeal existence, whereas in fact many of the bearers of names are bodies. The metaphysical notion that all properties must be dispositions of matter and thus attached to some body is paralleled linguistically in the doctrine that descriptions have no status in themselves: they must be predicated of an actually existing subject if they are to say something about the world which is true or false. Most of the surviving Stoic etymologies are of nouns, and it is possible that the 'primary sounds' were considered to be solely nouns or components of nouns. As signifying actual entities, nouns might be regarded as naturally representational in a way which the Stoics could less easily defend for verbs and other parts of speech. But this is a speculation. The fundamental point is their recognition that the meaning of a sentence is what it is used to say; that this is something which cannot be reduced to any physical or psychological state of affairs, though it depends on both of these. As we shall also see in the next section, Stoic formal logic, which is a system of relations between statements, requires *lekta* as its subject-matter.

One of the most interesting features of Stoic semantic theory is the fact that it allows a distinction to be drawn between sense and reference.[1] This distinction, which was first formulated in a technical sense by the German logician Gottlob Frege, has been extremely fruitful and it is best illustrated by an example used by him. In the statement 'The morning star is identical with the evening star' we are describing the same thing by the words 'evening star' and 'morning star'—a particular heavenly body. But the statement is clearly different from 'The

[1] Mates was the first scholar to make this point in his *Stoic Logic*. G. Watson also has penetrating remarks on the Stoic theory of meaning, *The Stoic Theory of Knowledge*.

morning star is identical with the morning star'. Frege explained this
difference by saying that 'morning star' and 'evening star' are proper
names which have the same reference but different senses. A number
of Stoic doctrines require us to make a similar distinction. It is one of
their axioms that 'good' and 'profitable' can be asserted only of virtue
and virtuous action (D.L. vii 94, 102). 'The good' and 'the profitable'
have the same reference. But the sentence 'The good is the profitable'
expresses a different sense (*lekton*) from 'The good is the good'. The
Stoics used the former sentence not to express a tautology but to assert
that whatever is denoted by 'good' is also denoted by 'profitable'
and vice versa. This statement proved to be controversial not because
of its sense but because of its denotation or reference to virtue. For it
is undoubtedly controversial to say that virtue alone is profitable.
But, returning to Frege, we should beware of assimilating his theory
of meaning and the Stoics'. The Stoics have no term which corresponds
clearly to Frege's use of *Bedeutung*, 'reference'. Its place in Stoicism
is taken by 'bodies' (the thing referred to) or the 'grammatical subject' (*ptôsis*).

The Stoics made a number of acute and influential grammatical
observations. By the time of Chrysippus, four 'parts of speech' had
been distinguished: nouns—common nouns and proper names were
given different terms—verbs, 'conjunctions', which included pre-
positions, and the 'article', which included pronouns and demonstrative adjectives.[1] Adjectives were classified under nouns, and later,
adverbs were recognized as a 'fifth' part of speech. Two of the Stoics'
greatest grammatical achievements were in the field of accidence. They
recognized and named the five inflections of Greek nouns and adjectives, and the terms they used (nominative, accusative, etc.), have
become canonical. Equally noteworthy is their analysis of tenses.
Here too they fixed the terms which we use (present, perfect, etc.),
analysing verbs as means of signifying different temporal relations. It
was a Stoic doctrine that 'only the present is real' but the present is
said to consist of past and future (*SVF* ii 509, 517). This is a way of
saying that time is continuous, and can only be broken up into different
relations by means of language. Time like *lekta* has no independent
existence but is rather something which rational beings make use of
in order to explain the movements of bodies.

Before we pass on to formal logic a general assessment of the

---

[1] The evidence is found in R. Schmidt, *Stoicorum Grammatica* (Halle 1839,
reprinted Amsterdam 1967).

Stoics' linguistic theory may be helpful. Like their predecessors the Stoics failed to distinguish clearly between grammar and semantic or logical theory (the term *logos* does duty both for sentence and statement). But they laid admirable foundations for future investigation. Given the premise that language is naturally related to objective reality, it was consistent on their part to look for connexions between linguistic phenomena and features of nature. If this led the Stoics astray in etymology and prevented them from treating syntax as something to be studied in its own right, we should give them credit for a subtle theory of meaning and for noting correctly and systematically a number of fundamental points of grammar. Of course the Stoics were nothing if not systematic. That is both their strength and their weakness. In this short survey I have already alluded to details which belong to 'natural philosophy' rather than to 'logic', and it will be necessary to consider the method of definition and the so-called Stoic categories in later sections. It is easier from our point of view to treat these as metaphysical topics, but their linguistic implications will be readily apparent (see p. 162).

(iii) Statements, methods of inference and arguments

We come now to the most complex and controversial topic which the Stoics treated in their science of 'rational discourse'. The term 'logic' has a much broader reference in Stoicism than in modern usage, but the Stoics undoubtedly treated some aspects of logic in a recognizably modern sense. Sections 65–82 of Diogenes Laertius' summary discuss four main subjects: different kinds of statements; rules for deducing one statement from another; truth, possibility and necessity as applied to statements; and finally, methods of argument. The presentation of these matters is highly systematic, and the Stoics were clearly aware—as their nineteenth-century interpreters were not—that verbal precision and formal consistency are essential properties of logic. Benson Mates has shown the errors which can arise when Stoic formalism is not reproduced in translation, and his *Stoic Logic*, which takes account of modern logical theory, is a valuable contribution to the study of ancient philosophy. But while much of his work is authoritative, some scholars have recently argued that modern logic may not be the best key to understanding this or any other ancient logical theory.[1] The debate continues, and the main point to bear in

[1] See W. H. Hay, 'Stoic Use of Logic', *Archiv für Geschichte der Philosophie* 51 (1969) 145–57, and Charles H. Kahn, 'Stoic Logic and Stoic Logos', ibid.

mind is the ramification of Stoic logic into epistemology, linguistics, metaphysics and even ethics. This does not undermine the formal similarities to modern theories which Mates and others have noticed; but it does affect the interpretation of certain details and any general assessment of the Stoics' logical enterprises.

Formal logic in Stoicism takes its starting-point from the *lekton*, 'the meaningful description'. In its complete form the *lekton* has a subject and a predicate as its components, and the Stoics recognized nine types of assertion which fulfil this condition. These include questions, commands, prayers and oaths, but the all-important one is the *axiôma*, 'statement'. An *axiôma* (often translated 'proposition') is the *lekton* to which the predicates true or false can and must be applied (D.L. vii 65). The noun *axiôma* is formed from a verb which literally means 'to lay claim to'. And the force of the etymology is maintained in this Stoic sentence: 'One who says "it is day" seems to lay claim to the fact that it is day' (D.L. ibid.). Such claims are validated according to their correspondence with actual states of affairs.

The statement 'It is day' was classified by the Stoics as 'simple'. 'Simple' statements comprise three positive kinds: first, 'definite'— 'this man is walking'; second, 'categorical' (or 'intermediate')— 'Socrates' (or [A] 'Man') 'is walking'; third, 'indefinite'—'someone is walking' (D.L. vii 70). The significance of this distinction is metaphysical and epistemological rather than logical. In statements of the first type the subject is denoted by a demonstrative adjective, a term which serves to 'point', or rather, since terms cannot strictly point, 'this' is the linguistic equivalent of a gesture of pointing. In understanding the Stoics here we need to remember that 'impressions' registered by the senses are prior to statements made about them. The existence or reality of things is established not by logic but by the empirical criterion of 'cognitive impression'. 'The simple definite statement is true when the predicate, e.g. walking, belongs to the thing falling under the demonstrative' (Sextus, *Adv. math.* viii 100). The 'thing falling under the demonstrative' is a physical object disposed in a certain way, that is, moving one leg after another and so walking. This is what a 'cognitive impression' reveals—bodies disposed in different ways. The special status of the definite statement seems to be due to the fact that it makes ostensive reference to an actual

---

158–72. My 'Language and Thought in Stoicism' (*Problems in Stoicism*, ch. 5) is a further attempt to develop some of the general implications of Stoic logic.

thing. It is as if we were to say in English 'this here'. Other ways of denoting the subject involve increasing degrees of indefiniteness (*SVF* ii 204–5). Hence the truth of the categorical and indefinite statements is dependent upon the truth of a corresponding definite statement.

A true affirmative statement in Stoicism requires the existence of that which it describes: 'It is day is true', if it is day (D.L. vii 65). We see a curious implication of this in the Stoics' treatment of statements introduced by a universal term such as 'man'. Holding as they did that all existing things are particulars, the Stoics reduced universals to thoughts or concepts; they denied that there is any thing in the world corresponding to the general term, man. What then were they to say about the truth or falsity of a statement like 'Man is a two-legged rational animal'? Apparently for the Stoics, this is not a 'statement' in the strict sense; it is a meaningful utterance, but the evidence suggests that it is neither true nor false. The reference of this assertion is to the content of someone's thought, and not an externally existing thing. In order to make general statements which would not conflict with their metaphysics, the Stoics rephrased sentences of the form 'Man is . . .' as conditionals, 'If something is a man, then it is . . .' (Sextus, *Adv. math.* xi 8). Such an 'indefinite' antecedent has some individual existing thing hypothesized as its subject, and the Stoics are saying: 'If the predicate "is a man" is actually *instantiated* by something, then we can say of this "something" that it is a "two-legged rational animal".'

The subject of conditionals brings us to a further logical classification: compound statements, of which the Stoics recognized seven types. A quotation from Diogenes' summary (vii 71ff.) will give an idea of the way in which logic was set out in Stoic hand-books:

> Of statements which are not simple the 'conditional' . . . is constructed by means of the conditional connexion 'if'. This connexion asserts that the second part follows from the first, for instance, 'if it is day, it is light'. The inferential is a statement . . . constructed by means of the connexion 'since' . . . for instance, 'since it is day it is light'. The connexion asserts that the second part follows from the first and that the first is true. . . . The disjunctive is a statement which is disjoined by means of the disjunctive connexion 'or', for instance 'either it is day or it is night'. This connexion shows that one of the statements is false.

This truncated quotation shows clearly enough that the Stoics were interested in the *logical form* of certain statements. Modern logic has developed a system known as 'truth-functions' which the Stoics are often held to have anticipated. Very briefly, the system of truth-functions is a way of representing the truth conditions which govern statements of a particular logical form. The logical form of these statements is expressed by a combination of 'variables' and 'constants'. The variables, generally symbolized by letters, stand for a statement and other symbols are used for the constants, *not, and, or,* etc. The value of the system lies in its generality. P. F. Strawson writes: 'Any statement of the form "*p* v *q*" ("*p* or *q*"), is true if and only if at least one of its constituent statements is true, and false if and only if both its constituent statements are false.'[1] This expression of a logical rule in the truth-functional system bears some resemblance to the Stoics' definition of a disjunctive statement. But some of their definitions are not truth-functional, and import what we may call extralogical notions.[2]

There are similarities between the Stoics' account of formal reasoning and Aristotle's syllogistic logic, but the differences between the two systems are far more significant.[3] Like Aristotle the Stoics devoted great attention to patterns of argument in which, from the conjunction of two propositions which are laid down as premises, a third proposition can be inferred as conclusion. But Aristotle's logic is a system of establishing relationships between the terms which form the subject and predicate of the premises and conclusion: e.g. 'If all men are mortal [major premise], and Socrates is a man [minor premise], then Socrates is mortal [conclusion].' In this argument 'is mortal' is inferred as a predicate which applies to Socrates by means of the 'middle term' man. Aristotle uses letters to symbolize the variables in each mood of the syllogism, but the letters represent terms. Stoic logic is a system of establishing relationships between the propositions expressed by the sentences which form the premises and conclusion. Variables in Stoic logic, which they represented by numbers and not letters, are to be filled in by complete sentences, not terms. An example: 'If it is day it is light; it is day; therefore it is light'. This pattern of argument was expressed in the form: 'If the first, then the second; but the first; therefore the second' (e.g. Sextus, *Adv. math.* viii 227). Aristotle expressed the principles of the syllogism in conditional sentences,

[1] *Introduction to Logical Theory* (London 1952) p. 67.
[2] See W. and M. Kneale, *Development of Logic*, p. 148.
[3] For ancient disputes between the Stoics and the Peripatetics over their logical systems see Ian Mueller, *Archiv für Geschichte der Philosophie* 51 (1969) 173–87.

'If all men are mortal . . .', but the form of reasoning in the Aristotelian syllogism is not hypothetical. We can drop the 'if' without altering the syllogism's formal validity, and Aristotle specifically distinguished syllogistic reasoning from 'hypothetical argument' in which a proposition q is established on the hypothesis that q is true if p (*Pr. an.* i 44). Aristotle's successor, Theophrastus, may have already anticipated some of the Stoics' formalization of inference patterns for hypotheticals, but whatever he actually did was based upon the Aristotelian logic of terms. Only some Stoic argument forms employ conditional premises, but every Stoic argument is valid if the conditional proposition which has the argument's premises as its antecedent and the argument's conclusion as its consequent is true, where true is explained as: 'never has a true antecedent and a false consequent' (Sextus, *Adv. math.* viii 415ff.).

The most interesting feature of the Stoic theory of inference is a claim that all arguments can be reduced to five basic patterns. These patterns are 'undemonstrated' or 'indemonstrable', which was interpreted to mean that their validity is 'self-evident' (Sextus, *Adv. math.* viii 223). They are (using letters rather than numerals to symbolize propositions):

1. If p, then q; p; $\therefore$ q.
2. If p, then q; not-q; $\therefore$ not-p.
3. Not (both p and q); p; $\therefore$ not-q.
4. Either p or q; p; $\therefore$ not-q.
5. Either p or q; not-q; $\therefore$ p.

It appears from the titles of Chrysippus' logical works that he proved a large number of theorems for the analysis of complex arguments on the basis of these five inference patterns.[1] Unfortunately little evidence about these theorems survives. Ancient critics of the Stoics found fault with them for their fussiness about logical form and rigorous analysis. But it is these qualities which have earned the Stoics the admiration of modern logicians.

But the Stoics were not modern logicians and this fact, combined with a recognition of the very defective state of our evidence, is important. A number of studies have recently drawn attention to difficulties in Stoic logic, if this is considered purely as logic. One particular problem concerns the criteria for a true conditional proposition. It has been argued, probably rightly, that Chrysippus did not distinguish sharply (or at all) between logical and empirical

[1] See Mates, *Stoic Logic*, pp. 77–85; Kneale, *Development of Logic*, pp. 164–76.

compatibility of antecedent and consequent.[1] Carneades too, as we have seen (p. 103), was able to criticize Chrysippus for assimilating logical and causal relationships. But Chrysippus would no doubt have replied to Carneades along the following lines: in a universe governed by *logos* causal connexions are in a sense logical connexions and vice versa. It is the universal *logos* which is at work both in the connexion between cause and effect and between premises and conclusions. The Stoics were certainly interested in logical problems and are justly admired for their achievements. But a Stoic would not have given interest in pure logic as the reason for his logical studies. Logic is part of nature, and this is why the Stoic sage is required to practise logic. The Stoics themselves probably regarded the self-evidence of their undemonstrated inference patterns as something 'natural' rather than logical in a modern sense. The relation between cause and effect is *necessary* in Stoicism (it is sanctioned by universal *logos*) and there is no evidence that a different kind of necessity is involved in Stoic logic.[2] We may speculate that the inference patterns are natural laws applied to the explanation of relationships between statements.

If these thoughts are correct, they substantially affect the interpretation of Stoic logic. The Stoic universe is a world determined by law, by immanent *logos*. This is a fundamental concept in Stoicism, and it runs through all three aspects of their philosophy. After all, these are only aspects, ways of presenting something which in the last resort is a unity—Nature, the universe, or God. In language these different aspects can be picked out, abstracted from their coexistence in reality, and it was the need to distinguish the thing (i.e. the world) from what we say about it that led the Stoics to foreshadow the distinction between sense and reference. But as I understand the evidence, no statement can be true unless it accurately represents some real state of things. The 'true' is the propositional counterpart of the 'real'. The foundations of logic for the Stoics are embodied in the universe at large. They are not merely a system, something constructed by the human mind. Deductive inference is possible because of the way things are. The natural connexion of cause and effect is represented at the

---

[1] Josiah B. Gould, 'Chrysippus: on the Criteria for the Truth of a Conditional Proposition', *Phronesis* xii (1967) 156–61.

[2] Two texts may be cited out of many to illustrate this point: Stobaeus (*SVF* ii 913) observes that 'truth', 'cause', 'nature', 'necessity' and *logos* all refer to different aspects of the same 'substance' (i.e. the universe). Marcus Aurelius writes of 'one god, one substance, one law, common (or universal) *logos* and one truth' (vii 9), describing 'truth' as the first cause of all that is true (ix 2).

level of thought and language by man's 'concept of connexion'. The universe is a rational structure of material constituents. In natural events and in logic the consequent follows from the antecedent if and only if the connexion between them is 'true'. The 'truth' of all connexions is the work of Nature, God or cosmic *logos*.

(*iv*) *The Stoics and Heraclitus*

As they themselves acknowledged, the Stoics derived many ideas from Heraclitus. By examining some of these borrowings it will be possible to tie together some of the different threads examined in this chapter and to introduce the subject-matter of the next.

Here are three Heraclitean fragments which contain the word *logos*:

Listening not to me but to the *logos*, it is wise to agree (*homo-logein*) that all is one' (fr. 50 Diels-Kranz).

Although all things happen in accordance with this *logos*, men resemble people who have no aquaintance with it, even when they experience the words and doings which I set forth, distinguishing each thing according to its nature and pointing out how it is (fr. 1).

Although the *logos* is common, the many live as if they have a private understanding (fr. 2).

From these passages it is clear that *logos* is something which can be heard, which serves to explain things, which is common to all, etc.

Another fundamental Heraclitean concept is Harmony. He seems to have viewed the world as a collection of things unified and regulated by the *logos* which is common to them. And this notion is of great significance in Stoicism. For Heraclitus it is *logos* which makes the world an orderly structure, a *kosmos*. But the Milesian philosophers had assumed something similar when they attempted to explain all things in terms of transformations of some single material principle. The Greeks did not have to speak of a controlling *logos* in order to express the notion of order in nature. Heraclitus, though he certainly held that the world is an orderly structure, meant much more than this when he spoke of all things happening in accordance with the *logos*. In my opinion he was suggesting that there is a fundamental relationship between cosmic events and human thought or discourse; that if men would only but see it they have, in their own capacity to think and to speak, something which relates them to the world and which can provide clues to the true nature of things.

Heraclitus' own style reflects the antitheses and relationships which he held to be characteristic of the world itself. Perhaps the best example of this is fr. 48: 'The name of the bow (*bios*) is life (*bios*), but its work is death.' To Heraclitus the ambiguity of the word *bios* symbolizes an ambiguity in nature itself: the strung bow or lyre constitutes a unity or harmony, but it is a unity produced by tension or strife between the string and the frame. Just as language may be riddling, ambiguous, paradoxical, so in the world opposites coexist, unity is a product of diversity, harmony a consequence of strife. I am not suggesting that Heraclitus arrived at his theories about the world by thinking about the Greek language. But *logos-legein* in the sense 'meaningful discourse', must be relevant to his claim that *logos* controls all things. He held that the world is a unity of opposites, a harmony of opposing forces which can be signified by such statements as: 'God is day night, winter summer, war peace' (fr. 67); 'The road up and down is one and the same' (fr. 60). These conjunctions of contrary predicates were designed by Heraclitus to exemplify connexions in nature which everyday language had obscured.

The Stoics did not make much use of Heraclitus' notion of unity in opposition, though we find traces of this. But they took from him the concept of a *logos* which directs all things and which is shared by all men. Fire, the symbol or vehicle of the *logos* in Heraclitus, was also adopted by Zeno as the basis of Stoic physics. Above all, the Stoics systematically developed the linguistic and logical implications of a universe directed by *logos*. It would be fanciful to try to find specific influence of Heraclitus in all of this. But the Stoic notion of living *homologoumenôs*, consistently with *logos*, which stresses the relationship that should exist between man and the world, is Heraclitean in conception.

The assumption that the universe is an orderly structure is characteristic of Greek philosophy. And in Plato and Aristotle, as in Stoicism, the notion of order is combined with the notion of goal or purpose. But neither Plato nor Aristotle agreed with the Stoics that this order is an order of cause and effect perfectly represented both in terrestrial phenomena and the movement of the heavenly bodies. There is nothing in Stoicism corresponding to Plato's Forms, nor again to Aristotle's distinction between the celestial and sub-lunar realms. Stoicism does not set up Plato's degrees of reality, nor Aristotle's distinction between necessity and contingency. The objects of perception in Stoicism are all perfect examples of 'what exists', that is, bodies; and they exist necessarily given the causal nexus which determines all things.

Part of the difference between Platonic or Aristotelian methodology and Stoicism is due to the Stoic concept of *logos*. The unification under a single concept of the cause of all happenings and the instrument of thought and discourse led the Stoics to abandon certain modes of philosophical analysis which in their view had nothing real corresponding to them. Language and thought, being natural, must be matched up with natural phenomena. Universals, having no objective existence, cannot be a subject of philosophical study. As concepts they provide us with a convenient way of classifying things, but they do not define the structure of reality. Nature reveals to us particular objects not universals. The value of language to the philosopher is its capacity to describe the world. In a world governed by *logos* what is needed is to connect, to find the right description, the description which fastens upon the appropriate bit of Nature.

IV. THE STOIC PHILOSOPHY OF NATURE

Nature is an artistic fire going on its way to create (D.L. vii 156).

No particular thing however slight can come into being except in accordance with universal Nature and its rationality (*logos*) (Plutarch, *Stoic. rep.* 1050b, quoting Chrysippus).

The nature of the universe possesses voluntary movements, efforts and desires . . . and its actions accord with these just like ourselves who are moved by our minds and our senses (Cic. *N.D.* ii 58).

Stoic natural philosophy is a very large subject which can be approached from many different angles. The one from which I shall view it in this book is primarily conceptual. The historical background of Stoic physics and the Stoics' place in the history of science are topics which have deservedly aroused interest in recent years.[1] But for the purpose of this book they are less significant than the question: 'What is the conceptual structure in terms of which the Stoics tried to understand the world?' In seeking to answer this question I will mention a number of historical considerations, and one particular phenomenon—man—must be studied at the end. But in the interests of a comprehensive picture, many details of Stoic cosmology, meteorology, theology and other subjects will be passed over.

[1] See especially S. Sambursky, *Physics of the Stoics* (London 1959).

Logos is the concept which has so far received the bulk of our attention but the balance must now be redressed in favour of *physis*, 'nature' (Latin, *natura*). First, some examples of the use of the term in Stoicism: (1) the power or principle which shapes and creates all things (*SVF* ii 937); (2) the power or principle which unifies and gives coherence to the world (*SVF* ii 549, 1211); (3) fiery breath (or artistic fire) self-moving and generative (*SVF* ii 1132ff.); (4) necessity and destiny (*SVF* ii 913); (5) God, providence, craftsman, right reason (*SVF* i 158, 176, iii 323). The Stoics themselves ascribed two primary functions to Nature which subsume some of these uses: Nature, they said, is both that which holds the world together and that which causes things on the earth to grow (D.L. vii 148). But this statement does not bring out the functions of Nature signified in our fifth category. Nature is not merely a physical power causing stability and change; it is also something endowed with rationality *par excellence*. That which holds the world together is a supreme rational being, God, who directs all events for purposes which are necessarily good. Soul of the world, mind of the world, Nature, God—these terms all refer to one and the same thing—the 'artistic fire' going on its way to create.

To the 'artistic fire' we shall return. But next a word about the relation between Nature (*physis*) and the other key concept of Stoicism, *logos*. Nature and *logos* are often said to be the same thing in Stoicism, and it is certainly true that they often have the same reference—God, artistic fire, and so on. But they are not terms which have exactly the same sense. (Here again we have to distinguish, as the Stoics did, between the meaning of a word and the *thing* it refers to.) 'Nature is *logos*' is not a statement of identity, an empty tautology, and the Stoics, as one of the passages cited at the beginning of this section shows, could write of 'Nature *and its logos*'. Each term has its own connotations, and it does not forfeit these when applied to the same thing. The significance of this point can be clarified by an example from biology. Plants, so the Stoics argued, have *physis* (nature) as their governing principle; that of irrational animals is 'soul', and the principle in man is *logos*, 'reason' (*SVF* ii 714). Here we are considering three types of living thing as discrete objects. In fact, all three are governed by Nature, but Nature manifests itself in a different relation with respect to each type of thing. Nature itself is rational through and through, but that which governs a plant or an irrational animal is not rational so far as these individual living things are concerned.

Only in mature men is the rationality of Nature present to them as something which belongs to *their nature*. It is not the nature of plants to act rationally, but it is the nature of man so to act. Here we glimpse some of the ordinary connotations of the word 'nature' and the force of the Stoic conceptual relation between Nature and *logos*. Taken as a whole, as the governing principle of all things, Nature is equivalent to *logos*. But if we consider particular living things, though all have a 'nature' only some possess reason as a natural faculty.

The existence of God, or what comes to the same thing in Stoicism, the divinity of Nature, is a thesis which the Stoics devoted great energy to proving. They agreed with Epicurus that the strength and prevalence of human ideas of divinity provide evidence of the necessary existence of God or gods (Cic. *N.D.* ii 5), but they used many other arguments which have had a long theological history. Cleanthes, for whom theology was a dominant interest, accounted for religious beliefs by reference to many factors, four of which are recorded by Cicero: the validity of prophecy and divination, the benefits which men enjoy from the earth, awe inspired by phenomena such as lightning and earthquakes, and the beauty and orderly movement of the heavens (*N.D.* ii 13–15). Among a number of the arguments which Chrysippus put forward we may note the following:

> If there is something in the world which human reason, strength and power are incapable of producing, that which produces it must be better than man. But the heavens and everything which display unceasing regularity cannot be produced by man. Therefore that by which those things are produced is better than man. And what name rather than God would you give to this? (*N.D.* ii 16).

Many Stoic versions of the argument from design are also recorded, all of which seek to show that this is the best of all possible worlds with divine purpose immanent in it and working for the benefit of rational beings.

Some of the difficulties which this optimistic theology engenders in Stoicism will be discussed later. Their strenuous defence of divine providence is a complete reversal of the Epicurean attitude. The Stoics also differ greatly from the Epicureans in their treatment of traditional Greek religion. They did not approve of its ceremonial aspects and rejected sacrifices, temples and images. But they found a place for the Olympian pantheon by interpreting the individual gods

as names of natural phenomena (Hera or Juno is 'air') which are
divine manifestations of the one ultimate deity, Nature, whose name is
also Zeus. Fundamentally, Stoic theology is pantheist. The divinity
of the stars and great heroes of the past represents the working of
cosmic reason in its most perfect form.

(i) Historical background

In positing a cosmic principle which is not only intelligible but also
intelligent the Stoics were sharply at variance with the Epicureans.
But in the Greek philosophical tradition it is the Epicureans who
stand out as exceptional. Most of the Presocratics, with the exception
of the Atomists, found evidence of reason in natural phenomena.
Anaxagoras posited Mind as the first cause of all things, and a slightly
younger thinker, Diogenes of Apollonia, tried to explain the world
by reference to air, assigning to air intelligence and identifying it with
God. He held that air *pervades* and *disposes* all things, being itself subject to variations of temperature, moisture and speed (DK 64B5). Like
Anaximenes, a hundred years his predecessor, Diogenes regarded the
human soul as air and thus, on his principles, it is a 'portion' of God.
In a fragment preserved by Simplicius he writes:

> For without intelligence it would not have been possible for everything to
> be so distributed as to maintain the measures of all things—winter and sum-
> mer, night and day, rains and winds and fair weather; and everything else
> one will find, if one is willing to reflect, disposed in the best possible way
> (DK 64B3).

Though their picture of the physical world is vastly more sophisticated
than Diogenes', the Stoics have much in common with him. They too
posited as their active principle an all-pervasive intelligent material
which is identical to God and accounts for differences in particular
things by differentiations of itself. Diogenes' air plays a similar biological and psychological rôle to Stoic fire or *pneuma* (fiery breath), and
they also regarded the human soul as an 'offshoot' of God. Above all,
they accepted like him that the orderliness of natural phenomena provides undoubted evidence of the world's excellence.[1]

One of the striking features of Stoic natural philosophy is its biological orientation. There is little doubt that the Stoics were influenced
here by Presocratic modes of thought. But the Presocratics were only

[1] At *N.D.* ii 16–39 Cicero records a number of Stoic arguments for the world's
excellence and rationality.

one influence on Stoic natural philosophy. This is not the retrogressive system that many earlier scholars have suggested. On the contrary, the Stoics drew on a wide range of material, including contemporary medicine, and there are notable similarities between their own natural philosophy and Platonic and Aristotelian concepts.

In late Plato we find many anticipations of Stoicism. Plato regularly appeals to the orderly movements of the heavenly bodies in support of his claim that the world is the product of intelligent direction. Whether he writes allegorically of a Craftsman, as in the *Timaeus*, or more literally of a 'world-soul' as in Book x of the *Laws*, Plato is convinced that the world is directed by intelligence for purposes which are good. One passage from the *Laws* is remarkably 'Stoic':

> Let us persuade the young men by arguments that all things have been arranged by the overseer of the universe for the security and excellence of the whole; and the parts of the universe each act or are acted upon appropriately according to their capacity. Each of these parts down to the smallest feature of its condition or activity is under the direction of ruling powers, which have perfected every minutest detail. And you, you stubborn man, are one of these parts, minute though you are, which always contributes to the good of the whole. You have failed to see that every act of creation occurs for the sake of the universe, that it may enjoy a life of well-being; creation occurs not for your sake but you occur for the sake of the universe.... You are peeved because you fail to realize how what is best for you is best for the universe as well as yourself (903b–d).

This passage would be quite in place in Epictetus or Marcus Aurelius. Plato's distinction between part and whole is of central importance to Stoic ethics, and it has the same cosmic grounding. When Chrysippus wrote that ethics requires 'universal Nature' as its starting-point (Plut. *Stoic. rep.* 1035c) he was talking the language of *Laws* x. From a physical point of view there are of course great differences between Plato's universe and that of the Stoics. For Plato soul is something incorporeal like the Forms. The Stoics reject the Forms and make soul along with their 'artistic fire' a corporeal entity. But such differences do not undermine a fundamental common ground both in the attitude towards the universe and in its ethical implications.

The links between Stoicism and Aristotle's cosmology are rather different. Like the Stoics, Aristotle is a thoroughgoing teleologist, and his notion of 'nature' as a cause 'for the sake of something', expounded in *Physics* ii, has a superficial resemblance with Stoic *physis*. But Aristotle does not conceive nature as a rational agent; nature for him is that factor within each individual organism which accounts for its efforts to perfect itself. Though Aristotle sometimes speaks of nature as 'divine' he cannot in his mature system identify God and nature, since God is not 'in the world'. For Aristotle, God—the prime unmoved mover—is a pure Mind which acts upon the world not directly but through the mediation of the heavenly bodies whose movements are responsible for change in the terrestrial sphere. The precise relationship between Aristotle's self-absorbed Prime Mover and goal-directed processes on earth is one of the more obscure elements in his system. The Stoics, by setting Nature/God within the world, have united under a single principle functions which Aristotle kept apart. Stoic Nature resembles the Aristotelian Prime Mover in being a rational agent which is the ultimate cause of all things. But the Stoics also regard Nature as a material substance—'artistic fire'—which pervades all things and accounts for their persistence and their change.

It is interesting to note that the Aristotelian, Strato, who died about the same time as Zeno, reacted to Aristotle's cosmology in a quite different way. Instead of identifying God and nature Strato took the opposite step of denying any function to God in the explanation of the universe. In Strato nature becomes the ultimate cause of all phenomena, and it is conceived in mechanistic terms (Cic. *N.D.* i 35): nature is the interaction of opposing powers, fundamentally 'hot' and 'cold'. The Stoics are at the opposite end of this spectrum but only in one sense. They agreed with Strato in looking for the ultimate cause of change within the world and the Stoic concept of *pneuma* was very probably influenced by Strato's hot and cold.

Stoic natural philosophy looks radically different from Aristotle's cosmology in some respects. But in many details his influence is apparent. The Aristotelian distinction between 'matter' and 'form', and his notion of 'elements' which are transformed into one another, are two ideas which the Stoics incorporated with modifications into their own system. On neither theory is empty space acceptable. As advocates of a continuous and purposive universe Aristotle and the Stoics are at one against the Epicureans.

(ii) The structure of things: body, pneuma, elements
So much by way of general historical background. Nature, the concept with which we have been chiefly concerned thus far, refers in Stoicism to a kind of body, 'artistic fire' (or *pneuma*). Unlike the Platonists and Peripatetics the Stoics confined 'existence' to bodies (*SVF* ii 525).

Their position was justified by the assumption that for something to exist it must be capable of producing or experiencing some change, and that this condition is only satisfied by bodies—three-dimensional objects which are resistant to external pressure (*SVF* ii 359, 381). Zeno used this criterion of existence to refute claims of earlier thinkers concerning incorporeal entities (Cic. *Acad.* i 39). If the mind were such an entity, Zeno argued, it would be incapable of any activity. This is an interesting reversal of a Platonic argument in the *Sophist* (246a–247e). There the Eleatic Stranger argues against those who 'limit existence to what can be touched', who identify body and being, by turning the discussion to moral qualities. The materialists admit that there is such a thing as soul, and that souls may be just or unjust. The Stranger then elicits the admission that a just soul is one in which justice is present and that whatever can come to be present in (or absent from) something must be a real thing. The materialists, reluctant to abandon their position, are now said by Theaetetus to equivocate, neither accepting the inference that moral qualities (which are intangible) are unreal nor that they are bodies. The Eleatic Stranger next proposes that the materialists should abandon their previous criterion of existence in favour of a new 'mark of reality'—'that anything which really exists possesses some power of causing a change in something else or of experiencing change' (247e).

The Stoics, far from being embarrassed by Plato's mark of reality, accepted it and its consequences. They seized the nettle which Plato's materialists shrank from touching and boldly asserted that justice and all moral qualities *are* bodies like anything else which exists. An argument of Chrysippus' is quoted by Plutarch (*Stoic. rep.* 1042e) which implies the criterion of existence, 'power of acting or being acted upon', in discussing the perceptibility of virtue: virtue and vice are objects of sense-perception; we are able to see theft, adultery, cowardice, acts of kindness, and so forth. Therefore, we may interpolate, virtue and vice have the power to act upon our senses, and sensation requires physical contact between the percipient and the object.

But clearly, virtue or an act of kindness is not the same kind of thing as a man or a table. In order to see how the Stoics could intelligibly treat virtue as a corporeal entity we must turn to consider their two so-called 'principles' or 'starting-points' and the relation between them.

One of these 'principles' we have already encountered: the 'active principle' is Nature or God. But it is permanently related to a 'passive

principle', termed 'matter' or 'substance without qualitative determination' (D.L. vii 134). Seneca gives a succinct description of these
two principles: 'Matter is inert, a thing which is available for everything but which will be dormant unless something moves it'; the
'active principle' or 'cause' is 'reason which shapes matter and moves
it whithersoever it wishes and fashions from it products of different
kinds' (*Ep.* 65, 2). The Stoic concept of 'matter' was borrowed from
Aristotle. In Aristotle's metaphysics 'matter' is the undefined substrate
'underlying' the form or properties which particular things possess;
it is that 'out of which they come to be'. Considered just by itself
matter in Aristotle is devoid of form, but it is never encountered in
the world without some qualification: we know matter by analogy
with the matter of particular things—the bronze of the statue, the
wood of the bed. Similarly in Stoicism, matter and the active shaping
principle never exist apart from one another. Together they constitute
all that exists, and they can only be drawn apart for the purpose of
conceptual analysis.

The physical relationship between the two principles or constituents of 'being' is mixture: 'God is mixed with matter, penetrates
the whole of matter and shapes it' (*SVF* ii 310). This notion of one
thing completely interpenetrating another is difficult, but for the
present we may let it stand. A more pressing question is why the
Stoics postulated two principles rather than one. No Stoic text provides
an explicit answer, but the best clue is their criterion of existence as
'capable of acting or of being acted upon'. If body satisfies this condition then body must be analysable into active and passive components. For it could not simultaneously as a whole both act upon
itself and be acted upon by itself. 'Matter' in Stoicism is therefore not
equivalent to corporeality: it is rather one aspect of corporeality which
in any particular body is conjoined with the active component.

Since matter is completely indeterminate it can become qualified by
any form or disposition imposed upon it by the active principle. It is
misleading to describe the Stoics as 'materialists'. Bodies, in the
Stoic system, are compounds of 'matter' and 'mind' (God or *logos*).
Mind is not something other than body but a necessary constituent of
it, the 'reason' in matter. The Stoics are better described as vitalists.
Their Nature, like Spinoza's God or Nature, is a thing to which both
thought and extension are attributable.

Zeno and Cleanthes identified the *logos* with fire. Their reasoning
was based upon the assumption that heat is something vital and active.

Cicero is drawing on Cleanthes when he presents this Stoic argument:[1]

It is a fact that all things which are capable of nurture and growth contain within themselves vital heat, without which they could not sustain nurture and growth. For everything which is hot and fiery is roused and moved by its own agency (*N.D.* ii 23).

Heat or fire was a fundamental concept in Presocratic thought, and its influence persisted in later times. Aristotle regarded heat as the cause of growth which is present in every seed, and the early Stoics extended this biological notion to explain movement and change in the whole universe. Nature is an artistic or creative fire; and the essence of this idea is expressed in the sentence: 'God is the "seminal" *logos* of the universe' (D.L. vii 136). Heat or fire never loses this pre-eminence in Stoicism. 'Fiery' is the one qualification which 'matter' is always endowed with by its association with *logos*.[2] But from Chrysippus onwards the Stoics identified the *logos* throughout each world-cycle not with pure fire but with a compound of fire and air, *pneuma*.

This modification of the earlier doctrine was almost certainly prompted by contemporary physiology.[3] *Pneuma*, which literally means 'breath', was regarded by medical writers as the 'vital' spirit transmitted via the arteries. Aristotle made use of this idea, and Zeno connected fire and breath in his definition of the soul ('hot breath'). The same reasoning which led to the identification of *logos* with fire was obviously applicable to breath as well, if both things are necessary to a vital principle. Chrysippus took this step, and made *pneuma* the vehicle of the *logos*.

The expression 'vehicle of the logos' is chosen because the active principle is not a simple chemical compound of air and fire. It is 'intelligent *pneuma*' (or 'artistic' fire in the earlier formulation), something which is both a physical component of the world and an agent capable of rational action. This ambiguity of function was characteristic of 'fire' in Heraclitus, but in Stoicism there is no conceptual confusion. *Pneuma* is a dynamic entity. Its continuous

[1] Not Posidonius, as has often been argued; cf. F. Solmsen, 'Cleanthes or Posidonius? The Basis of Stoic Physics', *Meded. der kon. Ned. Akad.* 24, 9 (1961).

[2] The *ekpyrôsis* ('conflagration') which ends each world-cycle is a resolution of all things into fire. During this phase the supreme deity, which is equivalent to *logos* or Nature, is 'wholly absorbed in his own thoughts', like Aristotle's Prime Mover (Sen. *Ep.* 9, 16).

[3] See Solmsen, 'The Vital Heat, the Inborn Pneuma and the Aether', *Journal of Hellenic Studies* lxxvii (part 1) 1957.

movement, which we must consider shortly, makes *pneuma* something more like 'force' or 'energy' than a material object, and the Stoics stressed the tenuity and fineness of its structure (*SVF* ii p. 155, 33f.). Perhaps 'gas' is the least misleading modern analogue.

In Heraclitus' cosmology the material constituents of the world are 'turnings' or modifications of fire (fr. 31). The Stoics were strongly influenced by this idea, but in their system there is a further concept unrecognized by Heraclitus, 'matter', and a qualitative theory of 'elements' which betrays Aristotelian ideas. In Chrysippus' account, the only 'element' which persists for ever is fire (*SVF* ii 413). But fire, being a dynamic disposition of 'matter', causes it to take on other qualifications besides hot, namely: cold, dry and moist. Matter so qualified becomes respectively air, earth and water. These four 'elements' (the traditional quartet of Greek philosophers) are thought of as constituting two pairs, one active (fire and air=*pneuma*) and the other passive (earth and water). Once the cosmic fire has given positive determination to air this derived element joins with fire to form the active component of body, while earth and water constitute its passive counterpart (*SVF* ii 418). Thus the conceptual distinction between active and passive or *logos* and matter is backed up by an empirical distinction between *pneuma* and the elements of earth and water. Of course, the latter pair is not mere matter, a logical abstraction, but a disposition of matter engendered by fire.

The two pairs of elements are differentiated in further ways. A property of *pneuma* is to 'give coherence', to 'hold together' the other pair of elements, earth and water (*SVF* ii 439f.). The universe itself is a sphere, and all its constituents tend to move towards the centre; but only earth and water actually possess weight (*SVF* i 99). The *pneuma*, unlike the passive elements, pervades the whole cosmic sphere and unites the centre with the circumference. It prevents the universe from collapsing under the gravitational pull of its heavy constituents by endowing the whole with coherence. This function of *pneuma* in the macrocosm is equally at work in every individual body. Organic and inorganic things alike owe their identity and their properties to the *pneuma*. Its two constituents, fire and air, are blended in different proportions in different things. One arrangement of *pneuma* is the soul of an animal; the structure of a plant is a further arrangement, and the coherence of a stone yet another (*SVF* ii 716). Whatever *pneuma* disposes it also holds together by the 'tension' which it establishes between the individual parts (*SVF* ii 441, 448).

Some obscurity attaches to the notion of 'tension'. It is a concept which the Stoics inherited from Heraclitus, though their interpretation of his 'back-turning' or 'back-stretched' harmony (Diels-Kranz fr. 51) no doubt goes beyond anything which he had in mind. 'Tension' in Stoicism describes a kind of 'movement', which is to be sharply differentiated from change of place. Alexander of Aphrodisias, who criticized the Stoics from an Aristotelian position, speaks of Stoic *pneuma* as 'simultaneously moving from itself and towards itself' (*SVF* ii 442). Likewise Nemesius writes: 'According to the Stoics there is a "tensional" movement in bodies, which moves simultaneously inwards and outwards; the movement outwards produces quantities and qualities, while that inwards produces unity and substance' (*SVF* ii 451). Sometimes tensional movement is described as an alternation of two opposite movements (*SVF* ii 450, 458), but this is probably a modification of the Stoics' own words prompted by the difficulty of attributing simultaneous contrary movements to the same thing.[1] In fact the problem of simultaneity is largely resolved if the movement of *pneuma* is analysed as a function of the movement of its two constituents.

Pneuma is a compound of fire and air, and the two directions of its movement are explained as a 'contraction' due to cold (air) and an 'expansion' due to heat (fire) (*SVF* ii 446). By virtue of its constituents *pneuma*, which is spatially continuous, is continuously active. It makes the universe into a dynamic continuum all the parts of which are interconnected, though they differ from one another individually according to the mixture and tension of the *pneuma* that pervades them. Matter is made coherent and stable by the balance of forces which act upon it through its association with *pneuma*. The world-picture which results from this concept of *pneuma* differs radically both from Epicurean and Aristotelian physics. The ultimate constituents of Epicurus' universe are empty space and atoms. All change is a consequence of the movement and other necessary properties of an infinite set of discontinuous indivisible bodies. The Stoic universe sets this system on its head. The movement and properties of individual bodies are a consequence of the dispositions of a single all-pervading dynamic substance. There is nothing like this in Aristotle's cosmology with its chain of movers of which the prime one, God, is not in any spatial relation to the universe. Movement for Aristotle requires the existence

---

[1] Galen put 'tensional movement' to interesting use as an explanation of muscular activity (*SVF* ii 450).

of a continuous spatial medium. But he does not attribute any active function to the medium itself.

A recent study of Stoic physics has pointed out some interesting analogies between the *pneuma* theory and modern scientific concepts.[1] Some of the functions served by Stoic *pneuma* were taken over by the ubiquitous aether postulated by scientists from the seventeenth century up to quite recent times. Or the *pneuma* may be compared with the notion of a 'field of force' activating matter. More generally, it is intriguing to notice two modern writers describing the nature of things in a manner which could not fail to have won the Stoics' approval:

> Matter and energy are simply different aspects of the same fundamental reality and in all their manifestations obey ineluctable cosmic laws. . . . There exists a single unified system from one end of the cosmos to the other; in the last analysis, everything is energy [the Stoics would write 'pneumatic force']. Its larger spirals are the galaxies, its smaller eddies suns and planets, its softest movement the atom and the gene. Under all forms of matter and manifestations of life there beats the unity of energy according to Einstein's law. Yet this unified stuff of existence not only twists itself into the incredible variety of material things; it can also produce living patterns of ever greater complexity—from the gas bubble in the original plasma to . . . the crowning complexity of the human brain.[2]

From a conceptual point of view, the most interesting feature of the Stoic physical system is the reduction of all qualitative distinctions between objects and within objects to states or dispositions of *pneuma* interacting with matter. The Stoics were not exact scientists, but their theory would lend itself in principle to an expression of physical states in terms of a measurement of pneumatic movement and an analysis of pneumatic compounds. On one detail however, and it is a significant one, ancient and modern writers have noticed a fundamental difficulty. According to Chrysippus, *pneuma* interacts with matter by permeating it completely (*SVF* ii 473). But both *pneuma* and matter are corporeal, and it is an elementary principle of physics that two bodies cannot occupy the same space at the same time. How then is it conceivable that *pneuma* can completely permeate matter? The Stoics were aware of the difficulty, and they sought to overcome it by distinguishing between different modes of mixture.

[1] Sambursky, *Physics of the Stoics*, pp. 29–44.
[2] Barbara Ward and René Dubos, *Only One Earth* (Harmondsworth 1972) p. 83.

(iii) Mixture

Aristotle had already discussed mixture in the treatise *On coming to be and passing away* (i 10). There he distinguishes between two fundamental kinds of mixture: first, 'combination' (*synthesis*) is the state which results when, say, grains of barley and grains of wheat are 'mixed' together. For Aristotle this is not truly a mixture since the constituents retain their own properties. The Stoics followed Aristotle here, using the term 'juxtaposition' to refer to such mechanical combinations. Secondly, Aristotle distinguishes 'blending' (*mixis* or *krasis*): the characteristic of this is that the mixed components combine to form something homogeneous the properties of which are determined by the interaction between the mixed components. Thus bronze results from the mixture of copper and tin. But if one component is much larger than another, no new compound results: the 'weaker' component, say a drop of wine, does not mix with ten thousand measures of water; the wine loses its vinous property and becomes part of the total volume of water. The Stoics differed from Aristotle here by distinguishing two further modes of mixture.

One of these, 'complete fusion', is described by Alexander of Aphrodisias as follows:

> When bodies are destroyed together throughout their substance and component properties, as occurs in the case of drugs, the simultaneous destruction of the things which are mixed produces a new body (*SVF* ii 473).

Some of the examples of Aristotelian 'blending' would fall under 'complete fusion' though Aristotle's doctrine is based upon distinctions between potentiality and actuality which the Stoics did not recognize. But more important and more puzzling than the first two Stoic modes of mixture is the third. Here is Alexander's account:

> Certain mixtures occur when bodies are completely extended throughout the substance and properties of one another while maintaining their original substance and properties in this mixture. Chrysippus calls this specifically a 'blending' of mixtures (*SVF* ii 473).

Like 'juxtaposition' the components of this mixture can be separated since they retain their own properties throughout. But in 'blending', the components so 'extend' throughout one another that every particle among them shares in all the components of the mixture.

The Stoics defended this theory of the complete interpenetration of two bodies by empirical examples. The mixture of wine and water, they argued, is more than a juxtaposition of wine and water droplets. But it is not a complete fusion of these, since if one puts an oiled sponge into such a mixture the two components can be separated (*SVF* ii 472). The idea is clearly that no volume of such a mixture, however small, can be reached in which the constituents fail to exhibit the same properties and relationship to each other. So Chrysippus contradicted Aristotle's claim that a drop of wine cannot mix with a vastly greater volume of water (*SVF* ii 480). In the Stoic view the relative size or mass of two components is irrelevant to their potentiality for mixing. And here we see how the Stoics tried to defend a theory of the complete interpenetration of one body by another. The case in which they are acutely interested is the relation of *pneuma* to matter. Both of these are corporeal, but *pneuma* is a body of extreme tenuity. Matter is supposed to be pervaded through and through by the *pneuma*. And in order to explain this it was necessary to consider the different modes of mixture. The Stoics seem to have thought that the fineness of *pneuma* is such that a volume of it can simultaneously occupy the same space as a volume of matter. Their theory is made more plausible by the assumption that the quantity of *pneuma* within any compound will always be extremely small in proportion to the quantity of matter: 'If wholes completely extend through wholes and the smallest through the largest right up to the limits of extension, whatever place is occupied by the one will be occupied by both together' (*SVF* ii 477).

The Stoics could have avoided the consequences of this ingenious but untenable theory of mixture if they had emancipated the notion of physical force from the notion of body. Yet this would have required a complete revision of their basic principles, since *pneuma* possesses its power to act and to fashion matter in virtue of the fact that it is a corporeal entity. The Stoics did not recognize the possibility of action at a distance. The model behind their theory of causation is that of one thing touching and so acting upon another. But we may leave the problem of mixture at this point and examine in further detail the concept of qualitative differentiation which the Stoics based upon *pneuma*.

(iv) Categories

Simplicius and Plotinus are the chief sources of evidence for a Stoic theory of 'categories'.[1] Aristotle has a set of ten 'categories' and his

---

[1] See the texts in von Arnim, *SVF* ii 376–404. It is generally and probably rightly assumed that Chrysippus was the first Stoic to formulate the doctrine.

use of these straddles logical and linguistic analysis on the one hand
and metaphysical analysis on the other. The same holds good in
Stoicism but there are significant differences between the two category
systems. Aristotle's categories are a supposedly exhaustive classification of the ways in which we talk about things: for instance, 'being
of a certain size', 'being in a certain place', 'being at a certain time',
'acting', 'being acted upon'. The Stoic categories—four instead of
Aristotle's ten—are more abstract. To put it briefly, they are a series
of headings for analysing and describing the two constituents of
reality, *pneuma* and matter, and their interrelations.

The first category is 'substrate' or 'substance', and this corresponds
to 'matter'. But 'matter' in Stoicism never exists without some qualification since it is invariably permeated by *pneuma*. This fact accounts
for the second Stoic category, 'qualified'. Anything in the world must
be a substance, that is a material object, but it cannot exist as a material
object without being qualified by *pneuma*. 'Substance' and 'qualified'
are general predicates which must characterize anything that exists.[1]
This applies macroscopically—the world is a single and unique
qualified substance. But it also applies to all particular things. Since
matter is continuous, particularity in Stoicism does not refer to discrete atomic objects. It refers to the shape or form which marks off
one stretch of matter from another. The qualification which *pneuma*
bestows upon matter as a whole is also the means of differentiating
between different parts of matter. These different differentiations of
matter are what we call individuals, this man, this horse. Each of them
owes its individuality to *pneuma*, which so qualifies matter that each
so-called individual possesses some characteristic shared by nothing
else in the universe and which persists as long as it persists.[2]

Each qualified substance therefore has an 'individuating quality'
(SVF ii 395). That is part of the analysis of what it is to be 'qualified'.
But the Stoics also recognized that some of the properties possessed

---

For a detailed discussion see J. M. Rist, 'Categories and Their Uses', *Stoic
Philosophy* (Cambridge 1969) pp. 152–72 = ch. 3 of *Problems in Stoicism*.

[1] As we have seen, incorporeals (*lekta*, time, void and place) do not exist, but
they are not nothing; they can form the content of a thought and may be said to
'subsist'. The Stoics nominated a 'class' called 'the something' which embraces
both substances (bodies) and incorporeals (*SVF* ii 117).

[2] The Stoics insisted that no two things are exactly alike, citing hairs and
grains of sand as examples (Cic. *Acad.* ii 85). For their anticipation of Leibniz's
principle of the identity of indiscernibles cf. Sambursky, *Physics of the Stoics*,
pp. 47f.

by one individual can be classified under the same heading as those possessed by another individual. Socrates shares with Plato the property of being two-legged, rational and animal. These 'common qualities' are so badly documented in our sources that it is difficult to form any clear idea of what the Stoics said about them. But there can be nothing in the world which directly corresponds to them, for in nature only particular differentiations of substance exist. 'Common qualities' are probably concepts arrived at by generalization which provide a way of classifying the qualification of particular things. This ties in closely with the Stoics' discussion of nouns. Proper nouns signify the individuating quality; common nouns have the common qualities as their reference (see p. 136). What answers to the latter is not an individual, but something which belongs to many individuals.

The third Stoic category, 'being in a certain state', is generally translated 'disposition' (*SVF* ii 399–401). From one point of view the Stoics seem to have described any differentiation as *pneuma* or matter 'in a certain state'. But they also used this expression to distinguish relatively impermanent or accidental dispositions of individuals. The soul is '*pneuma* in a certain state' but it is essential for every animal to have a soul. Virtue and vice are also *pneuma* in a certain state, but not everything which has a soul is virtuous or vicious. These predicates only apply to mature men. What they refer to is a 'disposition' of the *pneuma* which is already in the state necessary to constitute soul. In its usage as a category, 'disposition' is a way of analysing not the specific and permanent characteristics of an individual but what it is about some individual which permits us to describe it as being somewhere, being at some time, acting, having a certain size, being coloured and so forth. Of course, any individual must at any time be in a condition where such things can be said about it. But men begin and cease to walk, they learn new things and forget other things, they undergo moral improvement or not as the case may be. Such descriptions are possible in the Stoic system because the *pneuma* which pervades anything is both the cause of its persistence in time and also the cause of its different states at different times. In the sentence 'Cato is walking' a disposition of a particular material object is described. Cato's walking is a certain state of the *pneuma* which makes Cato Cato. The disposition is not separable from the man himself; but in language we can draw a distinction between the subject of a sentence and what is said about it. Cato's walking refers to a physical reality; but his 'walking' is not something which can exist without Cato.

It describes the disposition of a material object at a certain time and place.

The fourth and final Stoic category is 'relative disposition' (*SVF* ii 402–4). The function of this is to classify properties which one thing possesses *in relation to* something else. Thus a man may have the property of being a father, but this differs from his, say, being white, in that being a father entails a relationship with something else, his child or children. Right and left, father and son—each one of these pairs 'needs something external if it is to subsist' (*SVF* ii 403). Relative disposition provides a category for analysing the extent to which what we can truly say about one thing is dependent upon something else. But the reasons which led the Stoics to posit this category are probably metaphysical rather than logical. All parts of the universe are related to one another by the *pneuma* which pervades them. Relative disposition offers a category for describing the working of cosmic 'sympathy', as it was called.

For this reason the fourth of the Stoic categories has the widest and most interesting implications. Where all things are interdependent, an idea which has today taken on a particular ecological significance, the concept of relationships is a fundamental one. In Stoicism, to be a good and happy man is to be related in a certain way to Nature or God. The psychological need to relate—to oneself, to one's society, to the world—was sensed acutely by the Stoics. Like William James, or Jung, or Fromm, they detected an all-inclusive desire to 'feel at home in the universe'. The Stoic philosophy of Nature provides a cosmic orientation for personal identity which, far from neglecting human relationships, makes them implicit in life according to reason. 'We have come into being for co-operation' (Marcus ii 1); 'The good of a rational being consists in communal association' (v 16). Individualism, in its Whiggish sense, was as antithetical to Stoicism as it is to many modern psychologists and philosophers.

(v) Causation: determinism, human action, cosmic evil.
This reference to social and ethical theories is no digression. For they are intimately bound up with the Stoic concept of Nature. But a more strictly physical dimension of relatedness remains to be considered. Nature connects and determines all things, and it was this conception of Nature which made the Stoics the first philosophers who maintained systematically the law of universal causation. What this law states has been expressed by Russell as follows:

There are such invariable relations between different events at the same or different times that, given the state of the whole universe throughout any finite time, however short, every previous and subsequent event can theoretically be determined as a function of the given events during that time.[1]

Now consider the following quotations:

Prior events are causes of those following them, and in this manner all things are bound together with one another, and thus nothing happens in the world such that something else is not entirely a consequence of it and attached to it as cause. . . . From everything that happens something else follows depending on it by necessity as cause (*SVF* ii 945).

If there could be any man who perceived the linking of all causes nothing would ever deceive him. For whoever grasps the causes of future events must grasp everything which will be. . . . The passage of time is like the unwinding of a rope, bringing about nothing new (*SVF* ii 944).

As these passages show, the Stoics held strictly to the view that for everything that happens there are conditions such that, given them, nothing else could happen. Chance is simply a name for undiscovered causes (*SVF* ii 967). All future events are theoretically predictable, and astrology and divination were appealed to as evidence for the validity of the causal nexus. Possibility exists to the extent that, but only to the extent that, men are ignorant of the causal connexion between events (*SVF* ii 959). A possible event is one 'which is prevented by nothing from occurring even if it will not occur' (ibid.). But there is something which prevents all non-events from occurring—the causes of those events which do occur. It is only human ignorance of causes which entitles men to assert the absence of any impediment to the occurrence of non-events.

The Stoics based their determinism on the proposition, every event must have a cause. Holding the universe to be a unified system they argued that any uncaused event would undermine its coherence (*SVF* ii 945). They also argued mistakenly, as we saw in the last chapter, that every proposition could not be true or false unless all things are a consequence of a fixed sequence of antecedent causes. But apart from such specific reasons, the Stoics were committed to determinism by the properties which they ascribed to Nature itself. As the all-pervading *pneuma* or *logos*, Nature is the intelligent director of everything. If some events were fortuitous or fell outside the scope of

[1] *Our Knowledge of the External World* (London 1914) p. 221.

Nature's power, the world could not be analysed entirely by reference to Natural Law. But it is fundamental to Stoicism that this should be possible. Further, divine providence, which the Stoics strenuously maintained, presupposes a capacity in God or Nature to bring about good works. The Stoics held that this is the best of all possible worlds; notwithstanding apparent imperfections here and there, Nature so organizes each part that harmony is present in the whole. The psychological and moral implications of this notion are constantly invoked by Marcus Aurelius, and it seems to be a fact that many men have found considerable comfort in the belief that, come what may, their lives contribute to some grand universal scheme:

Nothing is harmful to the part which is advantageous to the whole. For the whole contains nothing which is not advantageous to itself. . . . As long as I remember that I am a part of such a whole I shall be well content with all that happens (x 6).

Everything that is in tune with you, O Universe, is in tune with me. Nothing that is timely for you is too early or too late for me (iv 23).

William James was unwilling to classify such statements as descriptions of religious experience. But that may be a quarrel about a phrase. At the very least, Marcus' sentiments display something close to exaltation at being in harmony with Nature. The Stoic attitude was advocated by writers like Shaftesbury in the eighteenth century, and it is not one of blind resignation. They believed that the essential attribute of human nature, rationality, is derived from and an integral part of the active principle in the universe. This is something which will need to be borne in mind when we come to consider what they had to say about evil and the causes of human action.

The Stoics did not follow Aristotle in distinguishing different types of causal explanation (material, formal, efficient and final), but the single cause which they posited can be regarded as something which brings together in one substance his four causes. Seneca writes:

We Stoics look for a primary and universal cause. This must be single because matter is single. We ask what that cause is? The answer is 'creative reason', that is God (*Ep.* 65, 12).

It is the 'creative reason' which ultimately accounts for all particular substances and all happenings. Like God in Spinoza's *Ethics*, the *logos* is the 'indwelling cause of all things'. A portion of the cosmic *pneuma* is present in each substance and thereby constitutes the substance as something particular, a stone, a man etc. But the environment in which each individual thing is situated is also accountable to *pneuma*. According to its different dispositions *pneuma* is both an internal cause and an external cause. This distinction between internal and external is crucial to Chrysippus' explanation of action. The detailed evidence which survives about his theory suggests that he was the first Stoic to explore the problem of causation in depth. He may have been persuaded to do so in order to answer the criticism that Stoic determinism did away with all human freedom of action. But the thesis which he advanced is also applicable to the movements of inanimate objects.

In elucidating his causal distinctions Chrysippus took as an example a rolling drum (Cic. *De fato* 39–44). We are probably to suppose that the drum is placed upon a flat surface. Its rolling according to Chrysippus must be accounted for by reference to two causes. First, some external agency: drums on flat surfaces do not start to roll unless something else gives them a push. But secondly, the drum would not roll unless it had a certain kind of shape. Square boxes do not roll however hard they are pushed. The drum's rolling is thus a consequence both of external pressure and its own intrinsic nature. Chrysippus termed the first type of cause 'auxiliary and proximate'; the second, the drum's capacity to roll, is a 'principal and perfect cause'. Neither cause is sufficient to bring about the effect unless the other is also present. But Chrysippus' terminology shows that he regarded the intrinsic properties of something as more significant for the purpose of causal explanation than external stimuli.

Chrysippus' distinction is clearly useful and important. If we are considering the movement of some physical object, say a motor-car, it is not a sufficient explanation of the engine's ticking over to say: 'Someone turned on the ignition and the self-starter.' The engine would not go without fuel, and it would not go unless it were a properly manufactured machine which has the capacity to convert the energy present in its fuel into rotary movement. When fuelled and driven it functions necessarily in a manner determined by the arrangement of its parts. Chrysippus argued that every natural substance has a structure which is a causal component of anything predicable of it. In order for anything to act some external stimulus is required. But the manner in which a natural substance reacts to such a stimulus is necessarily determined by its intrinsic structure (*SVF* ii 979).

Cicero (*De fato*) shows how Chrysippus applied this causal theory to the explanation of human actions.[1] The problem is to maintain some human autonomy within the causal nexus, and Chrysippus sought to achieve this by arguing that in every action we have to distinguish between the external stimulus and the mind's response. He seems to claim that external causes are responsible for the 'impressions' which present the mind with a possible course of action. But it is up to the man himself how he responds to the impression. The external causes are an expression of the working of destiny, but they are not sufficient to necessitate our actions:

> Although an act of assent cannot take place unless it has been prompted by a sense-impression, yet . . . assent has this as its proximate not principal cause. . . . Just as someone who pushes a drum forward gives it a beginning of movement, but not the capacity to roll, so the visual object which presents itself . . . will mark its image on the mind; but assent will be in our power and . . . once it has been given an external stimulus it will move itself for the rest by its own force and nature (*De fato* 42–3).

This argument leaves a great deal that is obscure. It does not, for instance, elucidate what is meant by 'in our power', and clearly not all 'impressions' which prompt action have external causes. But other evidence makes it plain that 'in our power' means not referable to anything outside ourselves (*SVF* ii 1000). This leaves it open to ask whether a man at the moment when he assented to something was in fact free to act otherwise. The Stoic answer is no. The drum's capacity to roll belongs to the drum and nothing else, but it is a *necessary* constituent of the drum's structure. In the case of man his own nature determines the response to external stimuli. Nature here is a complex notion. It refers both to factors which are common to all men, for instance the faculty of assent, and also the character of the individual. All men respond to stimuli by giving or withholding assent, but the assent which any particular man gives or withholds is determined by the kind of man he is.

In explaining a deliberate act as the combination of an impression and an internal response Chrysippus is in line with the general position of Aristotle (*De an.* iii 10–11). Like Aristotle the Stoics did not look for a criterion of voluntary action in 'being free to act otherwise *now*'

[1] For a more detailed treatment of this subject see my discussion in ch. 8 of *Problems in Stoicism*, 'Freedom and Determinism in the Stoic Theory of Human Action'.

(*SVF* ii 984). Their test of human power is not freedom to act otherwise but acting deliberately. In spite of the distinction between internal
and external causes, the character of the individual falls under the
general causal law. For character is a consequence of heredity and
environment. The capacities with which a man is born are 'the gift
of destiny' (that is, cosmic Nature) which fashions each individual
thing (*SVF* ii 991). Once a man is born he comes into contact with
the environment, and the character which he acquires is shaped by the
interaction between his innate capacities and external events.[1] In the
last resort both of these are determined by one and the same thing
since *logos* is all-pervasive. But that is only one perspective. From the
subjective point of view the *logos* which determines the structure of
each individual man is *his logos*. We might express this by saying that
the universal causal principle takes on particular identity within each
individual man. And since the individual's *logos* is his real self, the
distinction between external and internal is a meaningful one. To say
that a man's character is determined by *logos* is equivalent to saying
that it is self-determined. Spinoza's concept of freedom may be compared with the Stoics': 'That thing is said to be Free which exists by
the mere necessity of its own nature and is determined in its actions
by itself alone' (*Ethics*, part I, def. vii).

The Stoic philosophy of nature is an attempt to provide a rational
explanation for all things in terms of the intelligent activity of a single
entity which is coextensive with the universe. The history of the
universe is the history of one thing, which can be signified by many
different names. Uncreated and imperishable Nature, God, *pneuma*
or universal *logos*, exercises its activity in a series of eternally recurrent
world-cycles. Beginning and ending as pure fire each world-cycle
fulfils the goals of its active principle. Within each cycle Nature
disposes itself in different forms, animal, vegetable and mineral. To
one class of animals, men, Nature gives a share of its own essence,
reason, in an imperfect but perfectible form. Because Nature as a whole
is a perfect, rational being, all of its acts are ones which should commend themselves to other rational beings.

But, if 'the world is designed for the benefit of rational beings' is
there nothing bad within it? The problem of evil tested Stoic ingenuity

---

[1] This comes out very clearly in *SVF* ii 1000. The Stoics laid great stress upon
environment in explaining character development, and they traced the causes
of moral corruption to the 'persuasiveness of external affairs' and 'communication
with [bad] acquaintances' (D.L. vii 89, cf. *SVF* iii 229–36).

to the uttermost.[1] Chrysippus in particular offered a number of different explanations which are recorded and criticized by Plutarch.[2] On the one hand he argued that nothing is strictly bad except moral weakness, and the explanation of moral weakness raises its own problems, as we shall see (p. 181). But this confinement of evil to moral weakness provided no answer to questions about diseases, droughts, earthquakes and the like, none of which could be attributed to human depravity. Chrysippus did not deny that such things may legitimately be called bad in some sense, nor did he argue that they are caused by something other than Nature. But he claimed that they do not undermine Nature's providence:

> The evil which occurs in terrible disasters has a rationale (*logos*) peculiar to itself; for in a sense it too occurs in accordance with universal reason, and so to speak, is not without usefulness in relation to the whole. For without it there could be no good (Plut. quoting Chrysippus, *Comm. not.* 1065b).

Chrysippus, it should in fairness be said, was well aware of the difficulty of explaining away cosmic evil. The argument quoted above seems to be the best which he can put forward. From this it will follow that diseases and natural disasters are not *per se* the object of Nature's plan but an unavoidable consequence of the good things which are. An example of this which Chrysippus used is the fragility of the human head (*SVF* ii 1170). In order to fulfil its function the head is said to be fashioned out of very delicate and small bones. It is not a good thing for the head to be fragile, but better fragility and a good head than a bad but solid one. The illustration is well-chosen because it exemplifies the fact that Nature plays a double rôle in any causal explanation. To say of something that it is natural in Stoicism is to combine description with evaluation. Nature embraces both the way things are and the way they should be. It is important to remember that Nature is conceived as a 'craftsman' (artistic fire). To understand the work of a craftsman we need to know both what he is doing (e.g. planing a flat surface) and why he is doing it (e.g. to make a table). The craftsman works purposefully. Likewise Nature's works—which are matters of fact—are designed for a purpose, and because Nature has right reason its purposes are necessarily good. The Stoics regarded Nature's providence as something which it would be contradictory

[1] I have discussed the Stoic concept of evil in *Philosophical Quarterly* 18 (1968) 329–43.
[2] See especially *De Stoicorum repugnantiis* 32–7.

to deny: it is as natural as heat to fire or sweetness to honey (*SVF* ii 1118).

If Nature's providence is all-embracing then any event which causes injury or suffering has to be interpreted as something which, if all the facts were known, would be recognized as beneficial by rational men. As Pope, following Shaftesbury, wrote: 'All discord, harmony not understood, all partial evil, universal good.'[1] But all the facts cannot be known and therefore the supposed value of much that happens must be taken on trust. This optimistic attitude towards natural events, no matter how terrible they may seem, is one of the least palatable features of Stoicism. It is one thing to say that human vision is limited, unable to grasp the full cosmic perspective. But even at its noblest, in the writings of Epictetus or Marcus Aurelius, there is something chilling and insensitive about the Stoic's faith that all will turn out well in the end. They were the only Greek philosophers who tried to find a rationale for everything within their concept of a perfect, all-embracing Nature.

(*vi*) *The soul and human nature*

What is it about a man that distinguishes him from other physical objects? The traditional answer which philosophy has given is that a man has a mind. But what is the mind? To this question a bewildering variety of answers have been offered ranging from thoroughgoing mentalism on the one hand, which reduces body to mind, to thoroughgoing materialism, which reduces mind to body. Between these two extremes a large number of intermediate positions are to be found. Plato and Descartes regarded body and mind as two quite different kinds of thing, a theory which at once raises the problem of how one of them can act upon or be acted upon by the other. In his influential book *The Concept of Mind*, Gilbert Ryle set out to explode the 'Cartesian myth' by arguing that there is no internal substance which we are naming when we talk about the mind. To talk about the mind for Ryle is to describe a person's publicly observable dispositions to behave in various ways. More recently, attempts have been made to show that there are no good reasons for denying that mental processes are purely physical processes in the central nervous system.[2]

---

[1] Basil Willey has discussed the idea of Nature as a harmonious order proclaiming divine handiwork in *The English Moralists* (London 1964).

[2] A notable example is D. M. Armstrong's *A Materialist Theory of Mind* (London 1968).

These are just two notable examples of a continuing debate which, whatever its final outcome, is unlikely to produce much comfort for Platonists and Cartesians. The Stoics' theory of mind takes on a new interest in the contemporary philosophical climate.

Both behaviourist and materialist accounts of mind have affinities with Stoic ideas, but neither of these terms is an adequate description of their theory. In Stoic natural philosophy, as we have seen, mind and matter are two constituents or attributes of one thing, body, and this analysis applies to human beings as it does to everything else. A man is a unified substance, but that of which he consists is not uniform. A broad distinction can be drawn between his physical frame—flesh, blood, sinews—and his capacities to sense, to talk etc. In the last analysis all the attributes of a man are due to the interpenetration of matter by *pneuma*. But the Stoics applied their distinction between matter and *pneuma* to the traditional distinction between body and soul. The soul of man is a portion of the vital, intelligent, warm breath which permeates the entire cosmos (D.L. vii 156). That which it pervades, in the case of a man, is his body where body answers to matter.[1]

We should remind ourselves that *pneuma*, though it is the cause of all qualitative differentiations, does not endow everything with life. Life only arises for individual things if their *pneuma* has 'tension' of a certain kind, and the kind of life depends on the degree of tension. In those things which are alive *pneuma* disposes itself differently according as they are plants, animals or men; and only the two latter sets of living things have soul (*SVF* ii 714–16).

The Stoics spoke of parts, qualities or faculties of the soul. There are eight of these—the five senses, the faculties of reproduction and speech, and something called the 'governing-principle' (*hêgemonikon*) (*SVF* ii 827). This word is an adjective in grammatical form, used freely before the Stoics to mean 'capable of commanding'; but they were the first philosophers to form a noun from it which designates some component of the soul. As its name implies, the governing-principle is 'the most authoritative part of the soul' (D.L. vii 159), and it is situated, like the centralized sense faculty of Aristotle's *Parva naturalia*, in the heart. From the heart it dispatches the other parts of the soul as 'currents of warm breath' (*pneumata*) throughout the body,

---

[1] Most Stoics supposed that the soul, which is separated from the body at death, survives for a limited time. Cf. R. Hoven, *Stoïcisme et Stoïciens face au problème de l'au-delà* (Paris 1971).

governing them and through them the body itself. In one simile, Chrysippus portrays the governing-principle as a spider, with the threads of its web corresponding to the other parts of the soul (*SVF* ii 879). Just as a spider is sensitive to any disturbance of the web which it controls by its feet, so the governing-principle receives messages concerning the external world and internal bodily states by means of the air-currents which it administers.

The governing-principle is the seat of consciousness and to it belong all the functions which we would associate with the brain. One of these functions is what the Stoics called 'impulse', 'a movement of soul towards or away from something' (*SVF* iii 377). Impulse is a movement which the soul may initiate on receipt of some impression (*phantasia*). Together, impression and impulse provide a causal explanation of goal-directed animal movements.

But this is somewhat over-simplified. Granted that all animals exhibit goal-directed behaviour, why is it that they pursue some things and avoid others? The Stoics' answer to this question is most interesting. They argued that every animal is genetically determined to show just those preferences and aversions which are appropriate to its natural constitution (*SVF* iii 178–88). All creatures are so constituted by Nature that they are 'well-disposed towards themselves'. The word translated 'well-disposed' (*oikeios*) is commonly used in Greek to mean 'related/akin/belonging to'; but the Stoics are expressing a technical concept which can fairly be regarded as original, though Zeno, if Antiochus is to be believed, was influenced by the Academic Polemo (Cic. *Fin.* iv 45).[1] *Oikeiôsis* determines an animal's relationship to its environment, but that to which it is primarily well-disposed is itself (D.L. vii 85). Its self-awareness is an affective relationship, and all behaviour can be interpreted as an extension or manifestation of the same principle. Thus the direction of an animal's impulses is determined both by what it senses and by its innate capacity to recognize things which belong to itself. If we observe a dog making for a bone it is reasonable to infer that the dog has seen the bone and has an impulse to gnaw it. But the reason why it has impulses of this kind can be traced to a predisposition to recognize what belongs to itself as a dog.

A further factor is involved in the dog's behaviour. It has the sense-impression of a bone, but the source of this impression might have been a stone which looks like a bone. Suppose that the dog goes up to

[1] For a detailed discussion cf. S. G. Pembroke, *Problems in Stoicism*, ch. 6.

the stone and then turns away. This apparent change of intention is to be explained by a further faculty of the governing-principle, 'assent'. Our senses are reporting innumerable messages at any moment; we only attend to a fraction of these, namely those 'we assent to'. To assent to a sense-impression is to take note of a message and to identify its source. Hence assent is a necessary condition of impulse (*SVF* iii 171). We are not impelled or repelled by things which we fail to recognize as sources of advantage or harm. In going up to the bone-like stone the dog took what he saw to be a bone; he assented to the impression and experienced an impulse because of his predisposition to gnaw bones. A closer look was followed by a different response; the dog no longer assented to the stone's being a bone and his behaviour changed its pattern accordingly.

The faculties which have been described so far are common to animals and men alike (*SVF* ii 979, 991). The possession of a governing principle entails the capacity to select from the environment those things which are necessary for a creature's self-preservation. It does not necessarily entail the possession of reason.[1] Rationality is only characteristic of the governing-principle in mature men. The infant is 'not yet rational' (Sen. *Ep.* 124, 9) for *logos* takes seven (or fourteen) years to develop. Impulse, the primary determinant of animal behaviour, is also the faculty which governs human beings in their earliest years, so that their first thought is self-preservation. But gradually, as a child develops, its governing-principle is modified fundamentally by the accretion of reason, *logos*. In the words of Chrysippus, 'reason supervenes as the craftsman of impulse' (D.L. vii 86). The language is chosen deliberately to remind us that the universal causal principle is at work.

Reason, the late developer, is a faculty which shapes but does not destroy those faculties that precede its emergence. In the Stoic view of human development, innate impulses are so transformed by the flowering of reason that they cease to exist as an independent faculty. They are taken over by reason. Human nature is so constituted that it develops from something non-rational and animal-like into a structure which is governed throughout by reason. This conception is of the greatest importance in Stoic ethics. The development of rationality brings with itself a change in the direction of impulse. New objects of desire take precedence over the satisfaction of basic bodily needs.

[1] For the governing-principle of animals in general cf. Cic. *N.D.* ii 29; Sen. *Ep.* 121, 10.

Virtue is found to be something which 'belongs to a man' in a more fundamental sense than food, drink, shelter and so forth (Cic. *Fin.* iii 20ff.). But the processes at work are still the same, in the sense that man and beast alike act naturally when they seek out the things which 'belong' to them.

I leave over to our next section a full discussion of this 'natural' development towards a moral life. For it introduces a normative dimension which cannot be adequately grasped until we have completed the description of mental faculties. But facts and values cannot in the final analysis be kept apart from one another in Stoicism. This point emerges very sharply from a passage of Epictetus which is relevant to our immediate discussion:

> You will find many things in man alone, of which the rational animal had particular need, but also many things common to ourselves and non-rational creatures. Do they understand the relationship between events? Certainly not. Need and understanding are two quite different things. God had need of the animals to make use of impressions, and of us to understand the use of them. Therefore it is sufficient for them to eat, drink, to rest and procreate ... but for us, to whom God has given the faculty of understanding, these things are no longer sufficient. Unless we act correctly and in an orderly way and each in accordance with his own nature and constitution we shall no longer attain our own goals. For the acts and goals of creatures vary with their different constitutions. . . . God has introduced man to be an observer of himself and his works, and not merely an observer but an interpreter too. Therefore it is shameful for man to begin and cease where the animals do; he should rather begin where they do and end at the point where Nature has ended with respect to us (i 6, 12–20).

The observations about human nature in this passage are largely non-empirical. What it means to be morally aware, to experience hope, joy, awe, regret, to recognize that the world is multi-dimensional, these are not facets of human nature which can be established in any ordinary scientific sense.[1] But they form so much a part of what it is to be a man that any comprehensive theory of human nature which failed to accommodate them would be worthless. The Stoics were sensitive to this point. Their concept of human nature is both descriptive and prescriptive. On the one hand it includes a number of mental faculties which account for human behaviour in a factual sense. But

---

[1] A suggestive book which develops this point is *A Rumour of Angels* (Harmondsworth 1969) by Peter L. Berger.

it also stipulates a mode of conduct which is the use of faculties for the purpose designed by universal Nature.

(vii) Human rationality and the passions

The attainment of rationality is conceived as something which alters the whole structure of a man's governing-principle. Human behaviour in orthodox Stoicism cannot be analysed in terms of three independent psychic components as the Platonic model lays down. According to Chrysippus, 'there is no such thing as the appetitive and the spirited elements, for the whole of the human governing-principle is rational' (*SVF* iii p. 115). At first glance this looks an odd and highly unplausible statement, and so it has been interpreted by ancients and moderns alike.[1] Posidonius rejected Chrysippus' theory, largely on the ground that it failed to take account of 'irrational' elements in human experience.[2] Plato had provided for this, so it seemed, by treating appetite as a component of the soul which is distinct from reason though capable of submitting to and rebelling against it. Many scholars have chided Chrysippus for his excessive intellectualism.[3] There is some point to these criticisms, but they have been made too hastily. Chrysippus was a philosopher of the first rank, and before one dismisses any of his theories as senseless it is essential to take them seriously.

Much of the difficulty has arisen because the word 'rational' (or in Greek, *logikos*) is an imprecise and often an emotive term. The main charge against Chrysippus is that he flouts common sense by denying a distinction between, say, desiring or fearing and calculating or deliberating. But is this so? The answer depends on what is meant by rational, and it is pretty clear what Chrysippus means. The rationality of the governing-principle can be analysed as follows: all human acts—perception, procreation, speech, desire—are causally affected by the fact that man is a creature who sees relationships between things and has the means of expressing these in articulate thought.[4] Now let us consider how this affects Chrysippus' treatment of desire or impulse.

[1] Galen, drawing upon Posidonius, criticizes Chrysippus at length, *De placitis Hippocratis et Platonis* Books iv–v.
[2] *Posidonius* vol. i ed. Edelstein and Kidd, frs. 31–5.
[3] For a more sympathetic treatment cf. Josiah B. Gould, *The Philosophy of Chrysippus*, pp. 181–96, and J. M. Rist, *Stoic Philosophy*, pp. 22–36.
[4] See for instance the passages cited on p. 125.

Apart from being 'a movement of soul towards or away from some-thing' impulse can be described as 'an act of assent' and as 'the reason of man commanding him to act' (*SVF* iii 171, 175). The first descrip-tion is a physical account of something which presents itself to con-sciousness as a command. For elucidating the two further descriptions an example will help. Any act of perception involves assent, taking what I see to be, say, an orange. But suppose that I not only see an orange but also seize it and begin eating it. Chrysippus' explanation of the second fact is that in assenting to my seeing an orange I also issue myself with an imperative to eat it. Why do I do this? Because I am a man who likes eating oranges. My act of assent to what I see is not in this case a mere act of perception (though it perfectly well could be); it also contains an appetitive element. The orange strikes me as 'something good for me', and this 'striking me as something good for me' means that I desire it. My impulse is an act of the govern-ing-principle, and it is rational in the sense that it is an imperative implicit in a judgment *of the kind that moves to action*. That does not make my impulse only a bogus desire. To describe it as Chrysippus does is to analyse the notion of a desire. What will distinguish mere intellectual assent to the proposition 'X is good for me' from the proposition 'I desire X' is a movement of soul which follows in the latter case only.[1]

Chrysippus' doctrine of the passions follows similar lines.[2] A passion is defined as 'impulse' plus something else. Impulses become passions if they are 'excessive' (*SVF* iii 479), and their excess manifests itself in the movement of the heart (*SVF* ii 899). The 'excess' of a passion is comparable to the sense in which a man running 'exceeds' a man walking. Chrysippus also said that passions are false 'judg-ments' which have as their predicate very good or very bad (*SVF* iii 466, 480). Fear is 'judgment of an impending evil which seems to be intolerable'. In so far as passions involve value judgments they do not differ from impulses. The difference between them is analysed in terms of 'reason'. Passions, as distinct from mere impulses, are 'not-rational'.

[1] Impulse, unlike judgments in a wider sense, can only be prompted by some-thing which has absolute or relative value, *SVF* iii 118–21. Although all im-pulses are acts of assent, there is no reason to suppose the Stoics thought all acts of assent are impulses.
[2] This paragraph does not take account of the so-called 'good emotional states'—joy, well-wishing, and discretion—which are concomitants of a per-fectly rational governing-principle, *SVF* iii 431–42.

But here we seem to get a contradiction. If the human governing-principle admits of only rational dispositions how can passions as so described be possible? This difficulty is ostensibly resolved by distinguishing between 'right' reason and 'wrong' reason (*SVF* i 202). Anything which a man does is rational in some sense; this is an analytic truth since man is a 'rational animal'. But in another sense, the sage or good man is the criterion of rationality since he alone has 'right reason' (*SVF* iii 560). The soul admits of different degrees of tension, and any man whose *logos* is not consistently at the right degree of tension falls short of perfect rationality (*SVF* iii 473). To that extent his disposition is not-rational. He has an unsound *logos*. 'Passion is not other than *logos* nor is there dissension between two things, but a turning of the one *logos* to both aspects; this escapes notice because of the suddenness and swiftness of the change' (*SVF* iii 459). Here we have the Stoic explanation of the conflict between reason and passion. The difference from Plato is primarily a temporal one. As the Stoics would have it, a man is not simultaneously subject to the influence of two different forces. Rather, if he is not a sage whose life is on a consistently even keel, he is liable to sudden changes and fluctuations of his governing-principle. At one moment he may assent to the true Stoic proposition that pain is not a bad thing; but if this judgment is insecurely based it will not be strong enough to reject a contrary judgment, that pain is something very bad, which comes to mind and is accompanied by a bodily reaction as the dentist starts drilling his tooth. The Stoics distinguished good men from others by reference to the consistency of their *logos*. At worst a man might have a governing-principle which is never rational in the correct sense. But this is probably a very exceptional case. Most of us, Chrysippus would have said, are ruled by reason in a quasi-right sense part of the time; but we are also ruled by reason in its wrong sense part of the time and this absence of consistency with right reason marks us out as 'foolish' or bad men. We fluctuate between these two conditions and our desires may clash as one condition is followed by the other. Our moral progress is typified not by the extirpation of all emotion and desire, but by the occurrence of desires and feelings which are dispositions of a governing-principle increasingly consistent with right reason. The Stoics laid great emphasis upon the need to resist morbid emotions (see p. 206).

If the concept of 'right reason' strikes the reader as opaque, not to say arbitrary, it may be helpful, and would certainly be equally Stoic, to think in terms of mental health (*SVF* iii 278). This is a concept often in use today and most of us probably have some implicit criterion of normality with which we judge the behaviour of others. There is in our society a marked and probably increasing tendency to treat as personality defects dispositions which our grandparents would have termed morally reprehensible. A generation brought up on Freud and conscious of the damage which neglect can cause to a child's development is less confident in its ability to act as moral censor. Health and sickness are terms which have no necessary moral connotations. The Stoics, though they divided mankind into the two categories of wise and foolish, preferred this terminology to 'good' and 'bad'. Misunderstanding or ignorance not innate wickedness or sin is the characteristic of the foolish man, and the Stoics, as I have already mentioned, appealed to factors in the environment to explain the 'perversion' of reason. Equally, education and application can set a man on the road to virtue. No one is born a wise man, and there is no congenital elect. But human nature is such that a man can attain true well-being if he recognizes the full implications of his own rationality. Hints of these have already been given in our earlier pages, and they will be developed in the next section.

Clearly the Stoics' analysis of human nature may be faulted on several grounds. Their account of desire and passion, even if interpreted along the lines suggested, remains insensitive to aspects of human behaviour which cannot in any ordinary sense be reduced to rationality. One may also complain about the failure to describe mental faculties in language which is value-free. The second charge would also apply to Plato and, to a lesser extent, Aristotle. If we make it, we should recognize that we lack today anything which might be called a comprehensive theory of human nature. This may be a good thing, for theories of human nature have too often been used for purposes inimical to human welfare. But it is important to be aware of the fact that the special sciences of psychology, anthropology, sociology, biochemistry, along with philosophy and religion, are all attempting to say something about different aspects of the same thing, man. The Stoics, like other Greek philosophers, were able to be bolder than we dare to be. They did not suffer from the disadvantages of an ever-growing fragmentation of knowledge. In an exact scientific sense they knew extraordinarily little. But they certainly put what they knew to purposes which are still instructive.

V. STOIC ETHICS

The virtue of the happy man and a well-running life consist in this: that all actions are based on the principle of harmony between his own spirit and the will of the director of the universe (D.L. vii 88).

In one of the analogies which the Stoics used in order to illustrate the relationship between the sub-divisions of their philosophy ethics is compared to the 'fruit of a garden' (*SVF* ii 38). It is an apposite image. Logic and natural philosophy prepare the ground for ethics, and the reader will have noticed that moral doctrines have frequently been referred to in the treatment of the first two subjects. Nature, which the 'physicist' and the dialectician investigate from specific points of view, is also in Stoicism the ultimate source of everything which has value. So Chrysippus wrote: 'There is no possible or more suitable way to approach the subject of good and bad things, the virtues and happiness than from universal Nature and the management of the universe' (Plut. *Stoic. rep.* 1035c). Nature (God, *pneuma*, cause, *logos* or destiny) is a perfect being, and the value of anything else in the world depends upon its relationship to Nature. Accordance with Nature denotes positive value and contrariness to Nature the opposite.

(*i*) *The part and the whole*
But what is it for something to accord or fail to accord with Nature? This is clearly a fundamental question, and the analysis of it requires our making a number of distinctions. First of all, we need to specify what it is that we are talking about. If our subject is a plant then we know what it means to say that a plant flourishes. Similarly, it is relatively easy to distinguish among, say, a group of cats those whose condition is excellent and those whose condition is not. A plant or a cat accords with the nature of plants or cats when it grows and behaves in a certain way. That way defines what it is for something to be good of its kind, and by reference to this 'natural' norm things can be classified as appropriate or inappropriate for plants, animals and men. On this method of analysis, accordance with universal Nature is referred to the nature which is appropriate to the type of thing in question.[1] The concept of universal Nature is necessarily a complex one which has a diversity of references. Eating hay is natural to horses but not to men. It accords with universal Nature that horses should eat hay and that men should speak a language. But the former

[1] cf. the procedure in Cic. *N.D.* ii 120ff., Sen. *Ep.* 124, 7–24.

is inappropriate to men and the latter to horses. Universal Nature sanctions a norm for particular things—the nature of plants, animals and men—by reference to which they can be said to attain or not to attain their individual ends.

We may call this method of analysis the perspective of the part. But universal Nature accommodates all particular natures, and these can secondly be described and evaluated from the perspective of the whole.[1] It is an obvious fact that many creatures do not experience things which are appropriate to their particular nature. Disease, drought and famine create conditions which make it impossible for many individual living things to function successfully. Are such occurrences contrary to Nature? We have already noticed the Stoics' answer to this question. From the long-term point of view nothing of this kind is independent of Nature's ordering. If an event is considered independently of its relation to the cosmos as a whole it can be evaluated as natural or unnatural (or neither natural nor unnatural) to the creature affected by it. From the perspective of the part, poverty and ill-health are unnatural to mankind. But such an analysis is only made possible by abstracting human nature from universal Nature. From the perspective of the whole even such conditions are not unnatural, because all Natural events contribute to the universal well-being.

These two perspectives are brought together in many Stoic texts. 'Many external things can prevent individual natures from perfecting themselves, but nothing can stand in the way of universal Nature because it holds together and maintains all natures' (Cic. *N.D.* ii 35). The universe as a whole is perfect, but its perfection is compatible with and even requires a certain proportion of things which are unnatural if the perspective of the part alone is considered. Marcus Aurelius writes: 'Welcome everything which happens, even if it seems harsh, because it contributes to the health of the universe and the well-faring and well-being of Zeus. For he would not have brought this on a man unless it had been advantageous to the whole' (v 8). From the perspective of the whole nothing which befalls a man is disadvantageous either to himself or to the whole. Certain things can be called disadvantageous which are contrary to Nature from the perspective of the part. If Nature could have arranged a perfect world without such things this would have been done. Nature does not

[1] It is characteristic of Marcus Aurelius to analyse particular things from this perspective, viii 46, v 8 etc.

ordain suffering for its own sake, but it is necessary to the economy of the whole.

From what has been said so far it follows that 'unnatural' is an evaluation and description of events which can only be applied when Nature is referred purely to the faring of particular things. The Stoics seem to be committed to the claim that from the cosmic perspective everything which happens accords with Nature and is therefore right. But then nothing can be wrong (Marcus, ii 17). Yet the Stoics insisted most strenuously that the term 'bad' has a valid usage; that there is something which must on any analysis be judged contrary to Nature. Their attempt to resolve this apparent contradiction involves yet a further conceptual distinction, but before we study this some lines from Cleanthes' *Hymn to Zeus* will help to focus attention upon the dilemma.

> Nothing occurs on the earth apart from you, o God,
> nor in the heavenly regions nor on the sea,
> except what bad men do in their folly;
> but you know how to make the odd even,
> and to harmonize what is dissonant; to you the alien is akin.
> And so you have wrought together into one all things that are good and
>   bad,
> So that there arises one eternal *logos* of all things,
> Which all bad mortals shun and ignore,
> Unhappy wretches, ever seeking the possession of good things
> They neither see nor hear the universal law of God,
> By obeying which they might enjoy a happy life (lines 11–21, *SVF* i 537).

This point of view persists from the earliest to the latest Stoicism. Epictetus, writing almost four hundred years after Cleanthes, re-phrases it:

> Zeus has ordained that there be summer and winter, plenty and poverty, virtue and vice and all such opposites for the sake of the harmony of the whole (i 12, 16).

Much can be written about the pre-Stoic background of these sentiments, but I cannot pursue that interesting subject here.[1] According to Cleanthes, everything does accord with Zeus (or Nature) with one

---

[1] See especially Heraclitus fr. 67 'God is day night, winter summer, war peace . . .'; fr. 102, 'To God all things are fair and right, but men have judged some things to be right and others wrong.' Hugh Lloyd-Jones, *The Justice of Zeus* (Berkeley, Los Angeles, London 1971) should be consulted for the early literary background.

exception. 'What bad men do in their folly' is contrary to the will of
Zeus. But in the very next sentence Cleanthes qualifies this assertion.
Out of disharmony Zeus creates harmony. So it seems that everything
after all, including the actions of bad men, ultimately accords with
Zeus (or Nature).

It is difficult to resist the conclusion that the Stoics' desire to
attribute everything to a single principle has produced a fundamental
incoherence at this point. But to this they would reply that the harmony
of the universe as a whole is something which transcends any attempt
to view the world from the perspective of a particular part. If we view
Nature's activities as contradictory this is due to the limitations of
human vision. Moreover, Nature does not will the actions of bad men.
The harmonizing of dissonance, not the creation of dissonance, is
Nature's work.

What does this last assertion mean? Chrysippus argued that virtue
cannot exist without vice (*SVF* ii 1169f.), and one may comment
that it is hard to see what use there could be for one of these terms
unless the other is also applicable to something else. He also said that
it is more fitting to live with the possession of a corrupt reason than
not to live at all (*SVF* iii 760). These statements are essential to the
understanding of Stoic ethics. Unlike all other natural beings, man
alone is endowed by Nature with the capacity to understand cosmic
events and to promote the rationality of Nature by his own efforts.
But equally, he is the only natural being who has the capacity to act
in a manner which fails to accord with the will of Nature. These
antithetical capacities are what make man a *moral* agent, that is, someone of whose conduct and character 'good' or 'bad' can be said.[1] By
endowing man with reason (*logos*) Nature has ensured that every man
will be and do either good or bad. But Nature's own dispensation is
not morally neutral. Man is naturally equipped with 'impulses to
virtue' or 'seeds of knowledge', and this equipment is sufficient to
direct human reason in the right direction (*SVF* i 566; Sen. *Ep.* 120,
4). But Nature itself does not go further than this.[2] The achievement
of a good character calls for the most arduous efforts from any man
and, as we have seen, external influences can (and generally do)
prevent him from developing a rational disposition perfectly harmonious with Nature itself.

[1] For the thesis that *good* can only be realized in that which is rational, cf. Sen.
Ep. 124, 13ff.
[2] Cic. *Leg.* i 27; Sen. *Ep.* 49, 11.

In order that virtue shall be attainable the potentiality for vice must also be granted. Nature has established these conditions and given man the status of a moral agent by making him a conscious participant in the rational processes of the universe. The effect of this is to set before the majority of men a task which they are too 'foolish' to fulfil just in the manner which Nature would have them adopt. But their 'badness' is not inimical to the ultimate purposes of the cosmos if these purposes are to include the offer of a life chosen deliberately to harmonize with Nature. As the Stoics look at the world it is better to be vicious and to have the opportunity of virtue than to be denied the latter possibility.

In giving man reason Nature makes him, from the perspective of the part, an autonomous agent (see p. 168). The character which a man develops, though it falls under the law of cause and effect, is his own character, not Nature's. For the environment in which a man finds himself he is not responsible. But the way in which a man acts in relation to his environment is attributed to him. The Stoics stressed the importance of aiming at rather than achieving a desirable result.[1] Moral judgments and human well-being are related to the agent's inner attitude, his state of mind. This distinction between external results and intentions was illustrated by the simile of a dog tied to a cart. The cart represents a man's external situation. He cannot act independently of this, but, so it is argued, the man himself and not his environment can determine whether he will run willingly or be dragged along. 'Guide me, O Zeus, and thou Destiny, whither I have been appointed by you. For I will follow freely; and if, grown bad, I prove unwilling, I shall follow no less' (Cleanthes, *SVF* i 527).[2]

But here of course we touch upon another crucial difficulty. Many of the things which befall a man during the course of his life cannot be isolated from his own intentions. The Stoics often write as if all external circumstances are beyond the individual's power to alter. But if the notion of an appointed life is to be compatible with moral judgment, then it only makes sense to regard a very limited set of circumstances as the dispensation of God or Nature. It would certainly be un-Stoic to regard an habitual criminal as a good man. The acts of a criminal cannot be explained as tasks appointed to him with which he should comply willingly, since they will occur in any case.

---

[1] See further, p. 198.
[2] I have discussed this passage and its moral implications in *Problems in Stoicism*, ch. 8 pp. 192f.

In advocating acceptance of the external situation the Stoics did not intend to prescribe passivity, nor did they regard the results of a good man's actions as equivalent in value to those of a bad man. But the possibility of inner freedom and the distinction between good and bad, which Nature as provident guarantees, cannot be squared easily with the factual necessities which Nature as destiny establishes. The Stoics tried to overcome this problem by stressing the importance of education. The initial potentialities of a man are supposed to be such that, with rigorous training, he can achieve a disposition to act in complete accord with the factual and moral order of things. But success or failure seems to depend on Nature and external circumstances rather than anything for which the individual can reasonably be praised or blamed.

Having now sketched some of the characteristics and problems of Stoic ethics I turn to details, following Stoic methodology as far as possible. It will not be possible to discuss their historical background here (see p. 111), but readers familiar with Socratic, Platonic and Aristotelian ethics will notice many points of contact with Stoicism.

(ii) *From primary impulse to virtue*

Diogenes Laertius tells us that from Chrysippus onwards the Stoics divided the 'ethical part of philosophy' into a number of sub-sections (vii 84). From the arrangement which he cites Diogenes exempts the names of Zeno and Cleanthes, though he observes that 'they did divide (i.e. classify) ethics, logic and physics'. The earliest Stoics differed from later ones in treating ethics 'less methodically'. We know too little about Zeno and Cleanthes to make a precise assessment of Chrysippus' own ethical innovations. It is not likely that he differed greatly from them over matters of substance. The refinement and systematization of Stoic moral philosophy was probably his primary object in this field. Most of the evidence from which I will draw over the next few pages is certainly or possibly derived from the teaching of Chrysippus. And it may reasonably be assumed that the majority of doctrines discussed here are those which a Stoic in the middle of the Hellenistic period would have espoused.

The division of ethics attributed to Chrysippus specifies three broad categories: first, 'on impulse'; second, 'on good and bad things'; third, 'on passions'.[1] The first category is sub-divided into 'virtue'

---

[1] This interpretation of the ethical categories is also adopted by Zeller, *Phil. der Griechen*, vol. iii 2 p. 206 n. 1.

and 'the goal of action'; the second has as its sections, 'primary value', 'moral action' and 'appropriate acts'. Finally, after 'on passions', Diogenes lists a topic 'suasions and dissuasions' which is probably to be regarded as an appendix giving prescriptions and proscriptions based upon the theory already laid down. Diogenes' own summary and to a lesser extent Book iii of Cicero's *De finibus* and Arius Didymus' compendium in Stobaeus, correspond fairly precisely to this arrangement of subject-matter. It is a reasonable assumption that the extant hand-books of Stoic ethics reflect the Stoics' own order of presenting the subject.

Of our summaries the most informative from a philosophical point of view is undoubtedly Cicero's. Who his source or sources were we do not know, but Cicero refers by name to all the leading early Stoics and to Chrysippus in particular. The most interesting formal characteristic of Cicero's book is its logical, or would-be logical, coherence. The quality of argument is uneven, but this and a number of obscurities may be due to Cicero rather than any Stoic writer. What is undeniable is the attempt to present a set of moral truths which are so related that the last is entirely consistent with the first. Throughout the book logical connectives abound—'from which it follows that', 'since . . . it is necessary that', 'if . . . it does not follow that', etc., and the work as a whole seems to be designed to exhibit through language the coherence which the Stoics claimed to be characteristic of Nature. The procedure, like some of the thought itself, reminds one of nothing so much as the *mos geometricus* of Spinoza. Spinoza is of course still more formal, but his practice of setting down one continuous chain of reasoning consisting of propositions, proofs and corollaries would have won the firm approval of Chrysippus. The resemblances are not accidental. Like Spinoza the Stoics sought to deduce ethical conclusions from premises describing the all-inclusive attributes of a Nature which is perfect.

The starting-point of Stoic ethics is the 'primary impulse' of a new-born creature. Diogenes Laertius' evidence on this deserves to be quoted in full:

The Stoics say that an animal has self-protection as the object of its primary impulse, since Nature from the beginning endears it to itself, as Chrysippus says in his first book *On goals*: 'The first thing which is dear to every animal is its own constitution and awareness of this; for it was not likely that Nature estranged the animal from itself, nor that, having made it, Nature gave it no attitude of estrangement or endearment. It follows then that having constituted the animal Nature endeared it to itself; thus it is that the animal rejects what is harmful and pursues what is suitable (or akin) to itself.'

The assertion that pleasure is the object of animals' primary impulse is proved to be false by the Stoics. For pleasure, they claim, if it really exists, is a secondary product when and only when Nature by itself has searched out and adopted the things which are suitable to the animals' constitution; as such pleasure is like the flourishing of animals and the bloom of plants. Nature made no absolute distinction between plants and animals, for Nature directs plants too, independently of impulse and sensation, and in us certain processes of a vegetative kind take place. But since animals have the additional faculty of impulse, through the use of which they go in search of what is suitable to them, it is according to Nature for animals to be directed by impulse. And since reason in accord with a more perfect prescription has been bestowed on rational beings, life according to reason rightly becomes in accordance with their nature; for reason supervenes as the craftsman of impulse (vii 85–6).[1]

Something has already been said in this book about the concepts of impulse and self-endearment which are made use of in this passage (p. 172). Arguments concerning them were set out with great detail in more technical Stoic treatises, as we can tell from the fragmentary remains of Hierocles' *Foundations of ethics* (see p. 116). The writer of this work was at pains to demonstrate that the first thing of which a creature is aware is not something in the external world but itself. Self-awareness, he argues, is the precondition of perceiving externals; but to be aware of oneself is at the same time to picture oneself in relation to something else.[2] The infant's self-awareness is manifested by its relation to the mother's breast. Its perception of the latter is thus an integral part of its perception of itself. And if we ask, 'What attitude does a creature have towards the image of itself?' the answer must be affection. For all creatures, up to the limit of their power, strive to preserve themselves and to avoid things which are harmful.

The last statement may be treated as an empirical observation, but in the quotation which Diogenes preserves from Chrysippus it is also described as the work of Nature. This means that an animal's primary impulse to preserve itself is not only an objective fact but also something ordained by the being which is perfect in all respects. The primary impulse, because it has Nature's sanction, provides the

[1] For a detailed logical analysis of this passage cf. my paper, 'The Logical Basis of Stoic Ethics', *Proceedings of the Aristotelian Society* 1970/1, 85–104. My translation is reprinted from this paper.

[2] See further S. G. Pembroke, *Problems in Stoicism*, ch. 6 pp. 118f.

logical starting-point for Stoic ethics. Their procedure is of the greatest interest and has every claim to be called original.

If human beings possessed no reasoning faculty, self-preservation along the lines initially sketched out by Chrysippus would be the only natural, and hence the right or appropriate thing, for them to pursue. Food-gathering, fending off enemies, procreation, these are activities which an irrational animal perceives as belonging to itself, and in engaging upon them it acts naturally—that is, in the manner designed by Nature. It preserves itself—that is to say, what it recognizes as constituting itself—by doing such things. But are not such activities also natural to human beings? The Stoic answer to this question is complex, and our best approach to it will be through an extended quotation from the *De finibus*:

> Let us proceed therefore, since we have left these starting-points of Nature behind, and what follows must be consistent with them. One consequence is this primary classification: the Stoics say that that has value which is either itself in accordance with Nature or such as to bring about that state of affairs; accordingly it is worthy of being selected because it possesses something of sufficient moment to be valued, whereas the opposite of this is not to be valued. We have then established as basic principles that those things which are in accordance with Nature are to be acquired for their own sake and their opposites are to be rejected. The first appropriate function of a creature is to maintain itself in its natural condition. The second, that it should seize hold of the things which accord with Nature and banish those which are the opposite. Once this procedure of selection and rejection has been discovered, the next consequence is selection exercised appropriately; then, such selection performed continuously; finally, selection which is absolutely consistent and in complete agreement with Nature. At this point for the first time that which can truly be called good begins to be present in a man and understood. For a man's first affiliation is towards those things which are in accordance with Nature. But as soon as he has acquired the capacity for understanding or rather, a stock of rational concepts, and has seen the regularity and harmony of conduct, he values this far higher than everything for which he had previously felt affection, and he draws the rational conclusion that this constitutes the highest human good which is worthy of praise and desirable for its own sake. In this harmony consists the good which is the standard of all things; and so virtuous action and virtue itself, which is reckoned the only good thing, though later in origin, is the only thing to be desired through its intrinsic nature and worth. And none of the primary objects of natural affiliation is desirable for its own sake (*Fin.* iii 20–1).

This passage encapsulates the fundamental doctrines of Stoic ethics. Knowledge of 'what can truly be called good' and virtuous action are treated as the culminating stage in the development of a rational being. From infancy onwards a pattern of behaviour is sanctioned by Nature as appropriate to man (and other living creatures), but the pattern changes as man matures from a creature whose responses are purely animal-like and instinctive into an adult fully endowed with reason. Each of the five stages traced by Cicero assigns a function to human beings which is appropriate to them at particular periods of their development. Human nature, as so defined, is an evolving phenomenon, a concept which gives distinctive character to Stoic ethics. Things which are appropriate at an early stage do not cease to be such later. But their relation to the function of a man changes as he changes. Each new stage adds something which modifies the immediately preceding function. The goal of the progression is life in accordance with mature human nature, that is, a life governed by rational principles which are in complete harmony with the rationality, goals and processes of universal Nature.

The stages sketched out here give a normative account of the development of human nature. The majority of men never fully attain to the final stage, and many of them do not reach even the fourth. If this were a purely descriptive statement of evolution from infancy to maturity foolish or bad men would not exist. They do exist because, as we have seen, the perfection of human nature is not determined independently of a man's own efforts, as are his primary instinctive impulses. But the ultimate goal or function of a man *is* the perfection of his nature.

'Function' is a word which has occurred several times in the last two pages, and it may seem odd to designate moral behaviour as a human function. The problem is Cicero's term *officium*, the Latin translation of a Greek Stoic term, *kathêkon*. About this concept more will need to be said shortly. I will just remark here that 'function' seems to me to be the least misleading translation of the term in our present context. *Officium* is an ambiguous word. Like its English derivative, 'office', *officium* is regularly used in Latin for the task, function, or duty of an official—a consul, a legionary commander, and so forth. A consul is bound or obliged by his office to fulfil certain duties, but one cannot speak of the duties of an infant, much less the duties of animals and plants to which the Stoics also ascribed *kathêkonta*. A mature man, according to the Stoics, does have duties and this is an appropriate interpretation of *officium* from stages three to five. But what makes them duties is the fact that they are functions of a rational being. Nothing in the moral sense obliges a non-rational creature to behave in a certain way. It is therefore best to translate *officium* by 'function' throughout, while remembering that it carries connotations which are determined by the nature of the creature whose functions are under consideration.

(iii) The good and the preferable (natural advantages)

So much by way of general discussion. Cicero's text also provides an excellent jumping-off point for the treatment of a number of fundamental details, and we may take these in the order of his text. He begins with a brief statement of what it is for something to have 'value', and this has proved a problematic concept in the interpretation of Stoicism, but some of the difficulties which have been found in it are more apparent than real.[1] As Cicero explains, the value of anything in Stoicism is defined by reference to Nature. By capitalizing this term I wish to signify Nature in its universal sense but, as has already been explained, Nature can and often must be analysed as the structure and behaviour appropriate to particular things—the nature of a plant, the nature of an animal and so forth. Anything which accords with the nature of a creature necessarily has positive value, and anything which is contrary to a creature's nature necessarily has negative value (I refrain from using the obviously simpler words 'good' and 'bad' for a reason which will be stated later). The *nature* of anything is simply that structure and pattern of behaviour which universal Nature has ordained as appropriate or in the interests of the creature concerned.

Although anything, and above all virtue, has value because it accords with Nature, orthodox Stoics from Zeno onwards used the expression, 'things according to nature', to designate a particular class of valuable objects, the opposites of which were called 'things contrary to nature' (*SVF* iii 140–6). The class of such objects was also divided in such a way that some of them are marked off as 'the primary things according to (contrary to) nature'. Let us take the latter first. The word 'primary' refers to chronological priority, and we have seen that every living creature is credited with a primary impulse to preserve itself. Those things which it is instinctively impelled to pursue and to avoid are according to or contrary to its nature in this primary sense, and they include food of a certain kind,

---

[1] I. G. Kidd gives an illuminating discussion, *Classical Quarterly*, new series v, 1955, 181–94 = *Problems in Stoicism*, ch. 7.

shelter, and parental affection. But human beings, as they develop, experience a natural affiliation towards a wider range of things than irrational animals. In a list of things according to and contrary to nature we find technical competence, health, beauty, wealth, high repute, nobility of birth and their opposites (*SVF* iii 127). This list could be considerably extended, but the examples show that it includes mental and physical attributes and external possessions all of which were popularly regarded in antiquity, like today, as 'good' things. It accords with the nature of man that he should regard these favourably and reject their opposites. Cicero's second stage, the acquisition of 'things according to nature' and the rejection of their opposites, describes this function as it would be appropriately exercised by a young child. We do not expect young children to discriminate care-fully between items towards which they are favourably disposed. It is through trying out and rejecting things that a child learns what it means to select in a discriminating way.

Before we consider Cicero's third stage it should be noted that the method of classifying things according to Nature does not comprise everything in the world. It is a matter of total indifference whether someone gesticulates this way or that (*SVF* iii 118). Human nature is not so constituted that a man has any built-in preference or aversion towards this and comparable things.

A young child is 'not yet rational', but the development of ration-ality is a continuous process which must be assumed to be well under way, though not perfected, at Cicero's third stage. Things which it was the function of a young child to pursue and to avoid instinctively, and other objects which are *naturally* attractive to more mature human beings, now present themselves as material for rational selection and rejection. The word 'rational' does not occur in Cicero's text at this point, but other evidence entitles us to supply it. As a human being acquires rationality this modification of his nature prescribes a new mode of appropriate behaviour. The function of a man is now to perform 'appropriate acts' (*kathêkonta*) the starting-point of which is not mere impulse or instinct but reason (*logos*). An appropriate act is defined as 'that which reason persuades one to do' (D.L. vii 108), or 'that which when done admits of reasonable justification' (ibid. 107). Inappropriate acts are defined in the opposite way.

Diogenes Laertius (loc. cit.) gives examples of 'appropriate acts': honouring parents, brothers, and native land, taking proper care of one's health, exercising by walking, sacrificing one's property. The last of these is only appropriate in certain circumstances, whereas the proper care of one's health is said to be 'unconditionally appropriate'. But the appropriateness of all these things rests on the fact that they accord with the nature of a rational being. That is to say, a man from the onset of rationality is supposed to recognize that the performance of such acts is 'becoming' to him. As rationality develops within a man the range of actions which it is 'appropriate' for him to perform becomes considerably enlarged. Cicero reports the Stoic view that 'we have been bound together and united by Nature for civic association' (*Fin.* iii 66). The social principles of Stoic ethics are derived from this impulse implanted by Nature to form familial and extra-familial relationships (*De off.* i 12). But the principle determining such behaviour is not regarded as different in kind from that which prompts more obviously self-regarding actions. The starting-point of justice is *oikeiôsis*, that attitude of attraction towards things which belong to oneself (*SVF* i 197), see p. 172. In its simplest and most basic analysis, moral development for the Stoics is the recognition that community life and virtue are pre-eminently things which belong to human nature.

Are we then to say that anyone who performs an 'appropriate' act does well? The answer to this question is negative. Following the dictates of reason is the appropriate function of a mature man, but reason, as we have seen, admits of the predicates 'right' or 'wrong', 'healthy' or 'unsound'. Any man who takes steps to maintain his physical well-being does something which is defensible on rational principles. But the mere fact that he does this tells us nothing about his moral qualities. He might be keeping fit for the purpose of robbing a bank. Or again, a man might behave patriotically solely because he is after a knighthood. These of course are extreme cases, and it is doubtful whether the Stoics would have regarded such acts as appropriate in any sense. But they help to show why the selection of something according to nature by a rational being is only a midway point in the acquisition of moral knowledge. It is certainly a necessary condition of virtuous action. The good man does everything in his power to promote the welfare of his country; he too is favourably disposed to 'the things according to nature'. But about him much more can be said than the fact that he is a rational being who selects such things and rejects their opposites.

The good man's selection is 'continuous'. He does not seek to promote his health and honour his parents, but ignore the interests of his country. All his behaviour is a continuous series of appropriate selections and rejections. What begins as something intermittent and erratic has become a disposition to act continuously on the basis of Nature's rational promptings. But continuity does not guarantee absolute consistency for the future. The good man is 'in complete agreement with Nature', a stage beyond 'continuity'. This means in Cicero's formulation that his scale of values changes or takes on a new dimension. The ever-growing consistency of his selection of natural advantages (performance of appropriate acts) brings a recognition that there is something of far greater worth than any of these objects, singly or collectively. Virtue is not defined by the consequences in the world which it succeeds in promoting, but by a pattern of behaviour that follows necessarily from a disposition perfectly in tune with Nature's rationality. The disposition to behave in such a way is not inconsistent with earlier human functions. Like all men the Stoic sage is predisposed to look after his health and his property. But he does not regard such natural advantages as things which are desirable for their own sake. He selects them if and only if his reason dictates that this is the right thing to do. The right thing to do is that which accords with virtue, and this is equivalent to saying that it accords with the nature of a perfect rational being. Only virtue has absolute or intrinsic worth. Natural advantages can be used well or badly and the same holds good for natural disadvantages (*SVF* iii 123). The sage will make good use of poverty, if it comes his way; and a foolish man may use wealth badly. This does not undermine the objective fact that wealth is preferable to poverty. But wealth is not a constituent of virtue. The moral value of selecting wealth depends entirely upon the agent's principles and manner of acting.

The Stoics expressed this difference between the value of virtue and that of other things by a number of linguistic and conceptual distinctions. Both virtue and wealth accord with Nature, but they accord with it in different ways. Virtue accords with Nature in the sense that it is the special function or goal of a rational being to be virtuous (D.L. vii 94). This statement is not relative to circumstances. It applies absolutely and unequivocally to all mature men. Wealth accords with Nature in the sense that a rational being is naturally predisposed to prefer wealth to poverty if it is open to him to select either of these. Wealth is a state which is objectively preferable to poverty, but wealth is not something which it is the special function of a rational being to possess. The value of wealth is relative to poverty, but wealth has no value relative to virtue. Morally speaking, wealth and poverty are indifferent; for it makes no difference to a man's moral worth (or welfare) whether he is rich or poor (*SVF* iii 145–6). In order to make the value of virtue sharply distinct from that of natural advantages like wealth the Stoics confined the reference of the ordinary Greek words for 'good' and 'bad', 'advantageous' and 'disadvantageous', 'useful' and 'useless' to virtue and vice respectively. ['The good' and 'the profitable' are logically equivalent (see p. 138).] Everything else is indifferent so far as moral judgments are concerned. But within the category of 'indifferent' things, the natural advantages are marked off as 'preferred' or 'preferable' and their opposites are similarly classified as 'things to be rejected'. The same distinction is observed in other ways: only virtue is 'choiceworthy' or 'desirable'. Natural advantages are 'to be selected' or 'to be taken'.

Ancient critics of the Stoa regarded these as pettifogging and incoherent distinctions. But before we consider what can be said for and against them it will be useful to quote some passages which help to elucidate the Stoic point of view. The most Cynic of the Stoics, Ariston, refused to make judgments of value about anything apart from virtue and vice (*SVF* i 351–69). This unorthodox position is criticized in Cicero's *De finibus*:

> The next subject is a way of differentiating things without which life would be turned into utter confusion, as it is by Ariston, and no function or work for wisdom could be found. For (under Ariston's procedure) there would be absolutely no difference between those things which affect the conduct of life and it would not be incumbent on us to make any discrimination between such things. Thus, although it has been adequately settled that the only good thing is virtue and the only bad thing vice, yet the Stoics wished there to be something to differentiate those things which have no significance for the actual happiness or unhappiness of life, in such a way that some of them are to be valued positively others negatively, and still others neither positively nor negatively. . . . Suppose we imagine that the final goal of action is to throw a die in such a way that it stands upright; a die so thrown will possess something 'preferable' with respect to this goal, yet the goal itself is not affected by the die's 'preferability'; similarly, those things which are 'preferred' have reference to the goal of life, but they do not affect its own meaning and nature (iii 50–4).

A further analogy might express the point more clearly. Until now no man has set foot on the planet Mars, but scientists are working to make such an event practically possible. Their goal is to land a man on Mars, and some day this goal may be achieved. But the goal is what it is independently of anyone's achieving it. One can ask questions about whether the efforts in promoting the goal are worthwhile or not irrespective of anything that may result from success. The goal of life according to the Stoics is virtue and virtuous action, but in order to achieve this goal a man must aim at particular goals which can be specified precisely. The virtuous man, if he has the opportunity, will engage in political life, marry, rear children, take exercise, study philosophy, and so forth (D.L. vii 121f.). All these things are objectively 'preferable' to their opposites, and worth making effort to achieve. But in aiming at them the good man always has a more comprehensive goal than the object which defines his particular action.[1] His comprehensive or ultimate goal is consistently virtuous behaviour, and at this he can always be successful whether or not he achieves each particular goal. The comprehensive goal is achieved by the qualities of rational discrimination and effort which go into the attempt to secure particular goals. Natural advantages and disadvantages are not constituents of virtue. But they are a necessary condition of virtue for at least two reasons.

First, complete knowledge of that which is good (Cicero's fifth stage) presupposes and arises out of a disposition to select natural advantages and reject their opposites on the promptings of reason (*Fin.* iii 23, 31). Secondly, they provide the 'material' for the exercise of virtue or vice (ibid. 61). The objection to Ariston takes its force from this point. Any virtuous action must aim at bringing about some change in the external world, and merely to say that someone acted virtuously or from the best intentions tells us nothing about what he did or tried to do. The distinction between natural advantages and disadvantages is valid independently of an agent's intentions and it makes possible the specification of a set of 'intermediate' goals which will normally include anything aimed at by a good man (and many things aimed at by men who are not good). I say 'normally' because exceptional circumstances may justify the promotion of a goal which is not 'preferred'. Chrysippus had this in mind when he wrote:

> So long as the succession of events is uncertain to me I always cling fast to the things which are better adapted for the attainment of natural advantages; for God himself has given me the capacity to select such things. But if I knew that sickness was ordained for me now, I would pursue sickness (*SVF* iii 191).

[1] Later Stoics used two different terms to distinguish the 'comprehensive' from the 'intermediate' goal. I have discussed this in 'Carneades and the Stoic Telos', *Phronesis* xii (1967) 78ff.

Universal Nature's ordinances for a man may include a large supply of things which are natural disadvantages. The good man, if he knows or has good reason to believe in advance that these are in store for him, will accept them gladly. But without such knowledge he will adhere to Chrysippus' principle. If his pursuit of health is unsuccessful, well and good. The moral worth of the action is not affected, and lack of success does not show that he was wrong to try. It is preferable to succeed but not morally more worthwhile.

Diogenes of Babylon, who was Chrysippus' successor as head of the Stoa, defined the goal of life in the formula: 'to act rationally [i.e. with right reasoning] in the selection of natural advantages' (D.L. vii 88). This prescription clearly sums up the general doctrine which has just been outlined, and it is possible that some of Cicero's Stoic material in the *De finibus* is expressed in Diogenes' formulations which may not always have been those used by Chrysippus. But there is no compelling reason to assume any divergence of opinion between these two Stoics on the relation of virtue to natural advantages.[1] Apart from the quotation of Chrysippus just referred to, we find Plutarch criticizing the Stoics in general for trying to have it both ways:

> By their actions they lay hold on natural advantages as if they are to be chosen and good, but in their terminology they renounce and revile them as indifferent, useless and of no weight with regard to well-being (*Comm. not.* 1070a).

Plutarch also attacks Chrysippus personally on the same lines in a number of places (e.g. *Stoic. rep.* 1042c–d). Diogenes' definition of the goal is an explicit statement of the orthodox Stoic position. Natural advantages have no moral value in themselves, but they provide the material or the means to exercise rational discrimination, which is morally good.

There were many in antiquity who shared Plutarch's contemptuous attitude. The fundamental criticism began with Carneades. He argued that the goal of engaging in any rational activity must be the actual attainment of something which is not contained in the activity itself (Cic. *Fin.* v 16): the Stoics have a good candidate for this, natural advantages, but they insist that the attainment of these is not the ultimate object of activities which are defined by reference to them.

---

[1] A similar view is taken by I. G. Kidd (cited on p. 189), who argues, to my mind convincingly, that the Stoics did not at any time differ significantly from one another on the status of natural advantages. For other opinions Kidd's paper should be consulted.

In fact, a formulation of the goal by Antipater, Diogenes' successor, does include the words, 'the attainment of natural advantages'. Antipater is credited with this formulation: 'doing everything in one's power to attain the primary natural advantages' (*SVF* iii Ant. 57). I have argued elsewhere that this formulation of Antipater's was prompted by Carneades' criticism of Diogenes' definition.[1] By substituting the expression 'efforts to attain' for Diogenes' 'rationally select', Antipater, as I understand him, accepted Carneades' insistence that 'the attainment of natural advantages' is implied as a goal by the Stoics. But he stipulated that the value of this goal is subordinate to the value of trying one's best to achieve it. It is probable that Antipater with this formulation did not intend to deviate from the doctrines of his predecessors. But as an answer to Carneades it played into the Sceptic's own hands and left the Stoa in an even more equivocal position. In Diogenes' formula, which Antipater also used (perhaps at an earlier stage of his career), the moral value of selecting natural advantages rests upon the opportunity this provides for exercising right reason. But Antipater's new formula makes no explicit reference to right reason. The natural inference which an opponent can draw from the words 'making continuous and infallible efforts to attain natural advantages' is the unqualified desirability of possessing such things. Antipater did not mean this, since he devoted three books to proving that virtue is sufficient on its own to provide well-being (*SVF* iii Ant. 56). But he could fairly be taken to imply it, and a fellow-Stoic, Posidonius, was later to object that the notion of 'life consistent with reason' should not be contracted into 'doing everything possible for the sake of the primary natural advantages' (*SVF* iii 12).

The distinction between 'the good' and 'the preferable' was also attacked from several points of view by the eclectic Academic philosopher, Antiochus of Ascalon. 'The good', so Antiochus argued, ought to include the satisfaction of those natural impulses from which it is supposedly derived (Cic. *Fin.* iv 25–8). He charged the Stoics with treating man as if he were a disembodied mind needing nothing from the physical environment. Why, Antiochus asked, are natural advan-

---

[1] In *Phronesis*, cited on p. 194. The relative dates of Diogenes and Carneades, along with Plutarch's reference to Antipater's being 'forced into verbal quibbling by the harassment of Carneades' (*Comm. not.* 1072f.), make it most unlikely that Diogenes' formulation was prompted by Carneades. For an interpretation of Antipater's definition which differs somewhat from my own cf. M. Soreth in *Archiv für Geschichte der Philosophie* 50 (1968) 48–72.

tages to be selected if the possession of them is not something 'good'? (ibid. 71f.). He was fully prepared to grant pre-eminent value to virtue (*Fin.* v 38). But virtue is not the only good thing, even if it outstrips the worth of everything else. There are bodily 'goods' which make a difference, however slight, to the sum total of human well-being (ibid. 71f.).

Was Antiochus right? Are the Stoics, as he held, to be interpreted as smuggling in a variety of 'goods' under a new terminology? Or is the distinction between 'the good' and 'the preferable' a coherent and valid one? The answer to these questions must depend to some extent on the critic's own moral theory. A Kantian will find different things to object to in Stoicism from a utilitarian. But any philosopher is likely to have difficulty with one Stoic concept about which little has been said so far. The Stoics claimed that virtue, the comprehensive goal of human nature, is wholly constitutive of *eudaimonia*, happiness, welfare or well-being: in order to fare well a man needs nothing but virtue, and as virtue is something absolute, welfare admits of no degrees (Cic. *Fin.* iii 43ff., D.L. vii 96). Compare this position with the more realistic view of Aristotle. He defined *eudaimonia* as 'activity of soul in accordance with virtue', but recognized that it also requires adequate provision of possessions, health and other 'goods'. The concept of welfare seems to be logically tied up with notions like useful, beneficial, profitable, and the Stoics themselves recognized this.[1] Virtue, which constitutes welfare for them, is profitable to its possessor. But once welfare has been admitted as 'the good for man', it seems to be arbitrary and false to assert that nothing except virtue identifies the content of welfare.

An even more serious difficulty arises if we turn to consider the welfare of others. Take the case of a child which is in danger of burning to death in its bed. The Stoics would recognize that a virtuous man will do everything in his power to avert this happening. In this case we might be prepared to agree with them that a man who so acted would in some sense fare well, if virtuous acts are beneficial to their agents. But part of the value of the action must consist in the external object which is its goal, the welfare of a child. The Stoics agree that the object has value, but it is something 'preferred' and not 'good'. Many will think that it makes far better moral sense to say that both the action and its external object were good. Good was done by the virtuous man's efforts to promote another's welfare; still more good

[1] cf. G. H. von Wright *The Varieties of Goodness* (London 1963) p. 87.

would have come from success. The Stoics recognized rightly that the goodness of an intention or principle of action must be evaluated independently of a man's achieving some desirable result, and their emphasis on this point is one of the most important aspects of their ethics. But their terminological distinctions may be thought to introduce more confusion than clarification. What makes motives or intentions commendable is the good which the agent sought to produce. If we call that 'good' the 'preferable', following the Stoics, we obscure the relation between the value of a morally good action and the value of the change in the world at which it is aimed.

Furthermore, a man's moral worth, one could argue, is partly demonstrated by the attitude which he has towards success or failure at achieving morally desirable results. We would normally think less well of a man who felt no sorrow or regret that he was unable to save a child's life in spite of all his efforts to do so. The Stoics however argued quite differently. The virtuous man, having done everything in his power, does not feel pity or regret (*SVF* iii 450–2). He accepts what happens without reacting emotionally. This seems such a strange notion that it calls for a different approach to our problem. We shall misunderstand the distinctions of value which have just been discussed unless we place them in the context of Stoic ideas encountered earlier in this book.

A man, as I have repeatedly stressed, is an integral part of the Stoic universe. The external circumstances of his whole life are an episode in the life of universal Nature, and they are 'in his power' only to the extent that he can choose to accept them or not when they occur. If he is a convinced Stoic he will accept them all gladly, on the understanding that they contribute to the well-being of the universe as a whole. But even a convinced Stoic is not omniscient. After something has happened he can say, 'Be it so', but not before. He is not a mere spectator of events, but an active agent himself. Before he goes to bed the Stoic will consider what may be the circumstances of tomorrow, and in advance of their happening he is more favourably disposed to some events than to others. He would prefer all manner of things for other people and himself to their opposites, and so far as he is able he seeks to bring about these preferable states of affairs. His preferences are perfectly rational, that is, they fully accord with an objective assessment of the relative merits of external things as determined by Nature itself. But he does not regard the things which he prefers as good, nor does he desire them. Why not? The answer to this has been partly outlined already. Viewed as an event which forms part of Nature's universal harmony, anything that happens is good. But, in his imperfect knowledge, the Stoic may be perfectly justified in preferring something which does not happen. Yet it would have happened if Nature had determined that it should. Therefore it was not good that it should happen. Towards future events the Stoic maintains an attitude of preference or rejection. He is in no position to judge of their goodness, and therefore views the future with relative indifference. This is something of concern to Nature alone who embraces all things.[1]

For similar reasons, if the Stoic's own well-being is to be 'in his power' it cannot depend on the attainment of results which may not be realized. But something is in the Stoic's own power, namely his disposition as a rational man. Nature ordains that a man can and should attain well-being solely through what is in his own power. This means through virtue, the only good. Virtue is a 'consistently rational disposition' (*SVF* i 202), and its value is something different in kind from natural advantages. They are things which a man can take if he encounters them, but virtue is something he can choose irrespective of circumstances. Natural advantages supply a man with objective goals at which he can choose to aim, and the material for forming his own moral principles. They are necessary to virtue only as means by which it can be exercised, and not as things which it needs for their own sake.[2]

(iv) The content of virtue: perfect and 'intermediate' actions

Let us recall what has so far been said about virtue. First of all, it is the one thing to which 'good' belongs in a strict and necessary sense; nothing else, for example an action, can be good unless it 'participates' in virtue (*SVF* i 190, iii 76). In a definition of virtue with which the names of Zeno, Ariston, Chrysippus and Menedemus, a Cynic, are associated it is said to be a disposition and faculty of the governing-principle of the soul, 'or rather: reason itself, consistent, firm and unwavering' (*SVF* i 202). Secondly, virtue is the goal which Nature

[1] See further Victor Goldschmidt, *Le Système stoicien et l'idée de temps* (Paris 1969), who relates the Stoics' stress on the importance of each present moment to their idea that future consequences have no bearing on the virtue of an action, pp. 145–51.
[2] For a comparison of the Stoics' position and Aristotle's *vis-à-vis* external goods see my discussion in *Bulletin of the Institute of Classical Studies* 15 (1968) 74–6.

has laid down for man. Thirdly, the earlier stages of a man's development are necessary to virtue as providing patterns of appropriate
behaviour out of which it can arise. But this is a very abstract account.
Can we fill out the content of virtue and state more fully what it means
to be virtuous?

Virtue is a kind of 'knowledge' or 'art' (*SVF* iii 256, 202). It is a
unitary disposition of the soul which can be analysed into four primary virtues: practical wisdom, justice, moderation and courage.[1]
Each of these is defined in terms of knowledge: for instance, courage
is 'knowledge of things which should be endured' (*SVF* iii 285). To
have this knowledge or the knowledge which belongs to any particular
virtue it is necessary to have the knowledge constitutive of virtue as a
whole. The influence of Socrates and Plato is plainly evident here.

The virtuous man's knowledge is grasped by his intellect, but as
steps preliminary to its acquisition he uses the evidence of sense-
perception. After sketching out the stages of man's moral development Cicero amplifies his account of 'knowledge of the good' in the
following passage:

> After the mind by means of rational inference has climbed up from those
> things which are in accordance with Nature it arrives at the idea of the good.
> But we perceive the good and name it so not as a result of addition or growth
> or comparison with other things but through its own specific nature. Honey,
> though it is very sweet, is perceived to be sweet by its own taste and not
> through comparison with other (sweet) things; similarly that good, which
> is our subject, is something of the highest value, but this assessment is valid
> because of the kind of thing the good is, not because of its size (*Fin.* iii
> 33–4).

Cicero's language recalls the famous passage in Book vi of Plato's
Republic (509c–511e) according to which the philosopher ascends to
knowledge of the good by the help of 'hypotheses' about the objects
of sight and intellect. Cicero seems to be describing a comparable
methodology. The 'things which accord with Nature' serve as stepping-
stones to reach a principle which is *sui generis* and cannot be inferred
directly from them. They are the 'preferable' objects of instinctive
and, later, rational selection. The fact that 'the good' is not intuited by
a simple comparison with these natural advantages does not mean
that 'the good' falls outside things which accord with Nature. Cicero's

[1] These primary virtues each admit of sub-divisions. For example, justice
embraces piety, kindness, fellow-feeling and fair dealing (*SVF* iii 264).

illustration makes this clear. We can get a notion of sweetness by tasting a number of sweet things; but tasting an apple will not provide an idea of the sweetness of Turkish delight. Accordance with Nature takes the place of sweetness in the illustration. Different things can provide an idea of being in accordance with Nature, but 'the good' accords with Nature in a sense which is beyond anything else. Other things provide the mind with a ladder which can help it up to a position from which 'the good' is directly apprehended through its own nature. How are we to interpret this conception in practical terms? Clearly no account can be fully adequate. Only he who has seen 'the good' knows precisely what it is. But we can conjecture what it entails. To know 'the good' means discovering a principle of conduct which satisfies the general idea of 'accordance with Nature', formed by induction and introspection, and the particular facts of human nature— that man is a rational being with the capacity to understand and participate in the universal activities of Nature.

One of Seneca's letters allows us to be still more specific. Seneca poses the question: 'How do we attain our first concept of the good and virtue?' (*Ep.* 120). It is not an innate human endowment, and it would be absurd to suppose that man hit upon it by chance. Seneca next lays it down that the antecedents of moral knowledge are 'observation' and 'comparison' of repeated acts. Without explaining this statement he continues: 'Our school of philosophers claims that what is good and of moral worth is learnt by means of "analogy"', and this last term he does explain. By analogy with physical health, a (natural) condition which is familiar to us, we have inferred (*collegimus*) that there is such a thing as health of mind.[1]

There are certain acts of generosity, or of humanity or courage, which have amazed us. We begin to admire them as if they were perfect. But they conceal many faults which are hidden by their appearance of something brilliant; and we have overlooked these. Nature bids us to augment praiseworthy actions.... From them therefore we have derived an idea of remarkable goodness.

Seneca proceeds to illustrate his theory by examples. By analogy with bodily health we learn that there is such a thing as health of mind; but that is not sufficient to show what health of mind is. In order to give

---

[1] Seneca's account is consistent with the brief statement: 'something just and good is conceived of *naturally*' (D.L. vii 53). To reason by analogy is natural to man. It is also Plato's regular practice to describe conditions of the soul in terms of health and sickness, e.g. *Rep.* 444c–e.

content to our general concept observation is necessary: we form an idea of courage by observing and comparing the behaviour of individual men. Seneca then draws distinctions between 'prodigality' and 'generosity', 'courage' and 'foolhardiness'. 'The similarity between these forces us to take thought and to distinguish things which are related in appearance but are immensely different in fact. In observing men who have become famous through doing some outstanding act we begin to note the sort of man who has done something with magnanimity and great zeal, but once only.' We see men who show courage in war but not in other spheres of life. 'Another man, whom we see, is kindly towards his friends, unimpassioned towards his enemies, dutiful in his public and private behaviour.' This kind of man is 'always consistent with himself in every action, good not through policy but under the direction of a disposition such that he is able not only to act rightly but cannot act without acting rightly. In him we recognize that virtue has been perfected.'

According to this theory our general concept of virtue is refined by observation. We learn to distinguish isolated acts of quasi-courage from the conduct of a man who always shows fortitude. Does this mean that the moral concepts which men form are relative to their experience? The Stoics tried to avoid the problems of relativism by setting up the sage as a paradigm and giving detailed descriptions of his disposition and of the kinds of things that he does. Imitation of the sage or actual good men cannot ensure virtue, but it can certainly set a man on the right road to secure it. We might sum up by saying that all men naturally form general concepts of value. Nature's part is to give man the equipment to form such concepts and the ability to think analogically. But virtue or knowledge of what is truly good does not follow necessarily from these faculties. To know what is truly good a man has to consider what is involved in the performance of, say, a courageous action and to ask himself why a man who acts apparently well in one sphere can fail to do so in another. That is to say, he needs to grasp what is needed if a man is to act well in all spheres at all times. The conditions nominated by Cicero and Seneca alike are orderliness, propriety, consistency and harmony. To know what all of these are is to know what is good.

'The good' is prior in value to anything else, but so far as any individual man is concerned it is posterior in time to other valuable things. A man can only come to recognize 'the good' after he has learnt to select natural advantages and to reject their opposites in a regular and systematic pattern of action. We may remind ourselves that natural advantages include all those states of affairs which, though not constituents of virtue, are objectively (or Naturally) preferable to their opposites. In most circumstances natural advantages are the intermediate goals at which the good man aims, but it is not necessary to be a good man to aim at these things. On the contrary, the good man was aiming at them before he became good and all men do so to a lesser or greater degree. It is not the special mark of a good man to select natural advantages but to do so in a certain way and on the basis of certain principles (*SVF* iii 516). The changes in the world which the good man seeks to bring about are all prompted by virtuous motives. But viewed objectively or externally they do not differ necessarily from the goals of foolish men, the other category of mankind.

Suppose that we observe a man taking exercise. According to the Stoics this is an 'appropriate' thing to do, for good physical health is a natural advantage. But on the basis of our specific observation we cannot form a judgment about this man's moral character. Cicero makes a similar point taking the example of 'returning a deposit' (*Fin.* iii 58f.). This too is something appropriate; it is justifiable on rational grounds and to accomplish such a transaction is a 'preferable' state of affairs. But there is a great deal of difference between returning a deposit and doing this 'rightly'. The former is merely 'appropriate', whereas the latter is 'perfectly appropriate'. But both actions have the same 'intermediate' goal. The expression 'intermediate goal' was used earlier in our discussion to distinguish the sage's aim to select natural advantages from his comprehensive goal, virtuous action. But natural advantages stand as 'intermediate goals' in the further sense that they are 'neither good nor bad'.

If an appropriate action is considered independently of the character of its agent it must be judged 'intermediate'.[1] But in terms of the agent's character every action, whether appropriate or not, is either 'perfect' or 'faulty'. The 'faultiness' of an appropriate act can have nothing to do with its external object.[2] Only 'inappropriate' acts are

---

[1] cf. J. M. Rist, *Stoic Philosophy*, pp. 98ff.

[2] This should not be taken to mean that an appropriate act is faulty if it fails to secure the object aimed at. I. G. Kidd argues that 'the whole stress of *kathê-konta* lies in the object of the act being achieved' (*Problems in Stoicism*, p. 155), but no evidence seems to require this conclusion. It must in certain circumstances be sufficient to have tried but failed, though the efforts of a foolish man will be defective by comparison with those of a sage. My thinking on this point has been influenced by discussion with Professor P. A. Brunt.

faulty in this respect. But if an appropriate act is performed by someone who is not a sage it lacks the fundamental characteristic of fitting
into a pattern of actions all of which are completely harmonious with
each other. Of the man who has advanced to the point when he only
just falls short of wisdom or perfection Chrysippus wrote:

> He fulfils all appropriate actions in all respects and omits none; but his life
> is *not yet* in a state of well-being. This supervenes when these 'intermediate'
> actions acquire the additional property of firmness, consistency and their
> own proper co-ordination (*SVF* iii 510).

Here of course we have an extreme case. Most performers of appropriate acts will by no means fulfil all of them, and will thereby be
still further away from the absolute harmony characteristic of virtue.
In respect of *what* he does Chrysippus' man must be classified with
the sage, but in respect of his character he is to be judged still 'foolish'.[1]
In Stoic ethics a miss is as bad as a mile. There are no degrees of
goodness, though there are degrees of coming closer towards it. But
until a man is good he is bad (*SVF* iii 657–70). The minute element of
disharmony present in a man who has nearly reached the top is sufficient to disqualify anything that he does from the accolade of virtue.

This is a hard doctrine, and it is made all the harder by the Stoics'
own reservations on the actual existence of any man who has made the
grade. Chrysippus himself admitted the enormous gap which Stoicism
admits between theory and practical achievement:

> Wherefore on account of their extreme magnitude and beauty we seem to be
> stating things which are like fictions and not in accordance with man and
> human nature (*SVF* iii 545).

But if human nature is perfectible nothing short of its perfection can
be admissible as the ultimate goal. Stoic ethics is an epitome of idealism. The sage, to whom every commendatory epithet belongs, is not
found in everyday life. He is a perfect man, whose character mirrors
the perfection of Nature. Judged by the standards of the sage we are
all foolish or bad. But through assiduous effort and education the
theory is that we can progress to a condition which approximates to

---

[1] Seneca observes that 'precepts' can only lead to 'right actions' if a man's
character is compliant; they may tell one what to do but not *how* to live virtuously
(*Ep.* 95). It is of interest to compare the Stoics' view with W. D. Ross's claim in
The Right and the Good (Oxford 1930) that 'right' and 'wrong' refer entirely to
the thing done; 'morally good' and 'morally bad' to the motive of the agent, p. 7.

perfection. If virtue is to be something supremely worthwhile it deserves every effort on the part of man, and the ideal sage persists as a standard to which we may seek to conform ourselves.

The Stoics developed a radical political theory around this concept of the sage. I have already referred to Zeno's *Republic* in which the fundamental social and economic institutions of the Greek world are abolished (p. 110). In the ideal world the state withers away because each Stoic sage is self-sufficient and his own authority (*SVF* iii 617). But he is united with his fellows by the bond of friendship, for all wise men are friends to each other and it is only between them that friendship in its true sense can exist (*SVF* iii 625). A communal way of life which dispenses with all distinctions based upon sex, birth, nationality, and property—this is the pattern of social behaviour. The theory is utopian and was recognized to be such. But its interest lies in the criticism of contemporary society which it implies. Stoic political theory is not a blue-print for reform but a paradigm of the world as it might be if men could be united not by artificial ties but by the recognition in each other of common values and common purposes. Money, family, and hereditary status are all seen as divisive factors. They have nothing to do with being virtuous and virtue has everything to do with the ideal state.

Stoicism never lost its idealistic character. But over the years individual Stoic leaders gave increasing attention to the detailed analysis of practical moral principles for the guidance of day-to-day behaviour. The work which has proved most influential was done by Panaetius, but before we come to this it will be worthwhile to pause a little longer over the Stoic sage and his perfect actions.

(*v*) *The Stoic sage: tests of virtue*
The sage is defined by his moral expertise. He knows infallibly what should be done in each situation of life and takes every step to do it at the right time and in the right way. But suppose that we wish to form a judgment about the moral status of some man whom we are observing. Are there any tests which can be applied, independently of his own statements about himself, from which we may form a reasonable opinion? It is not sufficient that he should be seen to perform 'appropriate' actions, since these do not, on the Stoic concept of character or disposition, give any necessary indication of an agent's state of mind. Sextus Empiricus argues that the Stoics are unable to supply evidence from which the 'wise disposition' of the sage can be

established (*Adv. math.* xi 200–6). He considers a further test, 'steadiness and orderliness', and claims that this too is illusory since the wise man must be always adapting himself to changing circumstances (ibid. 207–9). But this criticism misses the point. It is perfectly possible to act differently according to changing events and maintain steady and consistent moral principles. One characteristic of the sage which Sextus fails to mention is 'timely' behaviour.[1] The Stoics justified suicide on the grounds that such an act might in extreme circumstances be the rational thing to do.[2] Suicide cannot be formulated in a general rule, such as the appropriateness of maintaining one's health. The preservation of one's life is what accords with human nature in most situations. But many of the things which accord with human nature are not unconditionally appropriate. 'Good timing' in the Stoics' sense has been well described as 'the point at which the process of a man's actions meets and coincides with those events which are the result of a series of causes called Fate'.[3] Suicide is an extreme example of conduct inimical to a man's own interests in most circumstances which might be rationally defended in certain situations. If we were to observe a man whose conduct had always satisfied all general principles of appropriateness—he had looked after his health, his family, his property, and the interests of others—voluntarily submitting himself to unjust imprisonment, torture or public vilification, or even taking his own life or that of a relative suffering from a most painful and fatal disease, there would be reason to regard such a man as a possible candidate for being a sage. The Stoics' defence of cannibalism, incest and non-burial, under exceptional circumstances (*SVF* ii 743–56), is to be placed in this context of 'timely' action.

But there is a more important test which we could perform. The Stoic sage is free from all passion. Anger, anxiety, cupidity, dread, elation, these and similar extreme emotions are all absent from his disposition. He does not regard pleasure as something good, nor pain as something evil. Many of a person's pleasures or pains are things which he can keep to himself, but it is difficult to conceive of someone subject to anger, dread or elation who never revealed his state of mind to an outside observer. The Stoic sage is not insensitive to painful or pleasurable sensations, but they do not 'move his soul excessively'.

[1] *SVF* iii 630; the Latin word is *opportune*, cf. Cic. *Fin.* iii 61.
[2] J. M. Rist has a good discussion of Stoic attitudes to suicide, *Stoic Philosophy*, ch. 13.
[3] D. Tsekourakis, *Studies in the Terminology of Early Stoic Ethics*, Ph.D. dissertation of London University (1971) pp. 91–2.

He is impassive towards them. But he is not entirely impassive, contrary to the popular conception of a Stoic. As I noted earlier (p. 176 n. 2), his disposition is characterized by 'good emotional states'. Well-wishing, wishing another man good things for his sake; joy: rejoicing in virtuous actions, a tranquil life, a good conscience (Sen. *Ep.* 23, 2); and 'wariness', reasonable disinclination. Like Aristotle the Stoics regarded the emotional attitude which accompanies actions as an index of moral character.[1]

The absence of passion and the presence of the qualities just enumerated provide an objective measuring-stick for sorting out possible sages from other men. Added to the tests already mentioned, they set up a canon of excellence which could within limits be vouched for by an observer if any candidates were forthcoming. It is not surprising that Stoic philosophers themselves did not pass the examination and knew of none who had done so.

The starting-point of this long chapter was a quotation which spoke of the 'remarkable coherence' of Stoicism. Unlike Aristotle the Stoics did not regard ethics as a science the subject-matter of which is imprecise by contrast with that of metaphysics. As moral philosophers the Stoics sought to establish a set of values and principles of conduct which would be as securely based as the laws of Nature from which they were derived. The concept of 'consequence' or 'what follows from what' is the lynch-pin of their entire system. The laws of the universe are manifested by a strict causal nexus. As a natural philosopher the Stoic describes the effects of this system, as a logician he analyses what can be said about it and the truths which it sanctions, and as a moral philosopher he looks at its implications for human well-being and conduct. We have seen that the system is incoherent, or verges on incoherence, at certain crucial points. Two fundamental and related difficulties are first, the usage of Nature both to describe objective facts and to sanction values, and second, the concept of 'rational assent' as something 'in our power' at the level of subjective consciousness and yet apparently determined objectively by the necessary sequence of cause and effect. The Stoics showed considerable ingenuity in attempting to resolve these dilemmas, but the result is not ultimately satisfactory.

But, for all that we know at the present time, free will is nothing more than a phenomenon of human consciousness. Possibly human

---

[1] For a comparison between the two, cf. pp. 79–82 of the article cited in n. 2 p. 199. More generally, J. M. Rist, *Stoic Philosophy*, ch. 3.

actions are causally related to antecedent events in a manner which could in principle be fully explained by the laws of physics and chemistry. If this is the case, it might have a marked effect on our concept of moral responsibility. But the need to evaluate actions and to designate certain states of affairs as better than others would still exist. Part of the contemporary interest of Stoicism lies in its attempt to square a highly elaborated moral theory with objective facts, facts which take account of innate human drives, environmental influences and laws governing all natural phenomena.

There are many other details, some of which I have remarked, that bear upon modern interests. Yet, in the last resort, Stoicism defies any simple comparison with developments which come before or after it. The Stoics offer a complete world picture and in a sense, as they themselves observed, one must swallow the whole thing or none of it. Points on which they seem to agree with other philosophers must always be considered in the context of the total system. If we ask which moral philosopher of subsequent times comes closest to the Stoics two candidates are particularly worthy of mention. Kant, who was certainly influenced by them, is a strong contender.[1] His 'categorical imperative', something 'conceived as good *in itself* and consequently as being necessarily the principle of a will which of itself conforms to reason' (*Ethics* 38), looks very like the Stoic 'right reason'. The value which the Stoics placed upon the subjective content of a moral action, and the relation of this to objective necessity or universal law, can hardly be accidental points of resemblance with Kantian ethics. But for Kant welfare or happiness is not a constituent of moral goodness, whereas Stoic virtue constitutes something which is in the interests of man *par excellence*. *Pflicht* (duty) and *Wille* (will) have nothing in Stoicism which corresponds to them with any precision, yet they are fundamental Kantian concepts.

Another strong contender is Spinoza. Consider his proposition: 'In the nature of things nothing contingent is granted, but all things are determined by the necessity of divine nature for existing and working in a certain way' (*Ethics*, part I prop. xxix). Or, 'All ideas, in so far as they have reference to God [sc. or Nature], are true' (part II prop. xxxii). But Spinoza renounced the conventional meanings of virtue and vice. More rigorously determinist than the Stoics, he totally rejected the idea of any purpose which a person is designed to

[1] cf. W. Schinck, 'Kant und die stoische Ethik', *Kant Studien* xviii (1913) 419–75.

fulfil. Like the Stoics he regarded happiness as wholly dependent upon understanding Nature and man's place in it. And he also stressed, as they did, the necessity of grasping the causes of man's passionate love and hatred of objects which have no relevance to happiness. But the 'freedom' of mind which such understanding can bring, though strikingly similar to the state of the Stoic sage, is not a goal which Spinoza's Nature sets man to achieve. Spinoza would have nothing to do with final causes. Pleasure and prudence, not Nature's disposition for man's active promotion of the world's well-being, are the motives which inspire Spinoza's philosopher towards fortitude and nobility.

CHAPTER FIVE

Later Developments in Hellenistic Philosophy

THE establishment of the Roman empire by Augustus in 30 B.C. ends the third and last Hellenistic century. For the history of philosophy this date has a general rather than a specific significance. Throughout the next two hundred years and more, Stoicism, Epicureanism and, to a much more limited extent, Scepticism found their adherents. Marcus Aurelius, Diogenes of Oenoanda and Sextus Empiricus are three writers who bear witness to this fact. But if we except the Sceptic Aenesidemus, who may have lived after the Augustan principate (see p. 75 n. 1), the movements described in this book had no representatives in the Roman empire who were outstanding for original contributions to philosophy. This does not mean that Hellenistic philosophy came to a dead end. Stoicism in particular was a force to reckon with for many years to come. As a moral doctrine its influence was pervasive long after 30 B.C. Indeed, the names of prominent Romans who were Stoics are more numerous from the first century A.D. than in any other period. They could include men as diverse as Seneca, the epic poet Lucan, the satirist Persius, and opponents of the tyrannical regimes of Nero and Domitian—Thrasea Paetus, Helvidius Priscus, Musonius Rufus, and others. Philosophy in antiquity was never a purely academic discipline, and the influence of Stoicism on Roman literature and social life is of the greatest interest and importance.

But in intellectual vitality Hellenistic philosophy reached its zenith before the fall of the Roman Republic. During its later years however (150–50 B.C.), three men flourished whose work deserves a short discussion. Panaetius, Posidonius and Antiochus are names which have only figured intermittently so far. Cicero was personally acquainted with Posidonius and Antiochus, and he drew on the work of all three philosophers in his own writings.

(i) *Panaetius*

The career of Panaetius has already been briefly described (p. 114). In one modern work he is said to have been 'very influential in his day . . . but his period of great influence was short'.[1] This is a relative judgment. Panaetius is not often referred to by writers other than Cicero, and this may indicate that he was little read in later antiquity. But few classical texts from the Renaissance to the nineteenth century have enjoyed the renown and influence of 'Tully's Offices', that is, Cicero's *De officiis*. It is certain that Cicero based the first two books of this work upon Panaetius, and through Cicero Panaetius might fairly be regarded as the most influential of all Stoic philosophers.

Because our information about Panaetius is relatively scanty it is difficult to gain a clear impression of his philosophical activities as a whole.[2] But the evidence does not point to a man who advanced strikingly new theories. Panaetius' importance rests largely on the manner in which he approached and developed the practical side of Stoic ethics. In earlier Stoicism, as we have seen, logic, physics and ethics are brought together to constitute a single coherent system. Panaetius disapproved of 'logic-chopping' (fr. 55), and though he did not abandon the central Stoic concept of a rationally directed universe, the doubts which he expressed about a number of orthodox dogmas relating to physics suggest that the emphasis on this subject was weaker in his work. Human nature rather than universal nature was Panaetius' primary interest.

Before considering this in more detail we may briefly review some of the orthodox theories on which Panaetius pronounced himself sceptical, or which he rejected altogether. Like all Stoics he took the universe to be imperishable, but he doubted or denied that it is periodically subject to a state in which all things are reduced to fire (*ekpyrōsis*, frs. 64–9).[3] This probably implies, as Philo of Alexandria asserts (fr. 65), that he rejected the related notion of a perpetual recurrence of the same events in successive world-cycles. Cicero also tells us that Panaetius was the only Stoic who 'repudiated the forecasts of astrologers' (fr. 74).[4] Earlier Stoics argued that the gods could not be

---

[1] J. M. Rist, *Stoic Philosophy*, p. 173.

[2] The texts in which he is named have been collected by M. van Straaten as *Panaetii Rhodii Fragmenta* (ed. 3, Leiden 1962).

[3] Boethus of Sidon, a Stoic contemporary with Panaetius, also rejected this tenet and made a number of further modifications to the orthodox doctrine which show the influence of Aristotle. Evidence in *SVF* iii 265–7.

[4] In this he agreed with Carneades, Cic. *De div.* i 12.

interested, as they are, in human welfare unless they give signs of
future events which men can interpret (*SVF* ii 1191–5). If the forecasts of diviners and astrologers are proved false, the fault lies with the
forecasters and not with the dreams, meteorological phenomena,
flights of birds, entrails, and other evidence from which the future can in
theory be foretold (*SVF* ii 1210). The Stoic defence of such forecasting
can easily seem ridiculous, but the principle itself was a fundamental
feature of the system. Unless signs of what will happen are available
in natural phenomena, the Stoic aim to live in accordance with
natural events has no secure foundations. Moreover, all events are
causally related to one another, and therefore anything that happens
must in theory be a sign of some subsequent effect.

Does Panaetius' rejection of astrology imply an abandonment of
these basic Stoic doctrines? Cicero also reports that he had doubts
about divination (frs. 70–1), and other sources say he rejected it
altogether (frs. 68, 73). But such attitudes are quite compatible with a
belief in divine providence, a subject on which Panaetius wrote a book
(fr. 33). Panaetius could hold that the world is arranged for the benefit of mankind, while denying that human beings as a matter of fact
are able to find evidence of the future in stars and other phenomena.
But he seems to have discarded astrology on stronger grounds than
the limitations of human knowledge. Cicero, who claims to be drawing
upon Panaetius, argues that the stars are too distant from the earth to
sanction the causal relationship which astrology must postulate
between celestial movements and human affairs (fr. 74). This certainly
suggests that Panaetius was less committed than his predecessors to
the necessary connexion between all events in the universe.

Panaetius' general attitude towards natural philosophy seems to
have been more Aristotelian than that of earlier Stoics. At the beginning of the *De officiis* (i 11–20) Cicero, drawing on Panaetius, derives
the four cardinal virtues from natural human impulses. This is a short-
circuiting of the orthodox Stoic procedure rather than a positive
modification of it, but Cicero proceeds to treat 'wisdom' as if its
province were primarily a disinterested pursuit of knowledge. The
other three virtues—justice, moderation and courage—are grouped
together with the task of 'providing the foundations for moral conduct
in the practical business of life'. Earlier Stoics gave purely moral
definitions of wisdom. It is clearly not Panaetius' view that there is
any sharp distinction between wisdom and the other virtues (*De off.* i
15 = fr. 103), but he did distinguish 'theoretical' from 'practical'

virtue (fr. 108) and this is unorthodox. Panaetius' most obvious precedent is Aristotle's Nicomachean and other ethical treatises.

Aristotle regarded the moral virtues as dispositions of the appetitive and emotional element in human nature (*E.N.* i 1102a23ff.). Panaetius, if Cicero is reporting his views (*De off.* i 101 = fr. 87), said:

> Souls have a double capacity and nature; one of these is impulse which drives a man this way and that; the other is reason which instructs and explains what should be done and not done.

Panaetius' analysis of the virtues may have been designed to fit an account of the soul which was more Aristotelian or Platonic than early Stoic. But too much should not be based upon the 'double' nature of the soul, as Cicero describes this. Psychological dualism is superficially incompatible with Chrysippus' doctrine that 'impulse' is a function of reason. Yet we know from Galen that Chrysippus was quite capable of using the term 'impulse' as if it referred to something which was in some sense distinct from reason.[1] Posidonius certainly abandoned Chrysippus' conception of the soul. Panaetius quite possibly did so too, but the modifications *explicitly* attributed to him are of much less significance.[2]

When we come to ethics Panaetius' position emerges with more clarity, but assessments of his orthodoxy have varied considerably.[3] There is little doubt that Panaetius placed less emphasis than his predecessors on the perfect but unexampled Stoic sage. The *De officiis* takes as its subject not 'perfect virtue' but 'likenesses of virtue'. The latter can be manifested by men whose wisdom is imperfect, and Panaetius' work *On that which is appropriate* (Cicero's source) dealt with 'duties' which should be the 'intermediate' goals of all men whether perfect or not:

> Since life is passed not in the company of men who are perfect and truly wise but men who act well if they show likenesses of virtue, I think it must

---

[1] cf. Josiah B. Gould, *The Philosophy of Chrysippus*, p. 183.

[2] Panaetius nominated six 'parts' of the soul, thereby making speech a part of 'impulse' and reproduction a part of 'nature' (fr. 86), see p. 171. The significance of this point is not clear. It is often said that he totally denied any survival of the soul after death, but no Stoic postulated unlimited survival or immortality. Panaetius may have adhered to the orthodox view of survival for a limited duration, cf. R. Hoven, *Stoïcisme et Stoïciens face au problème de l'au-delà*, p. 57.

[3] I agree in general with the position of I. G. Kidd, *Problems in Stoicism*, ch. 7. In my opinion Panaetius' ethical innovations were less significant than J. M. Rist supposes, *Stoic Philosophy*, pp. 186–200.

be understood that no one should be entirely neglected in whom any mark of virtue is evident (*De off.* i 46).

Earlier Stoics also took account of those who are 'progressing towards virtue', and they may have handled this subject with greater detail and sympathy than our fragmentary evidence suggests. But the probability is that Panaetius' readiness to admit 'likenesses of virtue' represents a methodological concession which made Stoicism both less rigid and more humane. The rigidity of early Stoic ethics is typified in the so-called 'paradoxes': there are no degrees of virtue or vice; all men except the sage are insane; all acts of wrong-doing are equally wrong. Panaetius would have agreed with his predecessors that such statements are correct from the perspective of perfect virtue. But we may presume him to have argued that they are wholly unhelpful for the purpose of everyday life and moral education.

Such a conclusion is justified not only by the content of the *De officiis* but also by a number of assertions which Cicero makes about Panaetius. 'He shunned,' says Cicero, 'the gloom and harshness of other Stoics and did not approve of the severity of their attitudes' (*Fin.* iv 79 = fr. 55). In his speech in defence of Murena Cicero contrasts the 'softening' effect of Panaetius' company upon Scipio with Cato's obduracy. But he adds: 'Panaetius' discourse and doctrines were just the things which please you' [sc. Cato] (66 = fr. 60). This last statement could not have been uttered if Panaetius' ethics were clearly out of line with the orthodox Stoicism embraced by Cato. Panaetius did not reject the ideal of perfection, any more than Chrysippus and Zeno ignored the performance of 'duties' as a mark of progress.[1] The duties covered by Cicero's treatise spring from natural impulses which are also the basis of perfect virtue.[2] It is the orthodox doctrine, as we have seen, that knowledge of goodness presupposes the ability to recognize and do the appropriate thing at the right time and in the right way. The *De officiis* looks at appropriate behaviour from the vantage-point of one who lacks this knowledge in its perfect form but aspires to possess it. Panaetius does not suggest even at this second-best level that virtue rests on the thing done or the external goal aimed at. 'That virtue, which we are seeking, depends entirely

---

[1] Zeno thought interestingly that a man's dreams provide him with evidence of his progress, *SVF* i 234.

[2] 'To live in accordance with the impulses bestowed on us by Nature' is Panaetius' formulation of the *summum bonum* (fr. 96).

on the mind's effort and reasoning' (i 79).[1] But guide-lines to the attainment of virtue can be laid down in general terms. Justice prescribes two basic principles: first, do no injury to another man; and secondly, see that the public interest is maintained (i 31). A man who acts upon these principles will act appropriately or fulfil his duty. What he ought to do can be and should be derived from these principles. But perfect virtue is more than the adherence to such principles and the attempt to do one's duty. The truly good man acts on the basis of knowledge, which is not reducible to a set of specifiable moral rules.[2] But moral rules can set a man on the right road, and Panaetius devoted considerable pains to the analysis of those attitudes and actions which characterize a man who is on this road.

It is this emphasis on what a man can achieve here and now which marks Panaetius' specific contribution to Stoic ethics. An approving comment by Seneca makes the point very clearly:

I think Panaetius gave a neat answer to a young man who asked whether the sage would be a lover: 'As to the sage we shall see. Your task and mine, who are still a great distance from the sage, is not to fall into a state which is disturbed, powerless and subservient to another' (*Ep.* 116, 5 = fr. 114).

The requirement to live free of passion is characteristically Stoic, but on the orthodox doctrine it distinguishes the sage from the rest of mankind. Panaetius, recognizing the fact of human imperfection, treats questions about the sage as irrelevant to life as we find it. He seems to have sensed the need for a criterion of moral judgment which was not satisfied by the orthodox dichotomy between sages and fools. Panaetius agreed with Zeno and other Stoics that the basis of moral conduct is man's rational nature (*De off.* i 107), but he also emphasized the fact that every man has particular attributes of his own. Self-knowledge, a concept which had a moral significance for the Greeks as early as the sixth century, was introduced by Panaetius as a criterion of 'propriety'. We should so act that our behaviour accords with human nature in general and our own nature in particular (i 110 = fr. 97). The *De officiis* lays down general principles, and it also seeks to show how these have been appropriately applied by different kinds

---

[1] In *De off.* iii 13ff. Cicero again distinguishes perfect virtue from the knowledge of 'intermediate duties'. But he makes it clear that even these latter depend on 'goodness of disposition' (*ingenii bonitas*) and 'advancement in learning'. See further p. 203.

[2] Cf. Sen. *Ep.* 94, 50f. referred to by Kidd, p. 164, cited in n. 3 p. 213.

of men in different situations. None of this is inconsistent with earlier Stoicism, but the cosmic dimension has virtually disappeared. It reappears in Marcus Aurelius and Epictetus, though the latter succeeds in combining it with the more humanist approach of Panaetius.

Panaetius was undoubtedly a Stoic, but he had an independent mind and was not afraid to modify or give a different emphasis to the doctrines of his predecessors. His cultural interests were possibly more diverse than those of Chrysippus, and he wrote about the authenticity of Socratic dialogues, Greek history and perhaps other non-philosophical subjects (frs. 123–36). A number of sources speak of his indebtedness to Plato and Aristotle (frs. 55–9), and historians of philosophy have often regarded 'eclecticism' as the defining characteristic of this period. Both Panaetius and Posidonius were eclectic in the sense that they were prepared to welcome ideas advanced by other philosophers if this suited them. And Antiochus of Ascalon manifests the same tendency still more strongly. This loosening of the boundaries between philosophical schools has been explained in various ways. The introduction of philosophy to Rome is sometimes thought to have had the effect of making the subject more pragmatic and therefore less concerned with theoretical niceties. But it is difficult to see anything specifically Roman in the philosophy of Panaetius or Posidonius. It was men like Cato who made Stoicism a Roman ideal. Philosophical dissatisfaction with certain aspects of Stoicism is the most likely explanation of the changes introduced by Panaetius, Posidonius and other Stoic philosophers of this period. Carneades' criticism must have made many Stoics all too well aware of weaknesses in the system, and it was not necessary to be an official Sceptic to have doubts about the usefulness or validity of certain doctrines. Orthodox Stoicism could not unfairly be charged with offering a way of life which fully satisfied neither everyday needs nor the yearnings of those whose temperament inclined them towards mystical and religious experience. The revival of Pythagoreanism in the first century B.C. is a symptom of interest in an other-worldly philosophy, quite unlike the Hellenistic systems, which was eventually to give rise to Neoplatonism.

(ii) Posidonius

Posidonius (see p. 115) has sometimes been regarded as a precursor of Neoplatonism, but with little justification. The subject of innumerable speculations for over a hundred years, Posidonius has concealed his significance more successfully than any ancient thinker of major stature.[1] We know that he was erudite, prolific, extraordinarily many-sided, renowned and influential. On some of his work, in history, geography and philosophy, we are quite well informed. But until 1972 there existed no authoritative and comprehensive collection of all the evidence in which ancient writers refer to Posidonius by name. That gap has now been filled, thanks to the invaluable work of the late Ludwig Edelstein, and of I. G. Kidd, who has completed what Edelstein began.[2] Yet this the latest addition to the Posidonian literature should ideally have been the basis of every previous detailed study. If it had existed in the nineteenth century we might have been spared the endless series of theories about this enigmatic figure. Instead, Posidonius has been found lurking behind countless statements in Cicero, Seneca, and many other writers who never mention his name. Not unlike Pythagoras, Posidonius has turned up to explain anything and everything. Stoic and Platonist, rationalist and mystic, superficial and penetrating, reactionary and original—these are but a few of the alleged contradictions which surround Posidonius.

Whether Posidonius as a philosopher had any highly original ideas is a question to which I would give a provisional negative. But firmer answers are best withheld until Mr. Kidd has published the commentary on Posidonius' fragments which he is now preparing. Even if my provisional answer should prove to be correct it would not undermine the influence and importance of Posidonius. Neither Francis Bacon nor Rousseau was a man who advanced fundamentally new theories of great significance, but few thinkers have exercised more influence on their contemporaries. Originality in any case is a quality which can be assessed in a vast number of different ways. A critical synthesis of existing knowledge may be highly original and a most fruitful source of new discoveries.

Posidonius was a Stoic but a most unusual one. The remarkable thing about him is not what he made of Stoicism but the range of his interests. He settled, as I have already mentioned, in Rhodes (p. 115), but he travelled widely over the Mediterranean world and took careful

[1] Marie Laffranque gives a useful survey of work on Posidonius in her *Posei-donios d'Apamée* (Paris 1964) pp. 1–44.
[2] *Posidonius: vol. i The Fragments* (Cambridge University Press). A second volume of commentary is in preparation. The only previous work which attempts to collect all the evidence was published by J. Bake in 1810. By modern standards this is a very defective collection, though valuable in its day. The fragments of Posidonius' historical and geographical work have already been edited by Felix Jacoby in *Die Fragmente der griechischen Historiker* 87 (Berlin 1926).

note of what he saw. Whether it was the social customs of the Celts in Gaul, the Atlantic tides at Cadiz, apes on the North African coast, rabbits on an island near Naples, Posidonius recorded his observations. Geography in the widest sense, vulcanology, astronomy, meteorology, mineralogy, oceanography, ethnography—he wrote and studied all of them. He compiled a huge series of 'historical' treatises, which will have included most of his geographical data, and the fragments cover events datable between 142 and 93 B.C. Posidonius is said to have started where Polybius left off (146 B.C.), but it is impossible to say how far the younger writer shared his predecessor's favourable attitude towards Roman imperialism. Add to all this Posidonius' work in the conventional subjects of Hellenistic philosophy—physics, logic and ethics—plus the fact that he was a mathematician competent enough to criticize and amend various points of Euclidean geometry, and we are left with the impression of a veritable polymath.

In the range of his studies Posidonius can be compared with Aristotle, Theophrastus and the great Alexandrian librarian, Eratosthenes. But these men flourished at a different time and under different social and political circumstances. Posidonius stands alone in the first century B.C. Why was he interested in so much? This may seem a foolish question but the facts oblige us to ask it. We must take it for granted that he was a man of prodigious ability and energy. But these qualities do not explain the universality of Posidonius' interests. Nor does the equally reasonable assumption that he was indefatigably curious. In Posidonius we find philosophy and science reunited as they had not been since the time of Theophrastus. Was Posidonius acutely conscious of the lack of rapport between Stoicism and the empirical sciences, which had developed so successfully in the early Hellenistic period? Can we say that his universalist procedure was motivated by a dissatisfaction with the narrowness and scholasticism of contemporary philosophy, above all, Stoicism?

I think that these questions are along the right lines. Strabo, himself a Stoic, contrasts Posidonius' interest in 'seeking out causes' with normal Stoic practice (T85). In the same breath Strabo describes Posidonius' activity as Aristotlizing, and adds that 'our school avoids this because of the concealment of causes'. Aristotle regarded 'knowledge of causes' as the basis of science, and Posidonius seems to have agreed with him. Both men devoted great energy to the collection and classification of factual data. But this was not characteristic of the Stoics. While insisting that nothing happens without a cause Chrysip-

pus argued that men cannot discover every cause (*SVF* ii 351; 973).[1]
Posidonius could with justification object that his Stoic predecessors
had used this as a pretext for not trying. He had no quarrel, so far as I
can see, with the basic axioms of Stoic cosmology, though he modified
a number of details.[2] Unlike Panaetius he defended astrology and
divination. But not without evidence. Posidonius' principle was that
theories must be seen to fit the facts, and he rejected orthodox Stoic
doctrines which seemed to him to conflict with this principle.

The case which is best documented is his quarrel with Chrysippus
over the structure of the soul and the causes of passionate emotion.[3]
As we have seen (p. 176), Chrysippus held that the passions are
'excessive impulses' and that there is no such thing as an irrational
faculty of soul. Posidonius objected that there must be such a faculty
if some impulses are 'excessive', for reason could not exceed its own
activity and limits (F34). This is not merely a logical objection.
Posidonius clearly thought that the facts of human behaviour can only
be adequately explained on the assumption that the soul does possess a
purely irrational faculty. If Galen is reliable, Posidonius preferred
Plato's tripartite psychology, with its clear distinction between
rational and irrational faculties, to Chrysippus' monistic conception;
and he also sought to show that Cleanthes and even Zeno were not
supporters of Chrysippus' doctrine (T91). Chrysippus had defended
his views by quotations from the poets and Posidonius cited counter-
instances (F164). He also argued that Chrysippus' psychology made it
impossible to account for human badness (F169). Unless this has its
source within our own nature, which Chrysippus denied, why are
men attracted to pleasure? Why do they experience excessive impulses?
Posidonius rejected Chrysippus' explanation of 'external influences'
and located the 'root' of badness within the soul. Man has 'natural'
affinities to pleasure and worldly success, which compete with his
natural affinity to virtue and knowledge (F160). This 'irrational' side of
human nature is the cause of our passions, and it must be made subservient to reason if man is to attain his goal (F148; 186).

[1] On this point and on Posidonius' methodology and ethics cf. I. G. Kidd,
'Posidonius on Emotions', in *Problems in Stoicism*, ch. 9. I am greatly indebted to
this study.
[2] The assessment of Posidonius' modifications to Stoic physics is a very
controversial subject. I can only say here that I ascribe even less significance to
them than J. M. Rist, whose account of Posidonius, *Stoic Philosophy*, ch. 11, is
more sober than most.
[3] Galen's *De placitis Hippocratis et Platonis* is our source, cf. Edelstein-Kidd,
especially frs. 156–69.

Posidonius recommended various 'irrational' procedures for 'curing' emotional disturbance which cannot be fully enumerated here.[1] They include music and poetry, and the basic assumption is that the 'irrational' can be purged and changed only by means which take account of the 'irrational', which appeal to our pleasures and sensuous experience. Reason itself has no competence to modify our passions. One is reminded forcefully of the place which Plato assigns to poetry, music and other arts in his educational curriculum of the *Republic*; Aristotle's claim that tragedy by the pity and fear which it rouses purges these emotions is equally relevant. Seneca's tragedies, for all their rhetoric and platitudes, may be regarded as a practical Stoic example of the poetic purgative which Posidonius had in mind.

There is much more to Posidonius' psychology and emotional therapy than I can deal with here. But I have said enough perhaps to justify a few general comments. Posidonius' criticism of Chrysippus undoubtedly focuses on a number of basic difficulties. And this tells us something important about Posidonius. Possibly he misinterpreted Chrysippus whose 'rationalism' can be viewed more sympathetically than Posidonius acknowledged (p. 175). But Posidonius was eminently justified in raising questions about it and offering an alternative theory which seemed to explain human behaviour more convincingly. The alternative theory does not appear in essentials to say anything that had not been said before. Plato's psychology seemed to Posidonius to provide a better basis for understanding behaviour than Chrysippus', and he adapted it to suit a framework of Stoic concepts and terminology. This is not eclecticism in any disparaging sense. Rather, Posidonius remains a Stoic, but a Stoic who is prepared to criticize his own school if necessary and to make use of extraneous ideas. We should not suppose that earlier Stoics did not criticize each other. Chrysippus criticized Cleanthes, and no doubt Diogenes of Babylon and Antipater criticized Chrysippus. But, so far as our evidence goes, we are justified in saying that Panaetius and Posidonius show an open-minded attitude towards orthodox dogmas which was not characteristic of earlier Stoicism.

Seneca reports that Posidonius credited wise men with the government of human society in its earliest phase and with technological discoveries in the broadest sense—house-building, metallurgy, weaving, husbandry, fishing and so forth (*Ep.* 90=F284). The first point

---

[1] F168. cf. Kidd (cited on p. 219), pp. 205f.; Edelstein, *The Meaning of Stoicism* (Cambridge, Mass. 1966) pp. 56–9.

is acceptable to Seneca but he rejects the second: the sage has never engaged in such mundane matters. This critical observation brings us back to the universality of Posidonius' interests. If, as I have suggested, Posidonius did not amend the fundamental doctrines of Stoic physics, he certainly showed that a Stoic could advance the understanding of particular phenomena on a very wide front. Earlier Stoics did not share Posidonius' passion for astronomy, mathematics or geography. But he wanted more than vague generalizations. Measuring the size of the earth, calculating the sun's size and distance from the earth, classifying quadrilaterals, these are but a sample of the activities of Posidonius. Mathematics had always been the queen of the sciences in the Greek world and Posidonius' concern to reunite philosophy and science is surely demonstrated by his devotion to mathematics. A contemporary Epicurean, Zeno of Sidon, had attempted to overturn the principles of geometry, and Posidonius attacked him in 'a whole book' (F46). Galen tells us that he was 'trained in geometry and more accustomed than other Stoics to following proofs' (T83). Of course Chrysippus was passionately interested in logic but not, so far as we know, mathematical logic. Galen's intense dislike of Chrysippus may have helped him to emphasize Posidonius' achievement. But Galen was himself greatly interested in geometry, and we must presume that he found an ability in Posidonius which other Stoics had not shown.

Our evidence for Posidonius is extremely fragmentary and only a part of it has been described here. Did he hold some unitary conception of all departments of knowledge? Did he wish to show that all facts are worth ascertaining in a universe rationally determined by immanent providence? Such views a Stoic could hold and justify, and Posidonius was a Stoic first and foremost. One German scholar regarded cosmic 'sympathy' [i.e. the interaction and connexion between all things in the universe] as the unifying theme of Posidonius' philosophical and scientific enterprise.[1] The doctrine is not, as he sought to show, indicative of Posidonius' individuality. But the fact that other Stoics espoused it does not remove its importance in Posidonius. Cicero many times refers to Posidonius' efforts to establish divination: 'He supposes that there are signs in nature of future events' (*De div.* i 129 = F110). 'That the dying foresee the future is established by Posidonius with this example: a Rhodian as he was dying named six of his contemporaries and said which of them would die first, second and so on' (ibid. 64 = F108). Or, what is perhaps the most revealing

[1] Karl Reinhardt, *Kosmos und Sympathie* (Munich 1926).

passage, 'The Stoic Boethus and our own Posidonius have studied the causes of prognostications; and if the causes of these things were not discovered yet the facts themselves could be observed and noted' (*De div.* ii 47=F109). Posidonius' dedication to the study of causes has already been discussed, and here it is related to prediction and the knowledge of facts.

The predictability of events and cosmic 'sympathy' go hand in hand. Posidonius, unlike Panaetius, was strongly committed to both of them. If we wish to find a concept which might explain Posidonius' multifarious activities, cosmic 'sympathy' is perhaps the best candidate. But even if this is correct—and I would not base a Posidonian *system* upon this concept—it does not warrant us in regarding this fascinating man as a mystic or, what would be even less true, as unscientific. The characteristics of mysticism are not attributable to Posidonius, and it is a defining mark of science to determine the causes of things. Undoubtedly Posidonius was too credulous in his commitment to astrology and divination. But he was hardly wrong to postulate a causal connexion between observable phenomena and future events. Like most forecasters however he studied material which was insufficient to establish the actual links.

By any standards Posidonius was one of the outstanding personalities of the Hellenistic world. He exercised influence on many areas of intellectual life for over a hundred years, and Cicero, Seneca and Strabo were all heavily indebted to him. Geminus, a Rhodian follower, wrote a summary of one of Posidonius' scientific works (F18). No doubt there were other disciples. What Aristotle was to Plato, so in a sense was Posidonius to the Stoics. These two men mark the beginning and the end of Hellenistic philosophy. It is unfortunate that we lack the evidence to make a true comparison of their achievements.

(iii) Antiochus

The third individual who must come within the purview of this chapter is Antiochus of Ascalon.[1] A Syrian like Posidonius, Antiochus (born *c.* 130 B.C.) is known to us chiefly through Cicero, who studied under him at Athens in 79/8 B.C., admired him and disseminated his views in the *Academica* and *De finibus*.[2] As a young man Antiochus

---

[1] Ancient texts in which Antiochus is referred to by name have been collected by Georg Luck, *Der Akademiker Antiochus* (Bern and Stuttgart 1953).

[2] For Cicero's presentation of Antiochus' views, cf. H. A. K. Hunt, *The Humanism of Cicero* (Melbourne 1954).

came to Athens where he attended lectures of the sceptical Academic, Philo of Larisa, and two Stoics, Dardanus and Mnesarchus, the latter of whom was a pupil of Panaetius (Cic. *Acad.* ii 69ff.). Under Philo's influence Antiochus became a Sceptic and a most rigorous proponent of the New Academy (Cic. loc. cit.). On the outbreak of the war against Mithridates in 88 Philo left Athens for Rome, and Antiochus probably went with him. If so, Antiochus then had an opportunity to become acquainted with Lucullus, an up-and-coming Roman states-man who owed his rise to the patronage of Sulla. In 87/6 Lucullus was in Alexandria as deputy-quaestor attempting to raise a fleet for Sulla, and according to Cicero (*Acad.* ii 11) Antiochus was with him there. This visit to Alexandria marks a turning-point in Antiochus' career. There he read for the first time two books by Philo which made him very angry (Cic. loc. cit.). They were so much at variance with Philo's earlier views that Antiochus found it difficult to credit their authorship. Philo had attempted in his new work to maintain that the distinction between the Old and the New Academy was erroneous (Cic. *Acad.* i 13f.). The details of his argument escape us, but it seems from Antiochus' reply (*Acad.* ii 13–18) that Philo tried to interpret the 'ancients'—Empedocles, Democritus, Socrates and Plato—as 'sceptics' in a sense compatible with the New Academy.

Why did this annoy Antiochus so much? The answer turns on Philo's reasons for assimilating the two Academies. Arcesilaus and Carneades had insisted that the true nature of things cannot be known. Philo, doubtless in the books which provoked Antiochus' wrath, claimed that 'things can be grasped as they really are' but not by the Stoic criterion of 'cognitive impression' (Sextus, *P.H.* i 235). How then do we grasp things? Philo, it seems, offered no criterion. But he apparently maintained that the absence of a criterion does not entail that things are by nature unknowable. In practice Philo defended the probabilist position of Carneades, but from a weaker theoretical basis. His support for the Old Academy is to be interpreted in this light. He can hardly have defended the positive doctrines of Plato, on the evidence of Antiochus' own mature standpoint. Rather, we must presume that Philo tried to defend his modification of Scepticism by appeal to the 'ancients'. Ignoring Plato's theory of Forms—which was of course challenged by Plato himself in the *Parmenides*—Philo no doubt invoked Plato's support for the view that knowledge is attainable in theory but not in practice (cf. *Acad.* i 46).

Antiochus objected to this on historical grounds. It did justice neither to the Old Academy nor to the New. Plato had a 'most excellent positive doctrine' (*Acad.* ii 15). The New Academy professed nothing of the kind. But Antiochus' renunciation of the New Academy cannot have been prompted by a purely disinterested desire for accurate history. If, as is likely, he had become disenchanted with Scepticism before the appearance of Philo's latest works, the feature which must have annoyed him most would be Philo's attempt to bring Plato and his predecessors under the Sceptical umbrella. Antiochus saw a very sharp distinction between the Old and the New Academy, and in the final stage of his life he devoted himself to restoring, at the expense of Scepticism, what he claimed to be the true Academic tradition.

The two fundamentals of philosophy, according to Antiochus, are the criterion of truth and the chief good or object of desire (Cic. *Acad.* ii 29). Theory of knowledge and ethics provide the basic subject-matter of his investigations. But the most interesting thing about Antiochus is not what he contributed to these topics but the sources of his ideas and his interpretation of the Academic tradition. He included as Academics not only Speusippus, Xenocrates, Polemo and Crantor but also the early Peripatetics, above all Aristotle himself (Cic. *Fin.* v 7). Even more strikingly, he claimed that the Stoics differed from the Peripatetics not in doctrine but in terminology (Cic. *N.D.* i 16), and that Stoicism, as founded by Zeno, was a 'correction' of the Old Academy rather than a new system (*Acad.* i 43). 'Zeno and Arcesilaus were diligent pupils of Polemo; but Zeno, who was older than Arcesilaus and an extremely clever dialectician . . . set out to remodel the system' (*Acad.* i 35).

Although Antiochus claimed to be an Academic, most of his doctrines conform to the 'remodelled system of Zeno's'. He took over and defended at length the Stoic theory of knowledge (Cic. *Acad.* ii 16–39). His ethics is primarily Stoic, though we shall observe a number of modifications in this field, and his philosophy of nature is more Stoic than anything else (*Acad.* i 26–30). How are we to evaluate Antiochus' conception of the Academic tradition? Cicero, who acts as the spokesman for the New Academy in his *Academica* ii, charges Antiochus with failing to follow his own 'ancestors' (Plato, Xenocrates, Aristotle) and never diverging a foot's length from Chrysippus (ii 142f.). The context is polemical—a Sceptical attack on dogmatic philosophers by reference to their disagreements—but history seems to be largely on Cicero's side. Neither Platonists nor Peripatetics defended a theory of knowledge based upon anything which resembles the 'cognitive impression'. This is a peculiarly Stoic doctrine. In ethics however Antiochus' main divergence from Stoicism, though less significant than his agreements, is compatible with one aspect of Peripatetic theory and also with a doctrine ascribed to Polemo.

The Stoics held that virtue by itself is sufficient to constitute happiness and nothing else makes any positive contribution to this goal. Antiochus, distinguishing in a non-Stoic manner degrees of well-being, argued that virtue is the necessary and sufficient condition of a happy life but not 'the happiest life' (Cic. *Tusc.* v 21ff.). As we have already seen, Antiochus rejected the Stoic distinction between 'the good' and 'the preferable' (p. 196). The value of good health, riches, reputation and so forth, though slight by comparison with that of virtue, is sufficient, in Antiochus' judgment, to make a virtuous life which is embellished by such things happier than one which lacks everything save virtue (*Acad.* i 22). Aristotle, similarly, observes that certain external goods disfigure happiness if they are absent (*E.N.* i 1099a31ff.). Some things, he writes, are needed as instruments for the performance of virtuous actions; others are 'adornments' which by their presence or absence can augment or detract from happiness. Subsequently Aristotle qualifies this assertion, and he can be read as adopting a position on external goods which is virtually equivalent to that of the Stoics.[1] But unlike them he regarded 'good' as a term which has multiple uses. Antiochus' claim that the Stoics and Peripatetics agree in substance and differ in terminology is superficially a fair comment on their respective attitudes towards external goods.

The position which Antiochus defended is also attributed to Polemo both in Cicero (*Fin.* iv 51) and elsewhere (Clement *Strom.* ii 22). This Academic philosopher, as I have already mentioned, is a most elusive figure (p. 112), and much of our meagre evidence about him is derived from Antiochus (cf. Cic. *Fin.* v 14). But there is no doubt that Zeno was personally acquainted with Polemo, and it is Polemo's specification of 'the natural starting-points' which, again on Antiochus' authority, Zeno is said to have inherited (*Fin.* iv 45). This statement may not be special pleading. In the *Academica* (i 19) Varro who is giving Antiochus' interpretation of Academic ethics says: 'They sought the subject-matter of good conduct from Nature and said that Nature must be obeyed, and that the ultimate good must be looked for in Nature

---

[1] I have discussed this point in *Bulletin of the Institute of Classical Studies* 15 (1968) 74–6.

alone. And they postulated that to have obtained all things which accord with Nature in mind, body and livelihood is the ultimate object of desire and the chief good.' This is Antiochus' position and what differentiates it from Stoicism is the characteristic assignment of positive value to bodily and external goods as well as virtue. As a summary of Platonic or Aristotelian ethics, as we understand these, it reads very oddly. But we cannot rule out the possibility that Polemo himself expressed such views as valid Academic doctrine. If he did, it would make the historical basis of Antiochus' interpretation and criticism of Stoic ethics more intelligible, though hardly sufficient to justify his view of the Stoa as simply an offshoot of the Academy. Cicero himself seems to have recognized the historical unreliability of such a thesis.

Historical reliability however is not the same thing as philosophical judgment. In order to appreciate Antiochus' interpretation of the Academic tradition we must remember that Stoicism had been a flourishing system for over two hundred years. For the same period the Academy had devoted itself to Scepticism. The Peripatetic school ceased to be influential after the death of Strato, whose devotion to science did not commend itself to Antiochus (*Acad.* i 34). In the first part of the first century B.C. Stoicism had more conceptual affinities with Platonism and Aristotelianism than any other philosophical movement. If Antiochus wished to combat Scepticism with the help of the current system which had most in common with the Academic tradition he had to turn to the Stoics. Under the guidance of Panaetius and Posidonius leading Stoics had begun to assimilate a number of Platonic and Aristotelian ideas. Platonism, as expounded by Plato's immediate successors, was dead. But interest in Plato's writings seems to have increased in the second century B.C., and a new stimulus to the study of the 'ancients' was to be provided, shortly after Antiochus' time, by the edition of Aristotle's treatises brought out by Andronicus of Rhodes.

Antiochus regarded the Stoics as the heirs of the Platonic and Aristotelian tradition. Within his loose terms of reference he was justified in doing so. But, as Cicero remarks, he was far more of a Stoic than a Platonist or Peripatetic. Whatever Antiochus knew of Plato, Aristotle and their immediate successors—and we must assume that he knew a good deal—he chose to make use of only those points which seemed to him clearly superior to the Stoics' views. His requirement that the highest good must take account of bodily well-being and things of material value is the most significant deviation from Stoicism, and he regarded the Stoics' 'indifference' to these as a contradiction of their own principles (Cic. *Fin.* iv 37–41). He also recognized correctly and seems to have disapproved of other 'innovations' by Zeno (*Acad.* i 35–9). The equality of all wrongful acts was 'most strenuously' rejected by him (*Acad.* ii 133), and he probably rejected the Stoics' rationalization of the passions and their refusal to admit an irrational faculty of mind.

In the realm of natural philosophy, judging from Varro's summary in Cicero (*Acad.* i 24–9), Antiochus interpreted the Academic tradition in almost exclusively Stoic terms. A passing reference to Aristotle's fifth element—the aether which is the material of the heavenly bodies— is the chief non-Stoic item, and it contributes nothing to the main train of thought. Later, Zeno is said, correctly, to have excluded the fifth element, and his rejection of incorporeal substances is also mentioned (39). But these play no overt part in the summary of 'Academic' physics.

The most puzzling subject is Antiochus' theory of knowledge. On the evidence of *Academica* ii he committed himself wholeheartedly to the Stoic doctrine of 'cognitive impression' and defended this, with some interesting arguments—many of them no doubt drawn from Stoic writers—against the criticism of the Academic Sceptics. Towards the end of the book, where Cicero is speaking as a Sceptic against Antiochus, he outlines a number of tests of truth advanced by various philosophers, concluding with Plato: 'Plato held that the entire criterion of truth and truth itself is independent of opinions and the senses and belongs to thinking and the intellect. Surely our friend Antiochus does not approve of any of these doctrines?' (142). Even if this is a rhetorical objection it does not undermine the fact that Antiochus' defence of the 'cognitive impression' commits him to the thesis that sense-perception can be distinguished as true or false, and that 'true impressions' are the basis of knowledge.

Yet in *Academica* i the Academics and Peripatetics are said to have regarded the intellect as the 'judge of things; because it alone perceives that which is always simple and just what it is' (30). Varro then adds: 'They call this "form", a name already given to it by Plato'; and he goes on to report Plato's distinction between the intellect and the senses, whose objects are always unstable. Here clearly we are a very long way from Stoicism. Subsequently, Aristotle is criticized for 'weakening' the theory of forms (33), and on the evidence of this context we would have every reason for supposing that Antiochus supported some version of this Platonic doctrine.

There seems to be a fundamental inconsistency, but it may not have been too great for Antiochus to swallow. The Stoics, as I have already noted, recognized 'rational' as well as 'sense' impressions. The 'general concepts', whose basis is sense-perception, are also included as a criterion of truth in Stoic theory. Further, the Stoics distinguished mere instances of accurate perception or 'grasping' from 'knowledge', which is 'secure and unshakeable'. And they also made their own use of Plato's distinction between knowledge and belief (p. 129). Antiochus himself, when defending the 'cognitive impression', speaks of the 'intellect itself as the source of sensations', and he seems to have regarded the acquisition of valid general concepts as a necessary condition of accurate perception (*Acad.* ii 30). I am not sure whether this can be called fully orthodox Stoicism. If Antiochus is describing what the Stoics called 'knowledge' then his emphasis on general concepts is orthodox. But as I understand the 'cognitive impression' in Stoicism, this does not require general concepts as a *test* of its validity (p. 128). Their function is to classify the objects of perception and to furnish material for the formation of non-empirical notions. However this may be, Antiochus' stress on intellect in his defence of the 'cognitive impression' is striking, and sufficient to suggest that he tried to marry up this Stoic concept with what he understood to be the Platonic theory of Forms. The Forms are not of course concepts, much less concepts derived from sense-perception. They are the ultimate realities which exist apart from our thoughts. But Seneca knew an interpretation of the doctrine which turned the Forms into the thoughts of God (*Ep.* 65, 7). Several scholars have suggested Antiochus as the source of this idea, and it is a promising hypothesis. The Stoics spoke of 'seminal principles' which God employs in his determination of the universe. Antiochus might well have interpreted these as Platonic Forms which men can intuit by their perception of particular objects.

Compared with Posidonius Antiochus was a thinker of minor stature.[1] His blend of the Stoic and Academic traditions lacks rigour, and it brings out the best in neither of them. But it would be a mistake to dismiss Antiochus as uninteresting or ineffective. As a renegade Sceptic he was well equipped to draw attention to theoretical and

---

[1] A much more detailed assessment of Antiochus will be found in J. Dillon's *The Middle Platonists*, a forthcoming volume in the Classical Life and Letters series.

practical difficulties in Scepticism. He succeeded in turning the Academy back towards a positivist philosophy, and when Scepticism was revived and supplemented by Aenesidemus (p. 75) it took the name of Pyrrhonism. Antiochus' criticism of Stoic ethics fastens upon genuine problems, and his recognition that human nature needs more than virtue for its perfect satisfaction is particularly important. More significant than his Academic teacher, Philo, Antiochus helped to prepare the ground however lightly for the revival of Platonism. This movement was to gather momentum over the next three hundred years until it culminated in the mystical and highly elaborate metaphysics of Plotinus.

(*iv*) *Cicero*

It would be inappropriate to conclude this discussion of later developments in Hellenistic philosophy without a further word about Cicero whose writings provide us with so much of our evidence.[1] Cicero never laid claim to any special expertise in philosophy, but no Roman of his time, with the possible exception of Varro, was better equipped to write about it. As a young man Cicero came into contact with leading Stoic, Epicurean and Academic philosophers who fostered in him an enthusiasm for philosophy which was by no means characteristic of ambitious Romans in the first century B.C. Rhetoric was the foundation of education for a young Roman with a public career to make, but Cicero combined the study of rhetoric with philosophy in the Greek fashion. With the help of his friends and voracious reading Cicero maintained his philosophical interests throughout a life crowded with activities of a very different kind. But it was not until 45 B.C., when he was over sixty, that Cicero took up philosophical writing on a large scale. These were the years of his greatest political disillusionment and personal unhappiness. Civil wars had finally destroyed the Republic and his beloved daughter, Tullia, was dead. In these circumstances Cicero found some personal consolation in a great burst of literary activity. The *Academica*, the *De finibus*, the *Tusculan Disputations*, the *De natura deorum*, the *De divinatione*, the *De fato*, the *De officiis*, and short popular works like *De amicitia* were all composed within less than two years.

As he makes plain on many occasions, Cicero had strong personal reasons for devoting this time to philosophy. But they were not his

---

[1] A. E. Douglas gives a helpful account of Cicero's philosophical writings in *Cicero*, Greece and Rome New Surveys in the Classics, no. 2 (Oxford 1968).

only motive. In the prefaces to his philosophical writings Cicero justifies his activity at some length. This extract from the *De natura deorum* may be taken as representative:

> If anyone wonders why I am entrusting these reflections to writing at this stage of my life, I can answer very easily. With no public activity to occupy me and the political situation making a dictatorship inevitable, I thought that it was an act of patriotism to expound philosophy to my fellow-country-men, judging it to be greatly to the honour and glory of the state to have such a lofty subject expressed in Latin literature (i 7).

Cicero was not a man who underrated his own achievements, but it would be a mistake to dismiss such references to patriotism as smug or insincere. Cicero genuinely believed that he was doing Latin speakers a service in making Greek philosophy available to them, and he was right. Before his time, it seems, Epicureanism was virtually the only philosophical subject which had attracted the attention of Roman writers and the works of the Epicureans, whom Cicero dismisses with such contempt (*Tusc.* iv 6–7), have vanished without trace. (Lucretius' poem, which Cicero never refers to in his philosophical writings, may not have been in general circulation at this time.) Cicero cast his net much wider. Professing to be an adherent of the moderate scepticism of Philo of Larisa, Cicero surveyed and criticized those doctrines of the Stoics, Epicureans and Antiochus of Ascalon which were probably most familiar to Greek readers and which he himself regarded as the most important. He is much less comprehensive than he claims to be. Ethics and theory of knowledge are treated in considerable detail. Physical theories are summarized only in broad outline and logic is scarcely handled at all. To some extent this reflects the activities of philosophers in the early first century B.C., but it is clear that Posidonius, to take only one example, had many speculative interests which find no mention in Cicero.

From a modern point of view Cicero's philosophical writings have other shortcomings. They are often verbose, sometimes obscure; and the subtlety of Greek thought tends to dissipate itself in his long periodic sentences. But we should judge Cicero by what he achieved and not what we should like him to have achieved. He had no ex-pectations that the philosophically expert would read his work in preference to Greek originals. His philosophy is largely derivative and acknowledged to be so. But Cicero had far more understanding of the Hellenistic systems than he has sometimes been credited with, and he was quite capable of pursuing a difficult train of thought rigorously. The fact that he wrote in Latin was itself a very considerable achievement, for he had to find new means of expressing ideas for which Latin was naturally ill equipped. He could not overcome this problem with complete success, but he pioneered the way to the later development of Latin as a highly effective philosophical language. And the sceptical criticism which he directed against dogmatic theorists, however unoriginal it may be, marks a significant contrast with Seneca's approach to philosophy and that of later Roman writers.

It would however be wrong to give the impression that Cicero was a rigorous sceptic. As a jurist he was well fitted to set out the pros and cons of a particular position, but there can be no doubt that the humane Stoicism of *De officiis*, his most influential work, represents views which he himself approved. It is the bearing of philosophy on human conduct which matters most to Cicero. Nor should one overlook the importance of his earlier political writings, *De republica* and *De legibus*, in which the Stoic concepts of natural law and justice are expounded. It was largely due to Cicero that such ideas gained the support of Roman lawyers and the Roman Church Fathers who gave them a new foundation in western culture.[1]

[1] cf. Gerard Watson, 'The Natural Law and Stoicism', in *Problems in Stoicism*.

CHAPTER SIX

Hellenistic Philosophy
and the Classical Tradition

CICERO'S influence on later antiquity and more recent times is just one aspect of the classical tradition to which Hellenistic philosophy contributed. The history of Stoicism, Scepticism and Epicureanism begins in fourth-century Greece, but it extends over the Mediterranean world through the Roman empire and into the Europe of the Renaissance and beyond. The influence of Plato and Aristotle has proved to be more profound and persistent, but in the widest sense less pervasive. Everyone has some notion of what it means to be stoical, sceptical and epicurean. First through Cicero and Seneca, later through Plutarch, Lucretius, Diogenes Laertius and Sextus Empiricus, the main ideas of Hellenistic thought were recovered in the Renaissance. These were the years when men looked to Hellenistic philosophy for moral guidance and for insight into the religious and scientific controversies of the time. The Middle Ages and the last two centuries, for clearly different reasons, are less noteworthy. But many of the ideas discussed in this book, especially Stoic concepts, have exercised a continuing rather than an intermittent influence.

The subject is so large and difficult to control that only an outline of some of its most significant features can be given here. It must be emphasized at the outset that an adequate critical and historical approach to the interpretation of Hellenistic philosophy has only been developed within the last hundred years. In this chapter I am concerned primarily with the writers and scholars who made Stoicism, Scepticism and Epicureanism a notable part of the classical tradition. We may take first the contribution of Hellenistic philosophy to thought and literature in the Roman empire, and second, its influence on the sixteenth and seventeenth centuries.

In the Roman world during the first two Christian centuries Stoicism was the dominant philosophy among educated pagans. The reasons for its success are not difficult to find. Stoicism was able to accommodate many traditional Roman attitudes about human excellence, and it also provided them with a theoretical basis in place of, or rather in addition to, custom and historical examples. The life and death of Cato the Younger showed what it might mean to be a Roman *and* a Stoic. Venerated by republicans for his patriotic suicide at Utica, Cato became the object of a long series of panegyrics. He was eulogized by Lucan in his epic poem *Bellum civile*, and undoubtedly helped to popularize Stoicism among Roman aristocrats during the first century A.D. The so-called Stoic opposition to the principate at this time has its sources in political conservatism and senatorial independence rather than moral theory. But it cannot be a coincidence that some of the most outspoken critics of the emperors were Stoics. Yet in the middle of the next century a Stoic, Marcus Aurelius, sat on the imperial throne. This is a remarkable development, though it must be admitted that Marcus was a Stoic as much by temperament as by conviction.

It is the Stoicism of Seneca, Epictetus and Marcus which has had greatest influence on later writers, and this is first and last a practical moral doctrine. 'The true philosopher,' writes Seneca, 'is the teacher of humanity' (*Ep.* 89, 13). In his best prose work, the *Moral letters to Lucilius*, Seneca sought to make good this claim by putting Stoicism to work in the moral education of his correspondent. The *Moral letters* are not a Stoic tract; Seneca frequently quotes an Epicurean maxim and he refers to other philosophers, most notably Plato. But the Stoics are *nostri*, 'our own philosophers', and Seneca deals in some detail with a number of central Stoic doctrines. Advice and exhortation, however, are his main concern. Stoicism is valued for the benefits which its principles can confer on a man's state of mind and the conduct of his life. Seneca has little time for logic and purely theoretical knowledge. 'To desire to know more than is sufficient is a form of intemperance. This pursuit of liberal studies makes men wearisome, wordy, tactless and complacent; they do not learn what they need because they have already learnt things which are superfluous' (*Ep.* 88, 37). Stoicism of course had always stressed the relevance of its subject-matter to practical ethics. But Seneca and the other Roman Stoics gave a more restricted and less rigorous interpretation to 'philosophy' than their Greek predecessors.

The process of toning down the rigid intellectualism of Stoicism had begun with Panaetius. Roman Stoics like Seneca and Epictetus followed his lead with their emphasis on progress rather than perfection, and concessions to human fallibility. Stoicism becomes warmer and more responsive to the emotional side of human nature. But it ceases to be an elaborate conceptual system. In the first century A.D. Stoics and Cynics came closer together. Cynicism seems to have been relatively insignificant during the second and first centuries B.C., but the literature of the early Roman empire indicates a strong revival of the movement. A Cynic called Demetrius, who castigated wealth and luxury, was admired by Seneca, and an idea of what it meant to be a genuine Cynic at this time—there were many charlatans—can be gained from some of the published speeches of Dio Chrysostom (A.D. 40–after 112). Dio began his life in prosperous circumstances, and won acclaim as an orator and sophist in Greece. Banished by Domitian for alleged complicity in a political conspiracy, he spent fourteen years wandering in the Balkans and Asia Minor before he was restored to favour by Nerva. He lived by taking menial work and perhaps also by begging. The themes of his speeches were the traditional Cynic programme, and Diogenes figures as a model in several of them. Dio saw his rôle as a spiritual doctor who cures mental ill-health by showing that happiness comes from self-sufficiency and strength of character, not property, reputation or bodily pleasure.

The mendicant way of life and the value which Cynics placed upon poverty and freedom of speech or, in some cases, squalid appearance and insulting manners, were frowned upon by the Stoics. But Epictetus, although he criticized the parade of 'shamelessness' in Cynicism, saw the 'true Cynic' as 'a messenger sent to men from Zeus to show them that they have gone astray over things which are good and bad' (iii, 22, 23). A Stoic like Epictetus did not adopt the external characteristics of Cynicism—preaching in the streets and travelling from town to town with staff and satchel—but the inner freedom which Cynicism sought to inculcate is one of his favourite themes. Equally Cynic is his emphasis on hardiness and asceticism.

It is not only the moral earnestness of Seneca and Epictetus which has influenced those who call Roman Stoicism a religion. The description imports some misleading connotations, but it would be insensitive to overlook the religious language and feeling in contexts of Seneca, Epictetus and Marcus where they speak of the 'universe' or 'nature' or 'god'. None of this is inconsistent with earlier Stoicism, and Cleanthes' verses show that the system could provide a basis for genuine religious experience. But among Stoics of the Hellenistic world Cleanthes stands out as exceptional, even allowing for the deficiencies of our evidence. Religious aspirations are notoriously difficult to define, but recorded pagan thought during the early Roman empire has a religious dimension which marks it off from philosophy in the Hellenistic world. Plutarch is typical of the later period in this respect. Stoics had traditionally attempted to harmonize their teaching on Nature and God with the divinities of Greek and Roman religion. But we find few traces of this in the writings of the Roman Stoics. Their conception of a supreme being is practically if not formally monotheist. Epictetus calls God the father of mankind. In Seneca God is a somewhat elastic conception, but he has no doubts about divine benevolence and the personal interest of God in humanity. 'God approaches men—no, the relation is closer: he enters men. Without God no mind can be good. In the bodies of men divine seeds have been scattered' (*Ep.* 73, 16). Such statements could not fail to make an impression on Christian writers, and there was much else in the Stoicism of Seneca and Epictetus which they found congenial and instructive.

The Stoa continued to exist formally until 529 when Justinian closed the four philosophical schools at Athens. Its effective life was over three centuries earlier. By this time Christianity was spreading rapidly throughout the empire, and the revival of Platonism among pagan intellectuals also threatened the survival of Stoicism as an independent philosophical movement. Plotinus (205–70) incorporated Stoic and Aristotelian concepts in his new interpretation of the Platonic tradition, and Neoplatonism became a significant rival to Christianity in the fourth century. But it was the Church which helped above all to keep Stoic ideas in circulation, and Stoicism in its turn had an important influence on the Christian Fathers, in association with the still more notable influence of Platonism.

To an early Father, like Clement of Alexandria (*c.* 150–216), it was essential to demonstrate the superiority of Christianity to Greek philosophy. But Clement's official denunciations of pagan philosophers are much less striking than the positive use which he makes of Stoic and Platonic doctrines. He assimilates Stoic *logos* to 'the word of God', approves of the suppression of emotional impulses, and while teaching salvation as the basis of ethics sees the life of the Christian as 'a collection of rational actions, that is, the invarying practice of the teachings of the Word, which we call faith' (*Paid.* i 102, 4 Stählin). The sinner, like the Stoic 'fool', is ignorant. And we find Clement using a Stoic style of argument to prove that man is loved by God (*SVF* ii 1123). Clement was steeped in Greek literature, and the Stoic doctrines which he refers to or incorporates are part of the orthodox tradition. Of all the Christian Fathers he is the most valuable as a source for Stoic theory.

Among the Roman Church Fathers the same equivocal attitude towards Stoicism recurs. Tertullian stresses the differences between a philosopher and a Christian, but he calls Seneca 'often one of us' (*saepe noster*). The legend of Seneca as a Christian convert probably developed only in the late Middle Ages, but he was sufficiently read and esteemed by Christians in the fourth century to make it seem reasonable that he knew and corresponded with St. Paul.[1] The letters which purport to be from Seneca are first cited by St. Jerome in 392. They greatly helped to propagate the notion of Seneca as a convert to Christianity. After Greek texts ceased to be widely available in the western part of the empire Cicero's *De officiis* also helped to keep knowledge of Stoic moral theory alive. Epictetus' *Manual* took the place of Seneca in the east, and traces of his work have been found in Arabic texts.

The fortunes of Epicureanism in the empire have already been briefly surveyed (pp. 17ff.). Up to the year 200 it probably remained the main rival to Stoicism, but its influence on literature and intellectual thought was very much weaker. Epicureanism was always an inward-looking movement in antiquity, and under the later empire it probably flourished more in the eastern provinces than the Romanized west. So far as our evidence goes, the school produced no individual at this time who stands comparison with Seneca or Epictetus. Throughout its history Epicureanism remained predominantly the philosophy of Epicurus himself, and his name is invoked by later writers far more frequently than Zeno, the founder of Stoicism. Knowledge of Epicurean doctrines was widespread, and the space which Diogenes Laertius allots to Epicurus in his *Lives and doctrines of the eminent philosophers*, though it does not prove Diogenes an Epicurean, suggests a third-century audience with considerable interest in the system. It is particularly noteworthy that Diogenes abandons his normal practice of chatty anecdotes or potted summary in recording three of Epicurus' own works along with the *Principal doctrines*.

Plutarch is the most voluminous pagan critic of Epicureanism and Stoicism alike. The Christian Fathers were also hostile to Epicurus, but less so than one might have expected. Both Lactantius and Augustine refer frequently to Epicurus, and they sometimes give him qualified

---

[1] cf. A. Momigliano, 'Note sulla leggenda del cristianesimo di Seneca', *Rivista storica italiana* 62 (1950) 325–44.

approval. Unlike most of the Renaissance critics of Epicureanism they understood enough of the system to realize that Epicurus was not an advocate of unbridled sensuality. But Epicurus' theology and his insistence on the mortality of the soul were sufficient grounds in themselves to rouse the opposition of the Church.

Intellectual life during the later Roman empire assumed very diverse forms. It is important to remember that scholarship existed alongside superstition, and that science was not suddenly ousted by religion. Galen, Ptolemy, Plotinus, Proclus, and the long line of distinguished commentators on Aristotle from Alexander of Aphrodisias to Simplicius—these were men whose writings helped to preserve and extend the classical heritage of Greek philosophy and science. But it was a tradition which never gained a firm hold in Rome, and from the fourth century A.D. the Byzantine world became the main repository of Greek learning and literature for the next thousand years.

The revival of Scepticism at Alexandria, which began with Aenesidemus (see p. 76) and culminated in the works of Sextus Empiricus about the end of the second century, must also be regarded as an episode in the intellectual history of the eastern empire. Sextus' detailed presentation of sceptical arguments and his criticism of the dogmatists implies a conception of philosophy which was very different from the moralizing preoccupations of Roman writers. Scepticism was never a popular movement in the ancient world, and Sextus Empiricus exercised far more influence in the later Renaissance than he seems to have enjoyed at any other time. But two of the Latin Fathers, Lactantius and Augustine, were familiar with Cicero's *Academica*, and it was largely from their very different assessments of Academic scepticism that men in the Middle Ages derived some knowledge of sceptical ideas. Lactantius found the Academic criticism of all positivist philosophy a valuable beginning for Christian belief. This position is expounded in the third book of his *Divinae institutiones*, and it prefigures the way in which many Renaissance thinkers used scepticism as a basis for fideism. St. Augustine on the other hand attacked scepticism in his *Contra academicos*, an early work written in 386. The answer to scepticism for Augustine was the Christian revelation, but his critical treatise, with its approval of Plato, does not conceal the fact that scepticism made a strong impression upon him as a young man.

Cicero, Seneca and the Latin Patristic writers were the principal sources through which western Europe in the Middle Ages attained some knowledge of Stoic moral thought. The number of ninth- and tenth-century manuscripts of Seneca gives a proof of the interest his work aroused, and many of Cicero's philosophical works were known at this time, though the great period of their influence began with Petrarch and other Italian humanists. William of Conches in the twelth century wrote a *Moralium dogma philosophorum* which he based largely on Cicero's *De officiis* and Seneca. These were the favourite ancient authors of Roger Bacon and some other notable medieval writers. But it was not until the Renaissance that Hellenistic philosophy reappeared as a major formative influence on western thought. By the beginning of the sixteenth century a combination of complex circumstances—they include the Reformation, the new humanist curriculum which emphasized rhetoric and moral philosophy rather than scholastic logic and theology, availability of printed editions, and the rediscovery of Plato and other Greek authors—contributed to more intense study of familiar writers such as Cicero and Seneca and the immediate popularity of many others who had been newly recovered: Epictetus, Plutarch and Diogenes Laertius are those most relevant to our main theme. The vogue of Lucretius and Sextus Empiricus came rather later.

Renaissance scholars were highly eclectic in their approach to ancient philosophy. Through Nicholas of Cusa, Marsilio Ficino and Pico della Mirandola Neoplatonism experienced a revival in Italy during the fifteenth century, and later, as we shall see, there were neo-Stoics, Epicureans and Sceptics. But it is generally misleading to apply such descriptions to sixteenth-century figures. They read Greek and Latin authors principally for moral edification, and Stoic, Platonic and Aristotelian ideas were frequently brought together and combined with Christian doctrine. In *The education of a Christian prince* Erasmus wrote: 'To be a philosopher and to be a Christian is synonymous in fact if not in name', and the philosopher might be Plato or Cicero, Seneca or Socrates.[1] Stoicism cannot be easily isolated from other constituents of Renaissance culture. But its importance at this time is conspicuous, and certain facts can be stated without undue danger of over-simplification.

Seneca enjoyed an enormous reputation, and the other principal sources of Stoic ideas were Cicero, Epictetus and Plutarch. Diogenes Laertius had been known through the Latin translation of Ambrogio

[1] Trans. L. K. Born (New York 1936) p. 150.

Traversari since the early fifteenth century,[1] but Diogenes' important summary of Greek Stoic doctrines was unpalatable compared with the rhetorical elegance and practical moralizing of the Roman Stoics. Erasmus, though he did not share Calvin's admiration for Seneca, published an edition in 1527, followed by a second two years later, which was reprinted several times before 1580. Calvin himself, who called Seneca 'a master of ethics', wrote a commentary on the *De clementia*. Epictetus was first edited complete by Trincavelli in 1535. The *Manual* was already widely known through Politian's translation, first published in 1495, and by 1540 it had been printed in Greek with Latin translation at Strasburg, Venice, Nuremberg, Basle, and Paris. The first edition of Marcus Aurelius appeared at Heidelberg in 1558.

The Stoics' emphasis on the rationality of human nature is frequently reflected by Renaissance writers. More's Utopians define virtue as life according to nature and the 'natural' life is interpreted in Stoic terms as one 'which in desiring and refusing things is ruled by reason' (pp. 121f. ed. Goitrim). Guillaume Budé drew on Seneca's *De tranquillitate animi* for his own work, *De contemptu rerum fortuitarum* published in 1520. Another sixteenth-century English work to which Stoicism made an important contribution is Richard Hooker's *Of the laws of ecclesiastical polity* (1594). But there were more notable attempts to harmonize Stoicism with Christianity. The Belgian humanist, Justus Lipsius, whose greatest scholarly work was an edition of Tacitus, projected a large commentary on Seneca which he did not live to complete. His interest in Stoicism had been declared in 1583 when he published *De constantia*, a work which proved extremely popular, and the completed parts of his Seneca commentary ran through five editions between 1605 and 1652. They include two essays on Stoicism, *Manuductio ad Stoicam philosophiam* and *Physiologiae Stoicorum*. In the latter work Lipsius gives an analysis of Stoic metaphysics and, where possible, he seeks to justify the Stoics by quoting biblical references. The *Manuductio* likewise is not an impartial account of Stoic ethics. Lipsius was concerned to show that Stoicism, by which he means chiefly the moral doctrines in Seneca and Epictetus, can be regarded as a valuable supplement to Christian faith. But in pursuing this aim Lipsius opened the door to natural religion

---

[1] R. Sabbadini refers to an earlier Latin version now lost which was in circulation from the tenth to the thirteenth centuries, *Le scoperte dei codici Latini e Greci* II (Florence 1914) pp. 262f. Mrs. A. C. Griffiths kindly drew my attention to this and several other points which I have incorporated in this chapter.

and secular morality. Holding as he did that a man imitates God by living in accordance with reason, Lipsius gave just the kind of rationalist interpretation of Christianity which men like Erasmus and Montaigne found objectionable.

Lipsius' Stoicism finds an interesting parallel in the work of a French contemporary, Guillaume du Vair. A lawyer by training, du Vair wrote three works designed to show the value of Stoicism as a philosophy of life: *La philosophie morale des Stoïques*, translated into English by Charles Cotton in 1664; *De la constance et consolation ès calamités publiques*, translated by Andrew Comt in 1602 with the title, *A buckler against adversitie*; and *La sainte philosophie*. Du Vair acknowledged that Stoic rationality must be augmented by faith and that perfection requires the help of God. But he traced the sources of moral error to false judgments, emphasized the need to free the soul of passionate emotions, and defined the good for man as 'a healthful reason, that is, virtue'.

Judging by printed editions of Seneca, Epictetus and Marcus Aurelius, Stoicism in the Renaissance was at its most popular in France, Germany and Italy between 1590 and 1640.[1] But its influence continued to be strong over the next hundred years. In his *Discourse of the pastoral care* (1692) Gilbert Burnet recommended the clergy to read Epictetus and Marcus Aurelius, whose works 'contain such Instructions that one cannot read them too often nor repass them too frequently in his thoughts'.[2] In England under the reign of Queen Anne a remarkable secular interest in Cato developed. Admiration for this Roman Stoic saint was nothing new. Through Plutarch's *Life* and other ancient sources Cato became one of the outstanding heroes of the Renaissance, but in early eighteenth-century England he was used as a symbol of political 'liberty' as well as moral virtue. Of Addison's tragedy, *Cato* (1713), Pope wrote to John Caryll, 'I question if any play has ever conduced so immediately to morals as this.'[3] Whigs and Tories alike claimed support for their principles from Cato, and Jonathan Swift seems to have consciously modelled himself on the Roman Stoic.[4] The English Augustan writers particularly admired the

---

[1] cf. J. Eymard d'Angers, 'Le Renouveau du stoicisme au XVI et au XVII siècle', *Actes du 7 Congrès Guillaume Budé* (Paris 1964) pp. 122–55.

[2] Quoted by M. L. Clarke, *Classical Education in Britain 1500–1900* (Cambridge 1959) p. 169.

[3] *Works* ed. Elwin and Courthope, vol. vi (London 1871) p. 182.

[4] cf. J. W. Johnson, *The Formation of English Neo-classical Thought* (Princeton 1967) pp. 101f.

Roman Republic and Cato provided a focus for their neo-classical ideals.

The philosophical influence of Stoicism, as I have already mentioned (p. 208), is evident in Spinoza and Kant. Two English philosophers whose work is worth studying from this point of view are the Earl of Shaftesbury and Bishop Butler.

Epicureanism had to wait longer than Stoicism for its own renaissance. The religious, moral and intellectual currents of the sixteenth century were largely against a philosophy which contained hedonism and empiricism as two principal features, and the usage of 'Epicure' to denote sensualist dates from this time. It is also worth observing that Lucretius unlike Seneca was virtually unknown in the Middle Ages. The oldest manuscript (Oblongus) dates from the ninth century, but it was Poggio's discovery of a text of Lucretius in 1417 which made the poet available to the Renaissance. The first printed edition appeared at Brescia in 1473, and Lambinus' important text and commentary was published in 1564. But it was not until 1675 that a Latin edition of Lucretius came out of England. Interest in Epicureanism and Lucretius grew more rapidly in Italy, France and Germany, but Laurentius Valla's sympathetic treatment (*De voluptate ac vero bono,* 1431) was exceptional before the seventeenth century, and Valla had not read Lucretius.

The man who did most to make Epicureanism respectable and who pioneered an important revival of interest in it was Pierre Gassendi. Gassendi (1592–1655) was a Catholic priest who ended his career as professor of mathematics at the Royal College in Paris. Like Descartes, Gassendi was a vigorous opponent of Aristotelian scholasticism, but the direction of his dissent was very different from Descartes'. In common with many of his French contemporaries Gassendi was influenced by ancient scepticism, and his 'Pyrrhonist' leanings helped to determine his search for a criterion of truth in the senses and not the rationalist's *cogito*.

In 1647 Gassendi published his *De vita et moribus Epicuri,* which he followed two years later with *Animadversiones in decimum librum Diogenis Laertii et philosophiae Epicuri syntagma.* The *De vita* was the most significant work of neo-Epicureanism. In it Gassendi sought to defend Epicurus' life and teaching against ancient and modern criticism. Most of the principal Epicurean doctrines were well understood by Gassendi and his commentary on the tenth book of Diogenes Laertius is a considerable work of scholarship. But Gassendi did not approach Epicurus as a disinterested scholar. Critical of Aristotle and Descartes alike, Gassendi found in Epicureanism a system which he could turn to good account in the dawning scientific enlightenment. As a Christian however he could not take over ancient Epicureanism without modification. The main changes which he introduced throw an interesting light on a man who was both a devout Catholic and a free-thinker. Gassendi rejected Epicurus' theology. The universe, on Gassendi's interpretation, is not a chance combination of atoms but an expression of divine goodness, and the atoms were created by God. Nor, as Epicurus claimed, is there an infinite number of atoms. Only God is infinite, and the movements of atoms reveal order and providence.

The actual effects of Gassendi's promotion of Epicureanism on seventeenth-century science cannot be assessed in this short survey. What is certain is his general influence upon an Epicurean revival which spread from France to England. Two years before the publication of the *De vita* another Frenchman, Jean François Saresin, brought out a work entitled *Discours de morale sur Epicure*, and these two books were drawn upon by Walter Charleton whose *Epicurus's morals* (1656) is the earliest surviving Epicurean publication by an Englishman. Charleton was a high-church medical doctor and his work gives a popular defence of Epicurean ethics. There was still however no English translation of Lucretius' complete poem. The diarist, John Evelyn, brought out a verse translation of the first book in the same year that Charleton's work appeared. But neither Charleton nor Evelyn provided the main stimulus to Epicureanism in England. The credit for this belongs to Thomas Creech, John Dryden and Sir William Temple.

Creech's importance rests on his translation of Lucretius which was published at Oxford in 1682. At last the most detailed account of Epicureanism was available in English, and Creech's translation in vigorous heroic verse was an immediate success. Creech concealed from his preface any overt sympathy for Epicurus. Like many who had previously written on Lucretius he professed that 'the best method to overthrow the Epicurean hypothesis . . . is to expose a full system of it to public view'. But the intellectual climate of Restoration England was for rather than against Lucretius and Epicurus. In 1685 Dryden included a selection of verse translations of Lucretius in his *Second miscellany*, and Dryden's reputation helped to stimulate still more interest in the Epicurean poet and his doctrines. Like Creech, Dryden was careful to distinguish between translating Lucretius and approving what he said. But in the same year, positive endorsement of Epicurean ethics came from the eminent and influential Temple. *Upon the Gardens of Epicurus; or, of Gardening, in the year 1685* is an odd mixture of Epicurean apologetics and a discussion of seventeenth-century gardening. The intention of Temple's apology can be shown by this enthusiastic quotation:

> I have often wondered how such sharp and violent invectives came to be made so generally against Epicurus whose admirable wit, felicity of expression, excellence of nature, sweetness of conversation, temperance of life, and constancy of death, made him so beloved by his friends, admired by his scholars, and honoured by the Athenians.[1]

For a short period, with the support of Charles II and his circle, a popular form of Epicureanism was fashionable in England. Shadwell's *The Virtuoso* contains praise of Lucretius. And the importance of distinguishing genuine Epicureanism from prevalent misconceptions is echoed in these interesting lines from Cowley's poem, *The Garden*:

> When Epicurus to the World had taught,
> That Pleasure was the chiefest Good,
> (And was perhaps i' the right if rightly understood) . . .
> Whoever a true Epicure would be,
> May find there [*sc.* in a Garden] cheap and virtuous luxurie.

But counter-attacks were soon forthcoming, including a turgid poem by Sir Richard Blackmore in 1712: *Creation: a philosophical poem demonstrating the Existence and Providence of God.*[2] Indirect references and influences are more difficult to detect. They have been postulated for many English writers from Hobbes to Gibbon, and John Stuart Mill regarded Epicureanism as an early, though inadequate, example of utilitarianism.

On the philosophical and literary influence of Stoicism and Epicureanism much work remains to be done. Ancient scepticism also enjoyed a considerable vogue in the Renaissance, and its direct influence on philosophy and religious thought has been demonstrated by Richard Popkin.[3] In the Hellenistic world it was the existence of conflicting

---

[1] *Works*, vol. iii (London 1757) p. 203.
[2] The French Cardinal, Melchior de Polignac, wrote a more distinguished verse polemic, *Anti-Lucretius*, published in 1745.
[3] *The History of Scepticism from Erasmus to Descartes* (Assen 1960).

positivist systems which provided conditions under which philosophical doubt could flourish. The sceptic solved the problem of judging between Stoics, Epicureans and others by developing arguments designed to show that certainty and truth were unattainable by any system. Later, as we have seen with Lactantius and Augustine, Christian thinkers asserted that the only adequate answer to scepticism lay in faith and revelation. But Lactantius unlike Augustine found it possible to approve scepticism for showing philosophical 'wisdom' to be illusory.

In the Reformation, which produced its own problem of the criterion of truth, scepticism was called upon, especially by Catholics, as a means of attacking the other side. Erasmus in *De libero arbitrio* (1524) gave a sceptical criticism of Luther's biblical interpretation advocating in its place a pious acceptance of the traditional Church doctrine. Luther's impassioned reaction in *De servo arbitrio* (1525) charged Erasmus with undermining Christianity: a Christian cannot be a sceptic; '*spiritus sanctus non est scepticus*'. What Popkin has called 'the intellectual crisis of the Reformation' gave a new interest and importance to ancient sceptical arguments. In *The praise of folly* Erasmus referred approvingly to the Academics,[1] but it was the Pyrrhonism of Sextus Empiricus, whose works only became widely known in the latter part of the sixteenth century, that proved particularly influential.

The first printed text of Sextus was a Latin translation of the *Outlines of Pyrrhonism* published by Henri Estienne (Stephanus) at Paris in 1562. Seven years later the French Counter-Reformer, Gentian Hervet, brought out a Latin edition of the whole of Sextus, which was printed at Paris and Antwerp. The Greek text was first printed in 1621 by P. and J. Chouet at Cologne, Paris and Geneva. This was not available to Montaigne who died in 1592, but the French essayist's familiarity with Pyrrhonist arguments is constantly evident in the work which had great influence on seventeenth-century scepticism, the *Apologie de Raimond Sebond*. Montaigne makes use of Pyrrhonism for its original purpose of casting doubt upon every objective criterion of judgment. He 'defends' Sebond in an oblique way by seeking to show that faith, not rational demonstration, is the basis of the Christian religion. Certainty is unattainable by theological reasoning and therefore Sebond's *Natural theology*, which had been criticized as unsound, could not be judged inferior to any other rational justification of Christianity. Two short extracts must suffice here to illustrate Mon-

[1] Trans. L. Dean (Chicago 1946) p. 84.

taigne's Pyrrhonism. The Pyrrhonist attitude of total doubt is approved because it

> ... presents man naked and empty, recognizing his natural weakness, fit to receive from on high any unknown force, stripped of human knowledge and all the more ready to accommodate the divine in himself, annihilating his own judgment to make greater room for faith.[1]

Here we see how Montaigne like Erasmus and other Catholics linked scepticism on the rational level with faith in religion, and saw the former as a means to the latter. Montaigne rehearses many of the traditional Pyrrhonist arguments against reliance upon sense-experience or scientific knowledge, and he concludes:

> In order to judge appearances which we receive from objects we need an instrument of judgment; in order to verify this instrument we need demonstration; in order to verify demonstration we need an instrument: there we are, arguing in a circle.[2]

It was not only religious controversy which stimulated the 'new Pyrrhonists' of the next generation in France. Opposition to Aristotelian scholasticism, alchemy, astrology, and the mystical systems of men like Paracelsus, Pomponazzi and Giordano Bruno also gave birth to scepticism. There was nothing in the early seventeenth century which could count as a scientific orthodoxy. Modern science was in its infancy and no one at the time could foresee its eventual development. It is impossible to survey the influence of ancient scepticism on the French 'libertins erudits' in this chapter. We must simply note that Sextus Empiricus was a most important influence on the writings of François de la Mothe Le Vayer, Gabriel Naudé and Gassendi. In the second half of the seventeenth century a new generation of sceptics rose to attack the new dogmatists, especially Descartes. Pierre Bayle represents the culmination of this criticism, and these remarks from his article on Pyrrho in the *Dictionnaire historique et critique* (1697–1702), even allowing for irony, throw a fascinating light on Pyrrhonism two thousand years after its inception:

> When one is capable of really understanding the tropes given by Sextus Empiricus, one feels that this Logic is the greatest effort of subtility that the human mind can make; but one sees at the same time that this subtility can give no satisfaction; it confounds itself: for if it were solid, it would prove that it is certain that one ought to doubt. There would then be some certitude,

[1] *Les Essais de Michel de Montaigne* ed. P. Villey (Paris 1922) p. 238.
[2] *Les Essais*, p. 366.

one would then have some Rule of Truth. . . . The reasons for doubting are
themselves dubious. One must doubt if one must doubt. What chaos and
what torture for the mind! It seems then that this unfortunate state is most
proper of all for convincing us that our Reason is a way to Bewilderment,
since when she deploys herself with the most subtility, she throws us into
such an abyss. The natural consequence of this ought to be to renounce the
guide and ask for a better one. This is the great step towards the Christian
religion, for it wishes that we obtain from God the knowledge of what we
ought to believe and do, it wishes that we make our understanding the
obedient slave of faith.[1]

While Bayle attempted to undermine all rational explanations of the
world, the laws of Nature were being proclaimed by Newton and his
followers. The laws of Nature were the laws of reason, and to many in
the eighteenth century the universe at large and the moral sense of the
individual revealed the handiwork of a divine artificer. Deism, or
natural theology, was a consequence of the contemporary scientific
and religious situation, but it has very strong conceptual, if not historical, links with Stoicism. It was the Stoics whose concept of
Nature as rational first sanctioned a clear connexion between physical
causation and universal harmony on the one hand and moral well-
being on the other. In the intellectual climate inaugurated by Newton
this idea took on a new significance. Newton himself at the end of his
Opticks wrote:

> If natural Philosophy in all its Parts . . . shall at length be perfected, the
> Bounds of Moral Philosophy will also be enlarged. For so far as we can know
> by natural Philosophy what is the first cause, what Power he has over us,
> what benefits we receive from him, so far our Duty towards him, as well as
> that towards one another, will appear to us by the Light of Nature.[2]

The Stoics would equally have approved the sentiments expressed in
this popular account of Newtonianism:

> Our views of Nature, however imperfect, serve to represent to us, in the
> most sensible manner, that mighty power which prevails throughout, acting
> with a force and efficacy that appears to suffer no diminution from the great-
> est distances of space or intervals of time: and that wisdom which we see dis-
> played in the exquisite structure and just motion of the greatest and subtilest
> parts. These, with the perfect goodness, by which they are evidently directed,

---

[1] Article 'Pyrrho', Rem. B, cited in Popkin, *Philosophy and Phenomenological
Research* 16 (1955–6) 65. For the impact of Pyrrhonism on historiography, cf.
A. Momigliano, *Studies in Historiography* (London 1966) pp. 10ff.

[2] *Opticks,* bk. iii, pt. i, qu. 31 (1st ed., 1704; reprint ed. E. T. Whittaker, 1931).

constitute the supreme object of the speculations of a philosopher; who, while he contemplates and admires so excellent a system, cannot but be himself excited and animated to correspond with the general harmony of Nature.[1]

Today such optimism seems out of place, but it was a reasonable attitude to hold in the eighteenth century and one which helps to show that Stoicism itself is of more than historical interest. The Stoics defended their system on rational grounds, but part of its attraction was aesthetic and emotional. The idea or ideal of an orderly universe to which men contribute as rational beings is one of its most important legacies to western culture.

The influence of Hellenistic philosophy on European literature and thought reached a high point between 1500 and 1700. Thereafter it becomes too diffused to be marked out briefly with any precision. The Roman moralists were still widely read up to the middle of the nineteenth century, but it was in the Renaissance that they were chiefly valued as guides to life. Epicurus and Sextus Empiricus helped to promote the development of modern empiricism, but this movement had acquired its own momentum by the early eighteenth century. For very good reasons academic interest in Plato and Aristotle increased, and the Hellenistic philosophers suffered by the comparison. In Germany, Hegelian idealism influenced the unfavourable assessment of Hellenistic philosophy given by Eduard Zeller in his *History of Greek Philosophy* (1st ed. 1844–52), and Zeller's authority determined many subsequent attitudes. But it was primarily German scholars, Zeller himself, Hermann Usener and Hans von Arnim in particular, who laid the foundations for a critical understanding of Stoicism and Epicureanism. A British scholar of distinction, A. C. Pearson, published *The Fragments of Zeno and Cleanthes* in 1891, twelve years before the appearance of Arnim's *Stoicorum Veterum Fragmenta*. And there were other notable British editions: J. S. Reid, Cicero's *Academica* (1885); Cyril Bailey, *Epicurus* (1926) and *Lucretius* (1947); A. S. L. Farquharson, *Marcus Aurelius* (1944). But in general, few British or American scholars who were active before the last war took a great interest in Hellenistic philosophy. Only two critical studies of lasting value were produced in Britain during this time: R.D. Hicks, *Stoic and Epicurean* (1910) and Bailey, *The Greek Atomists and Epicurus* (1928). Anglo-Saxon scholarship in this field

---

[1] Colin Maclaurin, *An Account of Sir I. Newton's Philosophical Discoveries* (quoted by C. L. Becker in *The Heavenly City of the Eighteenth Century Philosophers* (Yale 1932) pp. 62–3).

lagged behind the work which was being done in Germany, Italy and France.

The bibliography of this book, which concentrates on work in English, shows that the situation has changed during the last twenty years. British and American scholars have now done important new work on many aspects of Hellenistic philosophy, and as a result the subject has gained greater academic respectability in these countries. Under the aegis of cultural history Hellenistic philosophy has always commanded attention. But informed appreciations of its conceptual significance are still uncommon. More work is needed to illuminate unfamiliar topics and to demonstrate the intrinsic interest of Greek philosophy after Aristotle. Its limitations and achievements have much to tell us about ourselves.

Bibliography

THE principal ancient sources have been described briefly in the first part of Chapters 2, 3 and 4. Modern editions of these authors are listed in Part 2 of this bibliography, and some general works and background reading are referred to in Part 1. The rest of the bibliography is arranged according to the chapters of the book. Some works are cited here which are not referred to in the notes to chapters, and the bibliography is not designed to give details of every book or article mentioned in the notes. So far as possible the modern works which have been selected are in English, but some particularly valuable studies in other languages have also been included.

I. GENERAL

Philosophy and science

A. H. Armstrong (editor), *The Cambridge History of Later Greek and Early Medieval Philosophy* (Cambridge 1967); mainly devoted to Neoplatonism and later developments; good short treatment of the Academy and Lyceum in the Hellenistic period.

H. C. Baldry, *The Unity of Mankind in Greek Thought* (Cambridge 1965).

D. R. Dudley, *A History of Cynicism* (London 1937).

R. D. Hicks, *Stoic and Epicurean* (New York 1910); also deals with Scepticism; sometimes stimulating but also outdated in style and discussion of details.

W. and M. Kneale, *The Development of Logic* (Oxford 1962); very good discussion of Aristotelian and Stoic logic.

S. Sambursky, *The Physical World of the Greeks* (London 1956); includes an illuminating appraisal of Stoic and Epicurean physics.

E. Zeller, *Die Philosophie der Griechen*, vol. iii (5th ed., ed. by E. Wellmann, Leipzig 1923). An earlier edition translated by O. Reichel with the title, *Stoics, Epicureans and Sceptics* (London 1880); basically insensitive to the achievements of the Stoics, but still a useful synoptic work on Hellenistic philosophy.

History and cultural background

E. R. Dodds, *The Greeks and the Irrational* (Berkeley and Los Angeles 1951); includes a fascinating short account of philosophy and religion in the Hellenistic world which, in my judgment, does less than justice to the philosophers.

W. S. Ferguson, *Hellenistic Athens* (London 1911).

N. M. P. Nilsson, *Geschichte der griechischen Religion*, vol. ii (2nd ed., Munich 1961); the best book on Hellenistic religion.

R. Pfeiffer, *History of Classical Scholarship*, vol. i (Oxford 1968); a masterly work of synthesis on the scholars of the Hellenistic period.

W. W. Tarn, *Hellenistic Civilization* (3rd ed. revised by G. T. Griffith, London 1952).

T. B. L. Webster, *Hellenistic Poetry and Art* (London 1964).

2. PRINCIPAL ANCIENT AUTHORS

The editions specified include a full commentary unless otherwise indicated. Translations of most authors with facing Greek or Latin text are available in the Loeb Classical Library editions published by Heinemann and the Harvard University Press. Some more recent translations which have appeared in paperback are also mentioned.

Aurelius, Marcus (A.D. 121–80). *Meditations*, ed. and trans. by A. S. L. Farquharson, 2 vols. (Oxford 1944). Trans. in paperback by G. M. A. Grube, *The Library of Liberal Arts* (Bobbs-Merrill, Indianapolis and New York 1963).

Cicero (106–43 B.C.). *Academica*, ed. by J. S. Reid (London 1885).

— *De divinatione*, ed. by A. S. Pease (Urbana 1920–3).

— *De fato*, ed. by A. Yon, with facing French trans. (Paris 1950).

— *De finibus bonorum et malorum*, ed. by J. N. Madvig, with notes in Latin (3rd ed. 1876, Copenhagen; reprinted Hildesheim 1965). Books i and ii (summary and criticism of Epicurean ethics) ed. by J. S. Reid (London 1925).

— *De natura deorum*, ed. by A. S. Pease, 2 vols. (Cambridge, Mass. 1955–8). Trans. in paperback by C. P. McGregor, with introd. by J. M. Ross, Penguin Classics (1972).

— *De officiis*, ed. by H. A. Holden (3rd ed., Cambridge 1879).

— *De republica*, ed. by K. Ziegler (Leipzig 1960; critical text only).

— *Tusculan disputations*, ed. by T. W. Dougan and R. M. Henry

(Oxford 1905–34). Parts trans. by M. Grant in *Cicero on the Good Life* (along with *De amicitia* and other extracts), Penguin Classics (1971).

Diogenes Laertius (3rd century A.D.). *Lives of Eminent Philosophers,* ed. by H. S. Long, 2 vols. (Oxford 1964; brief annotation only). The best trans. is into Italian by M. Gigante (Bari 1962).

Epictetus (*c.* A.D. 55–135). *Discourses Recorded by Arrian,* ed. by H. Schenkl (2nd ed., Leipzig 1916; critical text only). Good Loeb trans. by W. A. Oldfather, 2 vols. (1925).

Epicurus, see Bibliography Part 3.

Galen (A.D. 129–*c.* 200). *De placitis Hippocratis et Platonis,* ed. by I. Mueller (Leipzig 1874; critical text only). No Loeb; Latin trans. in edition by C. G. Kühn (Leipzig 1821–33). A new edition is in preparation by Phillip de Lacy for the series, *Corpus Medicorum Graecorum.*

Lucretius (*c.* 94–55 B.C.). *De rerum natura,* ed. and trans. by C. Bailey, 3 vols. (Oxford 1947). Trans. in paperback by R. E. Latham, Penguin Classics.

Plutarch (*c.* A.D. 46–121). *De stoicorum repugnantiis* and *De communibus notitiis* have been edited along with Plutarch's anti-Epicurean treatises by M. Pohlenz in Plutarch *Moralia* vol. vi 2 (revised by R. Westman, Leipzig 1959; brief annotation only). Detailed discussion of the work *Against Colotes* (Epicurean) by R. Westman in *Acta Philosophica Fennica* VII (1955), written in German. The anti-Epicurean works are available in a Loeb edition by B. Einarson and Ph. De Lacy (*Moralia* XIV). A further Loeb edition of the anti-Stoic treatises is being prepared by Harold Cherniss.

Seneca (*c.* 5 B.C.–A.D. 65). *Epistulae morales,* ed. by L. D. Reynolds, 2 vols. (Oxford 1965; brief annotation only). A selection has been translated in a paperback edition by R. Campbell, *Penguin Classics* (1969).

Sextus Empiricus (second century A.D.). *Outlines of Pyrrhonism* and *Against the dogmatic philosophers,* ed. by H. Mutschmann and others (Leipzig 1914–54; critical text only). The Loeb trans. by R. G. Bury is sometimes seriously inaccurate. A selection of Sextus' writings trans. in *Scepticism, Man and God,* ed. by Ph. Hallie (Middletown, Conn. 1964).

3. EPICURUS AND EPICUREANISM

The standard collection of Epicurus' writings and other ancient evidence on his life and philosophy is H. Usener, *Epicurea* (Leipzig 1887, reprinted Stuttgart 1966). Usener arranged his material by subject-matter, beginning with Epicurus' own works, and the individual texts are numbered consecutively and referred to in this book as Us. 271 etc. No translations were given by Usener and he did not include fragments of Epicurus' works preserved in Herculaneum papyri. Much of the latter material has been incorporated in a collection by G. Arrighetti, *Epicuro Opere* (Turin 1960), who also gives an Italian translation and helpful annotation. This work, which is about to appear in a second edition, is a valuable supplement to Usener. The best text of the three *Letters* of Epicurus recorded by Diogenes Laertius is P. von der Muehll, *Epicurus: Epistulae tres et ratae sententiae* (Stuttgart 1923, reprinted 1966). A further text with translation and valuable commentary is C. Bailey, *Epicurus* (Oxford 1926).

General studies: the most authoritative work is C. Bailey, *The Greek Atomists and Epicurus* (Oxford 1928). N. W. de Witt, *Epicurus and his Philosophy* (Minneapolis 1954), and B. Farrington, *The Faith of Epicurus* (London 1967), are more stimulating but less reliable. J. M. Rist, *Epicurus: an Introduction* (Cambridge 1972), appeared after the first draft of this book was completed. It is a tougher work than its title suggests. For a bibliography of recent work and a collection of papers on many aspects of Epicureanism cf. *Actes du VIIIe Congrès Association Guillaume Budé* (Paris 1969).

Some recent studies of particular topics: on Epicurus' theory of knowledge cf. D. J. Furley, 'Knowledge of Atoms and Void' in *Essays in Ancient Greek Philosophy*, ed. J .P. Anton and G. L. Kustas (N.Y. 1971) 607–19, and A. A. Long, 'Aisthesis, Prolepsis and Linguistic Theory in Epicurus', *Bulletin of the Institute of Classical Studies* 18 (1971) 114–33; on cosmology cf. F. Solmsen, 'Epicurus and Cosmological Heresies', *American Journal of Philology* 72 (1951) 1–23 and 'Epicurus on the Growth and Decline of the Cosmos', ibid. 74 (1953) 34–51; on indivisible magnitudes, a controversial subject, cf. G. Vlastos, 'Minimal Parts in Epicurean Atomism', *Isis* 56 (1965) 121–47 and D. J. Furley, *Two Studies in the Greek Atomists* (Princeton 1967) first study; on theology cf. A. J. Festugière, *Epicurus and his Gods*, trans. C. W. Chilton (Oxford 1955); and K. Kleve, 'Gnosis

Theon', *Symbolae Osloenses*, suppl. 19 (1963); on psychology cf. D. J. Furley, op. cit. second study and G. B. Kerferd, 'Epicurus' Doctrine of the Soul', *Phronesis* 16 (1971) 80–96; on pleasure cf. P. Merlan, *Studies in Epicurus and Aristotle* (Wiesbaden 1960) first study.

Individual later Epicureans. (*a*) Philodemus: much of the extant material is extremely fragmentary. The most important philosophical text is the *De signis* (On signs) which has been edited, translated and discussed by Ph. and E. A. De Lacy, *Philodemus: On Methods of Inference* (Philological Monograph of the American Philological Association, no. x, Pennsylvania 1941). Cf. also M. Gigante, *Ricerce filodemee* (Naples 1969). (*b*) Lucretius: the best study of his treatment of Epicureanism is by P. Boyancé, *Lucrèce et l'Épicurisme* (Paris 1963). (*c*) Diogenes of Oenoanda: critical text by C. W. Chilton (Leipzig 1967), trans. and commentary by the same author, *Diogenes of Oenoanda* (London, O.U.P. 1971). New fragments have been discovered and published by M. F. Smith, *American Journal of Archaeology* 74 (1971) 51–62, 75 (1971) 357–89, and *Journal of Hellenic Studies* 92 (1972) 147–55.

4. SCEPTICISM

The best comprehensive study is V. Brochard, *Les Sceptiques grecs* (2nd ed. Paris 1932, reprinted Paris 1959). Less detailed but more interesting philosophically is C. L. Stough, *Greek Skepticism* (Berkeley and Los Angeles 1969).

Individual Sceptic philosophers: (*a*) Pyrrho and Timon: see Brochard especially; (*b*) Arcesilaus: an excellent concise study by H. von Arnim in Pauly-Wissowa, *Real-Enzyklopädie*, vol. 2, no. 1, article on Arkesilaos; see also O. Gigon, 'Zur Geschichte der sogennanten neuen Akademie', *Museum Helveticum* i (1944) 47–64; (*c*) Carneades: notes by A. Weische in Pauly-Wissowa, suppl. 11, article on Karneades; see also A. A. Long, 'Carneades and the Stoic Telos', *Phronesis* 12 (1967) 59–90; (*d*) Aenesidemus: for a persuasive account of his philosophical development see J. M. Rist, 'The Heracliteanism of Aenesidemus', *Phoenix* 24 (1970) 309–19.

Other useful modern studies: R. Chisholm, 'Sextus Empiricus and Modern Empiricism', *Philosophy of Science* 8 (1941) 471–84; Ph. De Lacy, '*Ou Mallon* and the Antecedents of Ancient Scepticism', *Phronesis*

3 (1958) 59–71; R. Popkin, 'David Hume: his Pyrrhonism and his Critique of Pyrrhonism', *Philosophical Quarterly* 5 (1951) 385–407.

5. STOICISM

The standard collection of evidence for Early Stoicism (Zeno to Antipater of Tarsus) is H. von Arnim, *Stoicorum Veterum Fragmenta* (*SVF*), 4 vols. (Leipzig 1903–24, reprinted Stuttgart 1964). This work has proved its value over the years, but it is now in need of revision. Some of the material which Arnim included is of doubtful validity for establishing Chrysippus' views, and certain writers, especially Cicero and Seneca, are under-represented. In using this collection it is always necessary to consider the context and characteristics of each author who is excerpted.

In this book, texts which are relatively accessible such as Diogenes Laertius and Cicero are normally cited by reference to their authors. Material which is most easily consulted by using von Arnim is cited by the fragment number in his collection, for instance *SVF* iii 121, that is, volume 3 and the passage or passages included as fragment 121. The text translated is not always that of von Arnim.

General studies: E. V. Arnold, *Roman Stoicism* (Cambridge 1911); lucid and well-balanced, though somewhat over-simplified and now outdated; especially valuable for its many quotations in the original. J. Christensen, *An Essay on the Unity of Stoic Philosophy* (Copenhagen 1962); the most philosophically sophisticated short introduction. L. Edelstein, *The Meaning of Stoicism* (Cambridge, Mass. 1966); a stimulating little book which is sometimes misleading. M. Pohlenz, *Die Stoa* (3rd ed., Göttingen 1964) 2 vols.; the most comprehensive book on Stoicism, very fully annotated in the second volume.

Zeno: K. von Fritz, Pauly-Wissowa, *Real-Enzyklopädie* suppl. 10A, article on Zenon of Kitium; a new study, particularly interesting on Zeno's philosophical background.

Chrysippus: E. Bréhier, *Chrysippe et l'ancien stoïcisme* (2nd ed., Paris 1950); a thoughtful and generally reliable book. J. B. Gould, *The Philosophy of Chrysippus* (Leiden 1971); some useful discussions but marred in part by rigidity in the selection of evidence.

Books which discuss specific topics in detail: Victor Goldschmidt, *Le Système stoicien et l'idée de temps* (2nd ed., Paris 1969). *Problems in Stoicism* (London 1971) ed. A. A. Long, with contributions by I. G. Kidd, A. C. Lloyd, A. A. Long, S. G. Pembroke, J. M. Rist, F. H. Sandbach and G. Watson. B. Mates, *Stoic Logic* (Berkeley and Los Angeles 1953). J. M. Rist, *Stoic Philosophy* (Cambridge 1969). S. Sambursky, *The Physics of the Stoics* (London 1959). G. Watson, *The Stoic Theory of Knowledge* (Belfast 1966).

Most of these works and a number of recent articles have been cited in the notes to Chapter 4. The following are also valuable: Ph. De Lacy, 'The Stoic Categories as Methodological Principles', *Transactions and Proceedings of the American Philological Association* 76 (1945) 246–63; R. P. Haynes, 'The Theory of Pleasure of the Old Stoa', *American Journal of Philology* 83 (1962) 412–19; M. E. Reesor, *The Political Theory of the Old and Middle Stoa* (N.Y. 1951) and 'Fate and Possibility in Early Stoic Philosophy', *Phoenix* 19 (1965) 285–97.

6. PANAETIUS, POSIDONIUS, ANTIOCHUS, CICERO

Source collections and some other works have been cited in the notes to Chapter 5.

Panaetius: the best comprehensive treatment is M. van Straaten, *Panétius, sa vie, ses écrits et sa doctrine* (Amsterdam 1946). He is rightly cautious about inferring Panaetius' views from texts in which the philosopher is not named. Apart from Panaetius' certain influence upon Cicero's *De officiis*, he was probably drawn on by Cicero for the *De republica* (cf. i 34).

Posidonius: a cautious and comprehensive study of M. Laffranque, *Poseidonios d'Apamée* (Paris 1964). Another useful work is 'The Philosophical System of Posidonius' by L. Edelstein, *American Journal of Philology* 57 (1936) 286–325. For a detailed bibliography Laffranque's book should be consulted. The Ciceronian works on which Posidonius' influence can be argued with some probability are *De divinatione* and *Tusculan Disputations*.

Antiochus: see the works cited in notes pp. 222–8 of Chapter 5.

Cicero: to Hunt and Douglas cited on pp. 222, 229 of Chapter 5 may be added: T. Petersson, *Cicero, A Biography* (Berkeley 1920); the introduction to J. S. Reid's edition of the *Academica* (London 1885) and the bibliographical surveys by S. E. Smethurst in *Classical World* li (1957), lviii (1964–5) and lxi (1967).

7. GENERAL AND LATER INFLUENCE

Good introductions to the Stoicism of Seneca, Epictetus and Marcus Aurelius in M. Pohlenz, *Die Stoa* (Göttingen 1964) and E. Zeller, *Philosophie der Griechen* vol. iii part 1, trans. by S. F. Alleyne as *A History of Eclecticism in Greek Philosophy* (London 1883). On the Roman Cynics cf. D. R. Dudley, *A History of Cynicism* (London 1937).

This list gives a short selection of books which deal with or touch on the influence of Hellenistic philosophy in antiquity and later:

E. Barker, *From Alexander to Constantine* (Oxford 1956).

M. L. Clarke, *The Roman Mind* (London 1956).

S. Dill, *Roman Society from Nero to Marcus Aurelius* (2nd ed., London 1905).

P. Gay, *The Enlightenment* (London 1967).

H. Haydn, *The Counter-Renaissance* (New York 1950).

J. W. Johnson, *The Formation of English Neo-classical Thought* (Princeton 1967).

P. O. Kristeller, *The Classics and Renaissance Thought* (Cambridge, Mass. 1955).

T. F. Mayo, *Epicurus in England* (New York 1934).

R. Popkin, *The History of Scepticism from Erasmus to Descartes* (Assen 1960).

C. B. Schmitt, *Cicero Scepticus: a Study of the Influence of the Academica in the Renaissance* (The Hague 1972).

M. Spanneut, *Le Stoïcisme des Pères de l'Eglise* (2nd ed., Paris 1969).

J. S. Spink, *French Free-Thought from Gassendi to Voltaire* (London 1960).

L. Zanta, *La Renaissance du Stoïcisme au XVI siècle* (Paris 1914).

Index

Academy, 12, 15, 111; early, 4–6; sceptical, 9, 88–106; pleasure discussed in, 62; and Antiochus, 223–9. *See* Plato, Platonism

action, causes of in Epicureanism, 55, 56–61; in Stoicism, 165–8, 172–4, 176, 219

Addison, Joseph, 240

Aenesidemus, 75–7, 106, 229

Agrippa (Sceptic philosopher), 75n

air, 51, 150, 155–7

Alexander of Aphrodisias, 116, 157, 159, 237

Alexander the Great, 1, 2, 3, 5, 80, 108

Alexandria, 1–2, 17, 223

ambiguity, 24, 30, 135, 146

analogy, 28, 124, 154, 201

Anaxagoras, 150

Anaxarchus, influence on Pyrrho, 80

Andronicus of Rhodes, 226

animals, and men, in Stoicism, 171–4, 185–189

Antioch, 1, 2, 17

Antiochus of Ascalon, 77, 186; criticism of Stoic ethics, 196–7; eclecticism, 216, 228–229; interpretation of Academy, 223–9; ethical goal, 225–6; on knowledge, 227–228

Antipater of Tarsus, 114, 115, 220; modifies Stoic ethical goal, 196

Antisthenes, and Stoicism, 7–8

apprehension, mental, in Epicureanism, 25–6, 54–6; in Stoicism, 90–1, 127–31. *See* cognitive impression

appropriate acts (*kathêkonta*), 187–8, 190–2, 203–4, 213–15. *See* officium

Arcesilaus, 9, 77, 88–95; sceptical criticism of Stoics, 90–1; and Antiochus, 223–4

Archimedes, 2, 119

aretê, 77. *See* virtue

arguing both sides of a question, in Scepticism, 82, 92, 104–6

Aristarchus of Samos, 2, 12

Aristippus of Cyrene, 8; and Epicurean hedonism, 5, 61

Ariston of Chius, 77, 193

Aristotle, 1–4, 6, 11, 103, 105, 110, 131, 133, 232, 247; career, 5; writings in Hellenistic period, 9–10; and Epicurus, 19–20, 23, 29, 36, 50, 60n, 62, 69; criticism of early atomism, 35, 37; teleology, 40–1, 151; theology, 43–4, 151–2; and Stoicism, 112, 142–3, 146–7, 151–2, 154, 155, 157, 159–61, 165, 167, 171, 178, 197,

207; logic, 121–2, 142–3; mixture, 159; categories, 161; happiness, 197, 225; and Panaetius, 213, 216; and Posidonius, 218; and Antiochus, 224, 225

assent, in Stoicism, 126–9, 167, 173, 176, 207; criticized by Arcesilaus, 90–1

astrology, 164; rejected by Panaetius, 211–212

astronomy, 2, 12, 45, 221; Epicurean approach to, 27; and theology, 42–3

Athens, 2, 3, 5, 13, 15, 88, 94

atomism, 20–1, 30, 39; and Gassendi, 241–2

atoms and effluences, 22, 24; compound bodies, 32–3, 37–9; chance combinations, 24, 40; atomic swerve, 37–8, 56–61, 101; minimal parts, 28, 33–5; properties of, 32–5, 36, 46; proved, 31–3; motion of, 32, 35–8, 58; and pleasure, 64. *See* Aristotle

Augustine, St., 133, 236, 237

Aurelius, Marcus, 107, 113, 115, 151, 170, 216, 233, 239, 240; religious experience, 165, 234; attitude to universe, 165, 180, 234

axioms, confirmation and non-contradiction in Epicureanism, 26–9, 31

Bacon, Roger, 238

Bayle, Pierre, on Pyrrhonism, 245–6

beauty, of human form, 46; of virtue, 204

belief, distinguished from knowledge in Stoicism, 78, 90–1, 129–30

Bentham, Jeremy, 69

biological approach, of Stoicism, 150, 155

Blackmore, Sir Richard, 243

body, concept of, in Epicureanism, 31–3; in Stoicism, 152–4

Boethus of Sidon, 211n, 222

Budé, Guillaume, 239

Burnet, Gilbert, 240

Butler, Bishop, 107

Calvin, John, 239

Carneades, 10, 88, 94–106, 114, 144, 195–6, 216, 223; background, 94–5; on knowledge, 95–9; on theology, 100–1; on free will, 101–4; on justice, 104–6

categories, in Stoicism, 160–3

Cato of Utica, and Stoicism, 113, 214, 216, 233; admired by English Augustan writers, 240–1